The
Sea Voyages
of Edward Beck
in the 1820s

The
Sea Voyages
of Edward Beck
in the 1820s

Edited by Michael Hay and Joy Roberts

The Pentland Press Limited
Edinburgh • Cambridge • Durham • USA

First published in 1996 by
The Pentland Press Ltd.
1 Hutton Close
South Church
Bishop Auckland
Durham

British Library Cataloguing in Publication Data.
A Catalogue record for this book is available
from the British Library.

ISBN 1 85821 435 1

Typeset by CBS, Felixstowe, Suffolk
Printed and bound by Antony Rowe Ltd., Chippenham

To my wife Sue and to old
friends who have shared yacht
cruising experiences with me.

PREFACE

by Captain Morin Scott MBE, FNI
(Master in Sail)

Having been involved in designing and commanding square-rigged ships for many years, and having been fascinated all my life by the true and fictional accounts of their voyages and battles, I have found it a delight to be allowed to read Edward Beck's diaries of his life at sea in the early 1820s.

His introduction to a seafaring life is in the form of joining the brig *CONSTANTIA* to trade to Ireland. He signed on as Captain's Servant, which brought him the additional duty of looking after the Captain's cabin and saloon and acting – as he says – as 'bottlewasher' as well as assisting with the sailing of the vessel, which later he much preferred.

He then joins the brig *LADY FRANCES* in London where she was discharging coal from Sunderland. She would have been one of the famous 'Collier Brigs' that kept the capital supplied with household coal from the North-East coast during the winter and traded to Canada or Scandinavia in summer. These brigs were renowned for being very handy and for being crewed by fine seamen who were not paid by the day but by the round voyage, which encouraged them to make fast passages.

Beck is a serious and observant diarist and we are treated throughout the book to various matters of interest which come to his notice – many of them by no means nautical. When in Sunderland, for example, he describes in great detail Great Iron Bridge which was built so high that ships could sail under it. Then he covers the local lifeboats and their crews, and winds up telling how he rode on a steam train while walking ashore and how it carried the coal from the colliery to the docks – and this was some years before passenger trains started operating.

After he joins her *LADY FRANCES* is taken off the coal trade and he makes two voyages in her to Quebec carrying passengers and general cargo outward and timber home. The first voyage commences in May 1823 and the second in April 1824.

He then joins the full-rigged ship *WOODFORD* as Third Mate for a voyage to India, his promotion being made possible by his applying himself to the learning of celestial navigation while on *LADY FRANCES* and quickly extended in *WOODFORD* as the Second Mate goes sick and the Captain elevates him to that rank which he manages to handle to the Captain's satisfaction.

It is interesting to read of them meeting the ship *BOMBAY* in the Indian Ocean and how that ship keeps her guns manned and trained on them during their 'speaking'. Later when the mate goes on board a Brazilian ship he finds that they are carrying slaves as well as cargo!

Of course we must remember that William Wilberforce did not succeed in getting slavery abolished in the British Empire until 1836 and the suppression of the slave trade was an important duty for the Royal Navy for another half century or more.

Further accounts of visiting Van Diemen's Land (now Tasmania) with a cargo of convicts and later transporting soldiers are equally fascinating while the last few pages find Edward Beck endeavouring to act as a doctor on board his shop and combatting an epidemic of cholera.

Altogether a fascinating contemporary account of life in a sailing Merchant Ship in the early part of the last century, fifty years before the advent of steam changed the pattern of life at sea.

Robin Salt

Editorial Notes

Edward Beck – my maternal grandfather's uncle – was a watch-keeper officer on merchant sailing ships trading in the 1820s. His childhood was spent at Dover, where his parents were prominent members of the Religious Society of Friends (Quakers). His mind had become fascinated by the sight of sailing ships passing through the Straits of Dover, and he felt a desire to experience the sea and visit foreign places.

His family was related by marriage to that of Lucas of Hitchin, also prominent in the Society of Friends. After he left the sea, he married Susanna Lucas in 1834.

He seems to have been a broadminded man, with wide-ranging interests relating to the voyages he made to Quebec, the Antipodes and Calcutta; this is apparent from his diaries and letters to his family. Prior to these longer voyages, he served his sea apprenticeship in a brig trading to Ireland, and his reminiscences of this are included here, as an introduction to the diaries he kept on the longer voyages.

Besides the problems of seamanship his duties included victualling and rationing, which in voyages lasting five months or more could be difficult, as his diaries show. As well as keeping routine watches, he had to help the paying passengers and see to their welfare. On the second Calcutta voyage, they had been commissioned originally to transport 100 convicts from the prison hulks at Portsmouth to Van Dieman's Land (Tasmania). These were the responsibility of a surgeon, who was a ruthless man. Inevitably there were medical problems, and even deaths on board, mostly from cholera. Treatment was limited, with bleeding or doses of opium the commonest treatments available.

In port, Beck had the job of supervising many of the tasks of repairing or replacing worn and damaged rigging.

Edward Beck was an observant man, who loved the sea and the play of light in the sky and on the water, and had the stamina to endure the inevitable vagaries of wind and climate. He loved to observe the birds, fishes and whales and to collect seashells when ashore. When tempers became frayed at the end of the second Calcutta voyage, he remained cool and philosophical.

To me he is a delightful, kindly and interesting person, probably unusual for his times, and he gives us a vivid picture of what a seaman's life in a trading ship was like in the 1820s.

Michael Hay

I have modernized Edward Beck's punctuation and spelling, to make for easier reading, but I have not changed any of his words. The occasional words in square brackets are simply minimal editorial additions, and the three dots (. . .) used once in a while, merely denote the exclusion of a word, phrase or (very occasionally) a short paragraph, which would be either unusually difficult or rather tedious for the modern reader. The intention throughout has been to make Beck's diaries thoroughly readable, truly accessible and highly enjoyable, while retaining his own, uniquely vivid, language and style.

We would both like to take this opportunity of acknowledging the invaluable contribution of Misses Anne and Mary Hay, who made a typescript from the original manuscript of Edward Beck's diaries and deciphered his handwriting.

Beck's original manuscripts are housed in the Maritime Museum at Greenwich.

Joy Roberts

CONTENTS

INTRODUCTION

How and when I first imbibed a wish to go to sea I cannot at this time possibly tell, any more than that it may principally be attributed to my being a natural [?]. Suffice it therefore to say that, after many a long deliberation upon the subject, and after all arguments had been used to dissuade me from it, I got my parents' permission to go with one Captain Moyse, who, from his being a member of our Society [The Religious Society of Friends] and also, at times, a minister, was considered as fit a one as could be found to have charge of me upon my entrance into my new profession. I shall not endeavour to picture to thee all I painted to myself in anticipation, how I looked forward to the close of the Yearly Meeting that I might see me on my way to Liverpool to join the good brig *Constantia* – how I occasionally put on my blue jacket and trousers and fancied the wind blowing me along, nor all those never to be realized pleasures, which at that buoyant time of life my fancy planned for the future. One thing was always uppermost with me, the seeing foreign lands and people, of which I had a pretty good share in the 9 years of which the following pages will contain a few reminiscences. In that time I visited Ireland, Scotland and Wales several times, Flanders once, North America twice, Calcutta 3 times, Madras as many, New South Wales once, Van Dieman's Land [i.e. Tasmania] twice, St Helena three times, Cape of Good Hope twice, Isle of France and others [?], so that I have not been disappointed on that head, but I must acknowledge that the novelty began to lose much of its charms, and towards the latter part of the time, on entering a voyage I lost the wish that I originally had, that it might be to a port I had not previously visited. I attribute this last principally to the care responsible situations brought upon me, the duties of which, being properly attended to, left but little time of leisure in harbour to devote to going on shore in the manner I had used to before, when, as soon as the work of the day was over, I had no more to think of, and consequently was glad of the opportunity of extending my observations.

Principally with a view to please thee, but partly that I may not entirely lose the recollection of those chequered days which are yet very fresh in my remembrances, I shall attempt to describe some of the incidents that occurred – to gild or gloom them, hoping, if they do afford thee much amusement, they may [amuse] me [at] some future day, when they might otherwise have been forgotten.

There was much to make me devoted to my profession, I was led on by the ambition of one day being the commander of a [n] India ship, which I hoped to attain by my own exertions and which I fully believed would make my fortune. It seemed a long ladder when I began at the bottom, but I always endeavoured to think myself destined for the top. I persevered, rose step by step in a manner that gratified and incited me, reached the summit, stood there 4 days in the long wished-for command – [which] was sold out – and am now a landsman – writing with the same moon shining through my window that has so often been my pleasant watch companion on the wide seas. She now wakes up, as she often does, a train of feelings, that I do believe are known to most; tho' few can describe them. Of the latter number I am not one. And now to my work.

Part I

How I Went to Sea

Chapter 1

THE START

The Yearly [Quaker] Meeting was over, and I was desired to be ready for a start the next day. My well-stocked chest (amply filled with necessaries of all kinds and many a kind present) was therefore securely lashed (alias corded) and sent to the canal office, to be forwarded by boat to Liverpool.

The night came, and I had to bid a long adieu, which was sore for us all, but particularly [for] my mother. In the morning I was up early, to adjust the final arrangements and to guard against leaving anything behind. I felt very low-spirited and my brother, who soon joined me in the counting-house, seemed much the same and bestowed a deal of good advice upon me – of which article, by the by, as may be supposed, I had received a great deal, more (I am sorry to say) than I ever made use of. I was so heavy-hearted that I almost repented, but the three quarters struck, off we marched to the Swan with Two Nicks,[1] Load Lane, when we parted . . . I found myself under the command of Captain Wm Moyse in the high official station of his cabin boy, to which I may perhaps without any pride also add, as is customary, bottle-washer. The two services generally rested in one person and, unlike many offices so held, with but little jealousy on the part of others towards their possessor.

The next day (having stopped one night at Birmingham) we arrived at Liverpool and I was committed to the care of a servant to be directed to my ship lying in St George's Dock, after having passed through an investigation at some Friend's house where we stopped and got tea, and I had been comforted by being well laughed at for my choice, and told I should soon be sick of it; to which latter I inwardly determined to give the lie. My conductor [i.e. the servant] I thought seemed to look upon me (as he had been present during the tea time) as some nondescript animal and seemed inclined to follow his master's plan [of laughing

---

[1] Two nicks or notches in the swan's beak denoted ownership of the bird by some sort of trade association.

at me], but as I had neither eaten nor drunk [anything] of his, I soon cut him short, in a manner that produced a speedy cessation to his enquiries of how I should like hard biscuits and whether I should fancy salt beef etc. – things [which] I may remark [were] at that time rather favourites of mine, for want of the intimate acquaintance we afterwards formed and which, when it had taken place, led me to share them as much as possible, as a man will a bad companion when unfortunately he finds he has formed a friendship with one, and detests him.

Chapter 2

THE JOINING

We soon arrived at the brig and the important circumstances [were] officially noticed in the log book thus. 'Joined as apprentice Edward Beck'. This constituted me one of the ship's company. I had been on board before in London and just knew enough of the 'phizes' [i.e. faces] to say 'How do', but I did not feel at ease till one J. Kekwick stepped up to me and we had talked a little together.

He had joined about 6 months before me, under pretty much the same circumstances, and had therefore got initiated and, being a prime, sensible fellow with a good education and stock of sense about him, I placed myself under his instructions as to my actions; for I soon found I was in a little world very unlike the rest I had yet seen. In it, tho', I soon found money had influence and, as I had a reasonable stock of the needful, by Jim's advice I parted with enough to convince them that I was an ignoramus and that I was willing to buy a little experience. And now, having introduced myself as afloat, I shall drop a connected narrating manner and resort to scraps.

I found, the first night I had to pass on board, that it was not [the daylight conditions] of the new little world alone that were so different to what I had been hitherto accustomed to: the following will show that the sleeping berth of a cabin boy in an Irish Trader is something unequal to a four-post feathered bed, by several removes! On my asking Robin Davies, the mate, where I was to sleep, he directed me to follow him down the cabin ladder, which I did, complaining of the darkness tho' as I descended. 'Oh,' said he, 'if you [intend to] make a sailor you must learn to [make] do in the dark as well as the light!' This hint I treasured up, and never after complained of this, the first deprivation. After we had been down [there] a few moments and got our eyes partially inured to the indistinctness of objects around us, he pointed to a small cupboard-like place, the base of which was the lower deck, as the spot I was to look upon as my dormitory for the time being. He was a good-natured fellow and assisted me in preparing it for the reception of my hair mattress, which was the work of a little time, as it was then occupied by old canvas, nails, twine, rolls of hogs' lard and, in fact, was the receptacle of all odd matters. When these varieties were all removed, I got my sleeping tackle into their place, and as past 9 was come (which was 'turning in time') and I was measurably fatigued, I pulled off my clothes to take possession. This I found rather a difficult job to my inexperienced limbs; however, by kneeling down and entering head first (with a good thump against a bolt that, in fastening its plank, was considerably above floor level), I accomplished it and tucked my clothes about me. Well do I recollect it – it was perfectly miserable; the collection of noxious smells, added to the cramped place and the stony hardness of the mattress on the deck, made it the very worst lodging by far I had ever occupied, and it was very long before I could get to sleep for my reflections upon it, but [as] I had calculated upon many deprivations of this . . . [kind], nothing daunted me. I knew there were worse to come, and I knew the truth – how often since would I with gratitude have accepted the offer of a four hours' nap in the same spot! I may just notice that lights are not allowed on board ships in the Liverpool Docks – of which more hereafter.

Chapter 3

THE FIRST WATCH AND FIRST EMPLOYMENT

My second night, after I had been asleep a few hours I felt myself shaken far from modestly, and, on testifying that I was awake, I was informed (in a manner that showed I was to have no opinion on the matter) that it was my watch. So out of my hole I crawled, and managed in the dark to put on my apparel somehow and to move on deck. Here I was let into the secret that I had to walk about in the moonshine for two hours, answer anybody that might hail the vessel, and take care she did not run away, of which latter there was little fear, from the secure manner in which she was fastened; but to a youngster such language only can be used that can be understood by him. Before it was over I felt quite satisfied that, of the two, my den was the most agreeable, and I felt glad when the ship's bell proclaimed the hour for claiming my relief – which I lost no time about, tho' from my delicacy in my manner of doing it, I had to repeat it several times, from which delay I soon learned to call as I was called. Thus, after a good shake: 'Come, fellow, turn out here! Past 12, it's your Watch!'

In my office of cabin boy I found I had a deal to do that I was a perfect stranger to, but into which I was soon initiated by Sam Fulton (I like to be particular in my remembrance of names) who on my coming was raised to the high office of cook.

The cabin was all mahogany, with a brass stove in it used for a fire in cold weather and as an ornament in the summer. My morning's work used to commence in harbour by scrubbing the floor with sand and a small square stone about the size of a quarto volume, then mopping and getting it quite dry. After which, the polishing the said mahogany and stove occupied me till breakfast time, which I set into and had ready by 8 o'clock. When it was over, I washed and put away the tea things, made the pudding for the cabin, gave the cook it, the meat and vegetables, swept up the floor, then worked with the men till time to get dinner, on which, . . . the washing and cleaning [of] the different utensils took me within an hour of tea (which meal was always as substantial as the breakfast and made to embrace also the benefit of a supper). This was the general routine of a duty I soon learned to detest. There was too little of the sailor in it to please me, and that I might the sooner escape from it, I strove hard to make myself useful on deck and to get all the information I could, which, as I had generally some half pence in my pocket and the men often wanted tobacco, I got through its [i.e. the tobacco's] charms.

Chapter 4

THE CONSTANTIA – *AN IRISH TRADER*

An Irish trader is about the size generally of one of the coal vessels that lie at Brighton, Hastings etc., commonly known amongst seafaring people by the name of 'beachers'. The *Constantia* was larger by 70 tons than most of these, had a figurehead and was altogether a smarter craft. We mustered 11 in all, thus, – the Captain, Mate, Captain's son (a sort of Second Mate), a carpenter, one man before the mast, and 6 apprentices – some of them as good as men, and indeed, but for the amount of their wages, the same 6 of us were Friends [Quakers], had received good educations and were (of course, omitting the Captain) very comfortable. Jem Kekwick was the best of the lot and he was the eldest apprentice; he and I soon formed a close intimacy which was never broken. (He is now afloat in command of a schooner trading about the Isle of France.) He gave me two or three hints, which after a time I soon learned to attend to. 'Never,' said Jem, 'lend halfpence; sailors never think of returning less than silver. Never answer till called by your name – "one of you" is everybody's and consequently nobody's. Stop no longer than you can help in the cabin; before the mast is the place to learn to be a British seaman. Attend to these, and you will save your money, labour and credit.'

On first attempting to go aloft I found it rather difficult, but as I saw many eyes were upon me, I determined to let them see as little awkwardness as possible, and here I found the kind of intimacy I had formed at Dover with vessels very useful to me, for tho' I felt strange at first, my observations of the way others acted enabled me soon to acquit myself much better than many, who might not previously have had any knowledge of a ship. In a boat I was perfectly at home and could do my part at any time; from the day I joined the *Constantia* this was a great use to me and was often during my cabin-boy-ship the means of my getting employed at boat work, whilst a less accustomed youngster was put to my duty on board. I may just remark that, at this time, those menial offices were of great use to me, as well as the discipline I was then under. I could before

9

scarcely brook [i.e. tolerate] control, took advice very impatiently and always spoke to anyone just what came uppermost. But I found very soon that, if I wished to get on, I must submit to the rules and regulations of the service I was in, and always pay marked deference to my superiors: this was, for a long time, hard work.

It was a fine afternoon that saw me going, for the first time, out of dock. I cannot describe my feelings, tho' I can fully recollect them – there was a mixture of pleasure and regret, with a great deal of fear, should I not be found fit for the calling I had chosen; however, I looked mostly at the bright side and, glancing at the confinement of Maidstone, I was delighted with the change and determined inwardly to acquit myself as well as I could. My old friend Joe Coventry, then a prentice [apprentice] with Thomas Thompson of Liverpool, came down to see me off and agreed to keep up our correspondence still, tho' farther separated; I shook him heartily by the hand, for he seemed the last link that bound me to old things, and we parted, he for Church Street, and we to lay off the town. As we hauled out, the pilot bestowed some hearty curses upon my unhandiness, to which I should no doubt . . . [have] soon replied, for the old leaven began to work, but Jem was at my elbow, 'Say naught, Ned,' said he, 'remember always the old sea saying "Curses cut no throats, bad words break no bones".' 'Well, but,' said I, 'would our Friend Williams [i.e. the Captain] allow me to be sworn at?' Jem laughed, and so would I have done since, at the simplicity of the question. Oaths, alas, I soon found at sea more plentiful than oakum. On the following day (a first day) [Sunday] after all was cleaned nicely and put to rights, our Captain came off and ordered a lot of us into the boats to fetch some timber alongside, which he had bought on speculation; and a pretty job we had of it, on account of a very strong wind and tide: however, we managed, and were done before dinner. I thought it rather queer in a Friend's [Quaker's] ship to work on Sundays, but soon had for an answer to my enquiries the laconic sea saying, 'There's no Sunday for sailors in 7 fathoms of water', the truth of which was very frequently afterwards exemplified.

In the afternoon the weather was beautiful; the atmosphere was quite clear, the River Mersey, in which we were at anchor, was prettily enlivened with all classes of merchant vessels with their colours flying, the town of Liverpool lay prettily before us like a picture, with its church bells calling the inhabitants to their afternoon devotions, and altogether I seemed to have got into another world . . . Well do I recollect, as I lay upon the skylight looking around me, repeating some lines I had picked up years before from the foot of an old engraving of this extensive port [?], and they seemed very applicable:

Behold the crowded port where rising masts
An endless prospect yield, and echoing docks
Re-echo to the hurrying shouts of seamen bold
Who hearty wave their last adieu,
And loosening every sail resign their spreading
Vessels to the wind.

Sundays in these vessels, when the men cannot go ashore, are generally spent by them in washing their clothes or repairing them in the forenoon, and after dinner in sleeping, reading or recounting the occurrences of bygone days. Sleep is a thing that, to men of such broken habits . . . is a kind of luxury, and one in which they invariably indulge whenever they have an opportunity. In an India ship it is quite curious to see all your men in their nice white, clean clothes lying about in all directions on a Sunday after dinner, and I am sure anyone unacquainted with their habits would imagine they had [had] no rest for a considerable time previous and that their fatigue alone could enable them to sleep so sound – whereas very often, in the tropics, they had been sleeping about the decks all night before. How often I have welcomed the day [Sunday], that I might (in sea language) 'bottle off a few doses of rest'.

We got under way the next day and tacked down the river; I was put to a station and, on asking what I was to do, 'Oh,' said my instructor, 'every time we are turning round, as soon as the pilot calls out, let go and haul; you pull that rope and try all you can to break it.' I acted up to the very letter and pulled with all my strength, which was what was required to turn the sail round in the direction of the wind, the consequences of which were soon apparent upon my hands by the appearance of a couple of good-sized blisters, of which, of course, I said nothing, knowing that use alone would remedy the tenderness of the skin. I was, however, heartily glad when we got out of the river and found the tacking part [was] over, from a fair breeze blowing towards the port we were bound for, Waterford in Ireland.

Oh, what a traveller I appeared to myself about to become, going actually on the way, to the land of which I had heard and read so much! But few are the pleasures of this life that are unalloyed, and over this pleasing dream a veil was soon thrown by a most uncomfortable feeling of my stomach – in fact nothing more nor less than seasickness.

There is in all vessels a smaller or larger quantity of water that the pumps cannot, from a variety of causes, discharge from the hold; this is called bilge water. Now, in an Irish Trader this said bilge water is generally very strong brine, that escapes from the cargoes of provisions brought in them from England; this, after it has laid quiescent in harbour for a considerable time, gets excessively fetid and putrid, so that when the vessel gets again tossed about at sea it emits ... [the] most disgusting, detestable stench that can possibly be conceived.

We had not cleared the mouth of the Mersey long, when I was called below to secure my sea furniture from rolling about, or something of the kind. I hastened to obey, but had scarcely reached the foot of the cabin ladder when the villainous combination of all that was nauseous invaded the olfactory region and almost knocked me down – 'tis years ago but I cannot forget it; the effect may be guessed. I reached the side just in time to save my credit, was saluted by a most intolerable horse laugh and a score of witticisms, tried to rally, could not do it [in] spite of all my exertions, and was obliged to yield to the Captain's directions to go to my crib.

'Get up, get up!' said the Captain's son, 'and eat something, mun, thee'll die there and she's quiet now, hardly any motion at all.' On this I crawled out, my clothes of course on (for I had devoted no time to pulling them off), and found I had been about 18 hours, in being partly awake and partly asleep, in fact half defunct, for my sickness was terrible and, strange to say, continued so as long as I was in the *Constantia*, from the time we started until we reached our port, and ... [mainly] from the detestable bilge water.

When [I was] out the Captain offered me some provender, but I bundled off into the fresh air as quick as possible, for my enemy was still below, tho' means had been used to get rid of it, from the annoyance it gave all on board. On deck all was fresh and beautiful, could I but have enjoyed it, but that was out of my power.

I had been boating about at Dover till I got rid of all approach to sickness, but I could not now do what I would. I went up aloft but it made me worse, I walked the deck but it would do no good, and to add to it I had to answer to such questions as these, 'Well, how do you like the sea? Do you ever mean to leave dry land again if you reach it? Are your accounts rightly settled?' etc., for which I could scarce find a reply.

My heart was right glad when we neared the high land of the coast of Ireland and when the white lighthouse on the Hook Point at Suir rose up out of the waters. I began to find a little appetite and could enjoy in a degree the barren boldness of that part of green Eire's coast. None would judge favourably of its fertility by its shores in this part, for they appear barren in the extreme. The long swell of the ocean here terminates in heavy breakers upon black rocks lying at the base of abruptly ending hills. The few huts that are here and there to be seen are whitewashed without and, [while] forming a little diversification to the coldness of the aspect, look anything but inviting, whilst to the mariner there are also many dangers in the way of rock and sand to be aware of. This is the appearance at the entrance, but uninviting as it was, I welcomed it with joy, and few people could be much merrier than I, when we let go our anchor to wait for the tide opposite the town of Passage – if it will deserve the name of town; certainly in England it would be called a very miserable village.

Just before we entered the river mouth a very pretty little vessel, called there a hooker, put off her small boat, in which was the pilot, and a boy to return with her. As soon as he was on the deck, the genuine Irish brogue in which he accosted the Captain assured me of the fact that I was in the boundaries of Auld Ireland. I will attempt to describe him, as I think he was a fair sample of his class, and I believe they are generally considered . . . effective and deserving [people] . . . He was rather an elderly man with white hair, tall and bony, with all the peculiarities of feature betokening his country; his dress was a thick blue 'dreadnought' flashing jacket and trousers, out of the pocket of the former peeping a 'dudeen' (short [clay] pipe), nearly black and, of course, proportionately valuable [because of its age]. His name was Pat Kelly and he was a great favourite, from his being a clever fellow.

Just before I left the *Constantia* he was drowned, off the wreck of a vessel he had boarded, in the hope of saving her from being lost on a very dangerous part of the entrance to the river. He attempted all that he could, but his efforts were unavailing – he perished, but not unregretted. The master of that vessel (*Martha*) I also remember well, a very respectable man with a wife and family resident at Swansea and dependent upon him. He had been on board the *Constantia* with our Captain only a day or two before. I had rowed him aboard the *Martha* on his leaving, and immediately almost after I was ordered down among the rest of the boat's crew to fetch up his corpse, that had been picked up after the gale that caused the wreck had subsided. We brought his remains on board the *Constantia*, where they were consigned to a coffin and then carried by us to the ground where they were interred. I kept one watch over him and can recollect being well pleased when it expired, for I had not at that time entirely overcome a repugnance that I had imbibed in childhood to the loneliness of a dark night, a churchyard and a variety of other things equally nonsensical – which soon, very soon, wore off when nightly duty led me to be much more acquainted with being alone. It is often proved to me, the culpability of servants terrifying children with tales, the effect of which many can never overcome in after life, tho' so fully convinced of their absurdity. (I long remember Sally Pribble the nursemaid.)

With a rattling breeze we soon ran up into the King's Channel, which is a very deep and dangerous passage on account of some rocks, to avoid one of which (the Golden Rock) a boat had to carry out a thick rope to haul the ship from striking it. It required quickness and quietness, but our skipper set up such a roaring that he frightened everybody about him. It was the first specimen I had heard of his abilities in that way, and if anyone had told me that the gentle, inoffensive man that sat so quietly in the corner of Tokenhouse Yard could have raised such a storm of words and with such astonishing volubility, I do not think that at that time I could have given credit to it, and I often smiled with Jem at the difference between his [the Captain's] voice at a Friend's teatable and aboard the *Constantia*. However, we got clear of the danger, and soon after anchored off the noble quay of Waterford, where many friends came off to see the Captain, to whom in my capacity [as cabin boy] I had the honour of offering, by the Captain's directions, a little biscuit and some whisky and water.

The new cabin boy and all about him soon came upon the carpet; I could hear many remarks made upon my looks, height etc. etc., which I should quite as soon have been spared, but my duty kept me at my post, which at such times was just outside the cabin door in the steerage (as it was termed in that vessel), where I stood, surrounded by many implements of my office, all ready when the call was made from within of 'Boy!' to pop in my head [and say] 'Sir!', for, be it understood, many of the friendly language was merged in the necessity of discipline and subordination.

Irish hospitality soon extended itself to me. I was kindly asked, in spite of my menial situation, (I think the first day) in the kind language of, 'Ha, wilt thee come and dine with us now, on First Day? Well, we'll be glad to see thee, come now!' to show their hearty welcome. Long will it be ere I shall forget the names of Daves, Strangeman, White, Penrose, Ridgeway and a variety more, from whose excessive kindness I never wanted [i.e. lacked] a place to go to, and mix with congenial spirits. I know not how much I owe them; their open doors gave me no occasion ever to risk forming improper acquaintances.

The first thing I did when I got ashore was to run to an old woman's stall and ask for two pennyworth of apples. They were so cheap that I was astonished at the quantity and could hardly believe she had made no mistake till with 'bad luck to her ragged old pocket' or something of the sort (with which the lower Irish are sure to accompany any delay of the kind,) she fumbled out a tenpenny [piece] and a couple of coppers [halfpence] in change, for at that time the English shilling went for thirteen pence. I put my apples in my hat and [was] off again on board, when I fully made up my lost time at sea by satisfying to the full all arrears due . . . [to] my appetite, by bestowing upon the beef and biscuits the most devoted attention, as also some very close embraces upon a pitcher of ale which had been drawn for somebody else but, not being wanted, was appropriated to its legitimate purpose, by him who views all such things as the little pickings of office. And let me say 'tis no such despicable thing to set to at the remnants of the cabin, after working and faring hard for any length of time.

But I must record the allowances per diem per man. We had, then, one pound of meat including bone, as much bread (at sea, biscuit is always [called] bread) at 14 shillings per cwt as we chose to eat, an ounce of butter, one teaspoonful of coffee (to make [either] a pint, or a quart, as we pleased), and 1 oz of sugar. The meat was always salt, except on Sundays, and alternately pork and beef, with at times . . . frequently though not always, potatoes. For drink we had as much water as we pleased to draw up from alongside, but nothing else. For plates each used his biscuit, cutting his meat upon it till it was consumed, the plan being to cut a mouthful of meat and then bite off a portion of the plate; by this means they were fairly equally consumed. Sometimes, when harbour duty was hard, we used to refuse, on being called, to come upon deck till we had more meat, and being always true to one another, the matter was generally adjusted by the Mate fetching some that might be intended for cabin use. It will therefore be no wonder that an occasional windfall [hospitality] of the kind I have described always came very acceptable, and I have rejoiced at a 'visit' as a vulture that sniffs [?] the battle from afar.

I dined one day with Joseph Strangeman at Lummerfield, and a most kind reception I met with; there was nothing like reserve, there was a kind of behaviour that made you feel insensibly at home, and from that time afterwards the doors seemed always open to receive me. How often have I heard the hearty salutation of 'Ha! Edward, welcome to Waterford!' and sat down after what (at that time of my service) seemed an enterprising voyage, and felt myself almost within my own family, enjoying myself to the full. Many a time, when thousands of miles from Old England, have I remembered their generous hospitality, and sighed to think there were none such in the land I was in – still, I must not give the idea that I was out of the way of enjoying myself, for I know not if the pleasure has not been fully as great when I have sat down of an evening under the lofty shrubs in Bengal with my cigar and lived, in fancy as it were, the days over again, that were spent in the society of far-away friends. Anticipation and retrospection often, I think, afford as much pleasure as the reality; at least I found it so, myself.

I had not been long in Waterford, when one evening the Mate directed me to cast loose [the warp] that made a lighter [i.e. a boat] fast to our ship's head. I went out upon the bowsprit to do it, when I lost my hold and overboard I went! The night was very dark and the tide was running under the ship's bottom at a very rapid rate, but I struck out and gained a boat that was attached to [the] stern of a vessel ahead of ours. I had thick clothes on, and on reaching her could do no more than throw one leg over her side, my clothes being so heavy with the water and being tired as well, . . . I found I could not get into her. I called for assistance . . . The Mate (who was walking the deck) hearing me, slid down a rope into the boat and hauled me in, and glad I felt when I got into the old *Constantia* again. This was my first essay at falling overboard, and it is to this day a wonder with me how I escaped. I fell upon our chain cable, that hurt me a little, but prevented my going down deep enough to be swept under the vessel's bottom before I rose to the surface; had I not, I cannot think I should have seen another day. It made me very careful for a long time afterwards to hold as tight as possible, indeed laughably so.

We had an old woman, Nelly we called her, who came with a 'kish' (or basket) at her back filled with greens every morning, and with her we used to play some most mischievous tricks. One of them I paid for, and nearly ever after repented. Our carpenter (Smith) was a very irritable man and therefore laid himself open to us boys in no small degree. She came one morning and, after leaving her quantum in the cookhouse (called 'caboose'), sat down and talked to old Davy, a Welshman and great crony of hers, for some time. Some of the boys took the opportunity and hid the carpenter's chisel under the remainder of her cabbages and, watching when the old lady shouldered it [her basket] to be off, told him she had got one of his tools, on which, he immediately desired her to give over thieving and restore his chisel that she had secreted. Nelly put down her 'kish' in a terrible rage (for I really believe she was honest) and exclaimed, 'Arrah search will ye yourself, ye limb of Satan ye, and do ye think now that I'd steel your tools, bad luck to you!' Smith searched and at the bottom, of course there it was; all burst into a roar of laughter, I among the rest, at her look of utter amazement, for I knew naught of the trick; but my laughter she soon stopped for, stooping down, she picked up the chisel and flung it at me with all her force, the corner cutting thro' my thick canvas trousers and making a deep incision in my thigh, from which the blood soon started out in fine style. When the poor lady saw the mischief she had done, down on her knees she went, and prayed to all the saints in heaven that she might be forgiven. 'Oh!' said she, 'I've kilt him dane, oh Mr Smith, why wid ye bodder Auld Nelly, bad luck to the auld fool that she is?' I stopped not longer but, with a handkerchief tied round tight, bustled off to Mr Dennis on the quay, and got it repaired with Diachlon [i.e. a form of dressing]. It was a mere flesh cut and had only bled profusely, but it was very well it had not been worse, which it would have been incalculably, had it gone to the right of the place and divided the artery. Poor old soul, many there are more refined, but few better hearted, I believe, than old Nelly. Every morning, as long as I laid there, she was constant in enquiring after my cut with her usual expression, 'Bad luck to me, but I'm an ould fool sure!'

On Sundays in the *Constantia* one always had to stop aboard as ship keeper; the price of a substitute was 6d, which I for one was always very glad to pay, for the relief of the job. In the afternoon all six, or at least five of us, used to meet in the Meeting [House] yard and, as soon as the Captain had passed by us, off we marched for a walk, taking especial care to be back in good time to pass muster [inspection]; after it [the walking] broke up, when friends used to ask one and the other to come to tea, some never went, but I always spent that evening ashore . . . glad of the opportunity and taking care, if I had the first watch from 8 to 10, to exchange with anyone who had the 2nd, so that I could make a long evening of it. About 10, Billy (as we called the Captain) generally came aboard, when he used often to walk to the forehatchway and begin calling [for] James Kekwick, which generally woke all – when we would, by mutual understanding 'snore' desperately loud [for] a bit. Edward Bath [gave] no answer but snoring. 'Ah!' he'd sigh, 'William Curtis, what, none aboard, eh?' 'Edward Beck, and he [it] is, too, who's got the watch.' Here the apprentice [Beck] would jump forward at once (from where he had seen and heard him all the time), and answer 'Sir!' 'Oh, it's thee . . . that has the watch – where's all the boys?' 'All aboard, sir!' 'Hum! That they can't be, I've been calling all of them, go and see!' As soon as he came to the hatchway and called over the names there was an unanimous answer at once and a, 'What do you want, eh? Who's to keep his watch if he can't sleep when he is below?' generally followed by a roar of laughter from us all, on which the old man, no doubt wishing us further [i.e. in hell], would get a light and go to his own bed. I really think we were a great trouble to him, much more so than all his money; there was no end to our nonsensical tricks upon either him or the Mate, who used to swear at us in Welsh, a language [neither] the Captain nor us . . . understood. He used to threaten to be worse than a seventh plague to us, but in the main he was a good fellow, but very double-faced, first 'pumping' us and then telling the result; to the Captain, knowing this, we took our measures accordingly.

The second time the vessel came to Waterford, three of us took it in turn, week and week apiece, to cook, and all wanted to be clear of it, so we agreed to run a race for it by running to the masthead, and the 2 that beat the one, he was to take the office entirely. At this [Edward] Bath and I rejoiced, being the lightest weight (Curtis was a heavy built, overgrown chap), and run for it we did. Bath was best man, I second, and poor Curtis last – consequently got the berth. But what did he do but, after all our labour, turn round upon us and say he'd a mind to try us, but he was sure he would not cook! This floored us completely: 'twas Bath's turn, he would not boil the pot. I would not, for a double reason, that it was not my turn and that Curtis had lost, and Curtis he would not and, on being threatened with 'cobbing' (a punishment I shall describe), clenched a fist like a leg of mutton and bid all the ship defiance. This latter argument there was no resisting but in a body; so we seized him and punished him, thus. We pulled his hands through two holes of the windlass and then tied them together, securing his legs as well. The oldest man then cried to the collected ship's crew,

All manner of men
Under three score and ten
That doesn't come to this cobbing
Match, we'll cob them!
A sheep's a sheep, an ox is an ox,
Which will you have, a pluck or a box?

As he would give no answer, we took the carpenter's saw and each gave him, with the flat of it, five whacks on the back, and then cut him loose. This made bad worse, he would not cook and there was a regular rumpus; the fire was out, the meat uncooked and each went to his pocket for his [cold] dinner. After a bit, Captain Moyse came aboard and ended the rumpus by shipping another boy for the express purpose of cooking, tho' not without a threat of returning us all upon our friends. Thus ended two of the most undesirable offices I ever held, in which I learned tho' to cook a beef steak, make 'lobscouse', a pudding, and to take special good care of myself, and many a time have I required my acquirements since that time.

I do not pretend to put anything these pages may contain in chronological [order] . . . they will be reminiscences and, as they occur to me, so will they be committed to paper. When the first cargo was out of the vessel that we took to Ireland, we got the satisfactory intelligence that we were to take an Irish band [crowd] to Bristol river, alias a freight of pigs; and [in] a short time we confirmed it, for as soon as the sufficient quantity of ballast was put on board, then [?] 380 of the first-rate porkers were brought alongside, to our great dissatisfaction. We soon hoisted them in (by hooking a rope round just behind their forelegs and walking them up to the yardarm) then, pushing them over the hatchway, lowered them into the hold, where they were regaled with potatoes, whilst in return they regaled us with their music. Three or four men came on board to conduct them to Bristol, after taking care of them [on board]: one of them was the master spirit of the pig-pokers, the rest your everyday gentlemen that are to be found at their task [?] upon the different routes they take towards the metropolis. They had not been long aboard before the stench became intolerable, whilst, from their rubbing together, a white dust flew continually up the hatchway, and yet the chaps that had charge of them lived constantly among them; that is, however, just raised a little above them. I, for one, was heartily glad when we started, and gratified no little by having a fair wind to waft us speedily towards our destination. On the passage [some] lads managed to get some whisky out of the Paddies, who were desperately seasick, by pretending they must either come up and pump for their lives, or send a drop of the . . . [whisky] up to those who did it for them; the latter they preferred, and the rogues exalted no little in the success of their scheme, drinking their health accompanied by shouts of laughter. The Captain's daughter was on board at the time and desperately sick; I was better than she, tho' I was bad enough; still, I was able to attend upon her as she lay in bed, tho' it was as much as even [?] my gallantry would enable me to do. When we got into Bristol river we soon began to land the pigs; we hustled them up and put them into a flat-bottomed boat managed by a wooden-legged man who, when he got them to the bank side, which was very steep (this was a place called Pill), screwed their tails till they leaped out into the mud, out of which they scrambled to the place where their conductors were collecting them together. When any [pig] would not scramble through, they were obliged to wade up to him and drive him out, which occasioned sometimes much fun, as it made the men in such a desperately muddy condition. As soon as we had got them all out and the Captain had received his freightage, we weighed anchor and proceeded over to Swansea to go into dock for repairs, as the old brig showed some dropsical symptoms. The entrance into Swansea Bay was very delightful, heightened by the beauty of the weather, and from being pretty free from seasickness I enjoyed it very much. I well can recollect that day the pretty ballad:

> For England when with favouring gale
> Our gallant ship up channel steered.

About this time, the poetical talent of some tar of the 'barky' [barque] (common appellation of the ship we sailed in) was put forth to, at that time, the tune of the coronation song that was in every boy's mouth:

> Against the quarter rails
> The noisy captain stands
> Attention to the sails
> And to his loud commands
> And hark he loudly speaks
> And every tongue is mute
> 'Turn up the hands on deck
> And put the ship about!'
> Too, ral, loore, loo.

> Turned up each takes his place
> With many wry grimace
> And with a sleepy face
> Claps on the leeward brace
> 'Main top sail quickly haul!'

Are the commanding words
But strongly as we pull
We cannot fill the yards.
    Too, ral, loore, loo.

The sails lie flat aback
The seas they overwhelm
Whilst on the selfsame tack
She keeps against her helm
'For shame, for shame you boys'
He cries with hideous faces
'What sail with Captain Moyse
And cannot work the braces!'
    Too, ral, loore, loo.

'Another crew I'm sure
Must quickly fill your stations
This work I'll ne'er endure
I must stop half your rations!'
But this he need not tell
We heed not such lee lurches
We all know very well
There's more ships than parish churches!
    Too, ral, loore, loo.

Of a dark night we used to sing it quite loud; as soon as he [the Captain] heard it, there would be a call of, 'Less noise, boys, thee Edward Bath or Beck, be still, will thee! James Kekwick, it's very curious there's so much noise there forward, one would think we were a floating public house!'

I was delighted with Swansea, 'tis a beautiful place in my recollection, and one I should like to see again. It was something very agreeable to me to be there; within a short distance, I could take such very interesting walks. Often, after the day's work has been over, I have started off upon liberty and extended my excursion till it has been quite late. One favourite spot of mine was to the Jews' burying ground, from which there was a most extensive view all over the bay, which has often been considered similar to that of Naples. Sitting there, how used I to long to extend my trip to a farther land, tho' at the same time I would have given anything to have been able to get an hour or two at home with those I loved. In these lovely walks, with a book for my companion, I used to shake off much rubbish which would otherwise have clung to me from my associations of the day, and return with fresh resolves to gain all information I could and as quick as I could, that I might the sooner merge into a more congenial sphere; but that I wanted [lacked]. I wanted to become [?] a good practical seaman.

The first time I went into the market I was very much amused with the Welsh girls in their hats, as they were just as much at me; indeed I could not tell what there was in me particular[ly] to smile at, till I was asked, if I always wore my shirt outside? The thing was, I had on a blue striped frock [smock], made very much like a shirt and a novel article of dress in that part of the country, where the sailors wear nothing of the kind; as I found I was an object of so much notice, I afterwards left it off when I went ashore. Here we went into dock, and rare work we boys had; all the seams of the brig's bottom were caulked (filled with oakum) and then rubbed over with hot pitch, which, when cold, we had to scrape off level with the wood; now, as the way to get at it comfortably was to sit on something low and to scrape above us, it may be guessed pretty well the mess we were in. To prevent it sticking, we used to grease all over our face and hands and the hair, where uncovered by the cap . . . at night purified by a good wash with soap. This was a work of some labour, and glad we were when the job was completed.

Richard Philips, now the minister at Wandsworth, then lived at Swansea and was a great favourite of ours. One day they (some other Friends [Quakers] as well as himself) sent us down near[ly] a barrow load of fruit pies, things to which we were but little accustomed, but which vanished like smoke before such a set of hardworking fellows as we were. I cannot just recollect what was the occasion, but I think there was some reason for this present of creature comforts, some marriage, Monthly Meeting or something of the kind; however, they came very welcomely, though we did not fail to blame their folly in not adding a bottle of wine to them. This was soon remedied; we made a collection and adjourned to the little parlour of the 'Welcome to Town' (a house of refreshment in our neighbourhood), and there discussed some, in which we did not fail to remember our Friends of the pies. 'Tis strange to look back on those days, it almost seems to me a dream: since then, where has not my lot been cast and under what circumstances, and all in the same line of life.

Whilst we lay at Swansea I got leave of absence for a few days, which I spent very agreeably at Bevington Gibbons's at Neath, and very much delighted I was with the scenery about that part. One thing particularly pleased me, the pretty appearance of a churchyard in the neighbourhood; each mound was cultivated and planted with small shrubs and flowers, if I recollect right, and kept as tidy as any garden could be. I cannot recollect the name of the village, but it was some[thing]-ferry. The view from the high ground about it was very extensive and grand; the particular points of its interest have faded away in the lapse of the few years since I was there, and mingled into a recollection of its general beauty. I should like to tread that ground over again, whose charms were all enhanced in their value by the kindness of my host who, when my liberty was expired, mounted me upon a horse and saw me part of the way on my return, which [was] safely accomplished, tho' I well recollect being nearly over my nag's head several times from his stumbling and my awkwardness.

Old Davy (the only seaman aboard) got into a most unfortunate affair while here, that caused us much fun. A matronly-looking person one day enquired after him and, on meeting, began upbraiding him in the most unqualified terms with being a most unfaithful fellow, calling him double-faced etc. etc., concludingly saying she was almost broken-hearted, all of which seemed to trouble Davy very little. When she was gone we found it was an 'old flame' of his to whom he had said many tender things, had often written by proxy to,[2] and in fact promised marriage, whenever he might reach Wales. But in London he had met with another, a widow, who seemed to him quite as suitable, and as there seemed no prospect of his then visiting Wales for a considerable time and he sighed for the married state, he buried in oblivion the fair maid of his native land and took unto himself 'the Dutchman's relict' [widow], with whom he received the whole wardrobe of him whose place he then took, which, when altered by her to the size of her new spouse, fitted the old man very well. The disappointed one made matters up before we sailed, but she could never forgive the scribe, who could be a party to so much business as she thought he had lent himself to. This was no other than Jem Kekwick, who had found fine fun in writing things as tender as he was tough, and in reading the ridiculous replies she sent, but who, so far from countenancing his unfaithfulness, had remonstrated most strongly against it.

Davy was proof to me of what a sailor may be with a good, careful wife. She was industrious and earned a living by washing for some Friends' families, and on his part [Davy] became saving of his wages, which he carried home to her. Whenever he left London his clothes were always in perfect repair, and in his bag was sure to be some addition to his comfort for a cold night. His evenings, that before had been spent, I was told, at the public house, were always, from the time I knew him, devoted to his wife. He was one that had seen much service, been in several actions, and in all classes of ship; in fact on all nautical matters a complete oracle, and all subjects of dispute amongst us were always referred to old Davy.

Before we left Swansea, rather late one evening when we were loaded with coals for Waterford quite deeply, our head ropes broke and we swung across the

---

[2] Evidently Davy was illiterate.

river, one end of the vessel lying very awkwardly pointed across, instead of facing, a strong ebb tide that was running down, considerably swollen by some heavy rain; it had fallen a day or two previously. She laid so, for some hours, in a position that subjected her to a very great strain, and to it we attributed all the misfortunes that befell us on the following passage.

The next day we went to sea, and the most lovely day it was, in the middle of summer; the bay of Swansea never showed to more perfection, I am satisfied, than it did then. The breeze was very light and we had orders from the Captain to go into the Mumbles and anchor . . . opposite to a pretty village upon the shore – about, I think, three miles from the harbour where, after he had settled his business, he would join us. When all necessary sail was set, old Robin the Mate said, 'Come, we will pump her out', a most unintelligible phrase to any but a seaman, but implying we were to pump the water out of the well of the ship – now this well is a part adapted for the reception of the pumps and so contrived that all water that leaks into a vessel shall find its way there – accordingly one pump was set in motion. When no prospect was appearing of that doing the business effectively, the well was sounded and a depth of four feet in her, which so alarmed Robin that he immediately had an apparatus rigged that worked by a wheel the 2 pumps at once, and sent ashore to acquaint the Captain of it. It was a long time before we got the pumps to suck, a term applied to the water being exhausted that supplied them; but we found we could not leave them, and therefore took our turns all round at keeping her free. In the afternoon the Captain came aboard and he and the mate had a deal of talk . . . the results of which conference [were] only known to us by the order, as the wind was fair, to heave up the anchor and be off, which was accordingly done, and we left the Mumbles – as beautiful a moonlight evening as we could ever have been sent, to match so fine a preceding day.

It fell rather light airs after we got a little distance off the land, and as there was a pretty large fleet of us about, we got foul two or three times (tho' without sustaining or doing any damage), indeed we must have gone back if we had received any, for our leak afforded the watch full employment without anything else and, judging from my experience . . . , I have no hesitation in saying that, had we met with a moderate gale of wind only, that would have distracted our attention from the pumps to the sails, that the ship would have foundered, and we must have left her for our chance in the boats. The Captain had the kegs all filled with water and put into the launch, and similar precautions as to provisions in case we needed them, which fortunately we did not. The night before we reached our port we fell in with the *Martha* of Bideford, who asked if we wanted any assistance, offering us a hand or two; this the Captain declined by asking him to keep company with us, as he was also bound for Waterford, which he said he should do; unfortunately for us, his idea was that we were steering too northerly a course, and [he] persuaded our master to alter his to lee. That led us about 30 miles to leeward of the harbour, down in fact to Goughall Bay or near it, so that instead of getting in about 8 in the morning we did not [reach our destination] till about 11 or 12 at night, having the terrible addition to pumping of constantly tacking ship, to beat up to windward all our lost ground. This was vexatious enough and set all of us in a very poor humour, so that we agreed among ourselves that, as we had brought the old leaky ship so far by dint of main pumping and hard work, on our arrival we would let the Captain find who he could to pump. With this understanding, we anchored in the river Suir, and glad we were to get to bed, where we had not been long before I heard my name called by the Captain pretty lustily, and on answering, he asked me, why I did not come up to the pumps? 'Oh,' said I, as it had been previously agreed upon, 'I've pumped all the way here and I am too tired to have any more of it,' thinking for sure all the rest were in bed, which error he soon dispelled by saying, 'For shame of thee!' (his usual expression), 'Here's all the rest of us up, and why can't thee? When I was a young man like thee, I should have been ashamed to have said I was too tired!' Up I jumped directly, stung to the very quick, told him I could do as much as any of them, and let him into the whole secret of the previous agreement. On asking my shipmate Jem Kekwick how it was they had run from their words, 'Oh,' said he, 'Old Davy [who] first put us up to it was the first to go and tell old Billy that we would not turn out, when the pilot's people who kept her afloat a few hours left the ship.' This taught me a lesson and I never after entered into any confederacy of the kind again. As it was, I must have been most desperately sleepy, for I never heard the call nor knew they were up, till the Captain first roused me from my short (but most delightful) nap. We had no men hired and whenever the rest grumbled, which they often did, I laughed at them and told them it served them all right, tho' for my own part I wished most heartily she would go to the bottom – which, if her pumps had stood but a few hours still, she would very soon have done.

When we got up to Waterford and were moored at our berth at the quay, I received a very kind invitation from David Malcolmson Clonmell to accompany his daughters home in his carriage, as he intended to go home by the regular conveyance next day. Captain Moyse gave me leave of absence and I did not want any pressing, but very joyfully took my seat between his two kind daughters, where (alas for my gallantry!) I fell asleep, and that as sound as a top – indeed, so far rude was I, that I afterwards understood I snored and talked as if I was on board the *Constantia*. About halfway to Clonmell they woke me, on account of one of the horses shying and becoming restive on the road, when I thanked them most kindly for their care in putting a handkerchief over my head, and begged a many pardons for my sad want of manners, which they freely granted when I told them of our slavish voyage and recounted all of our hairbreadth escapes from foundering, which at that time of my seafaring life seemed so many marvels. On hearing all this they wanted me to sleep again, but that I could not do, and it will be long before I can forget the kindness they showed the wearied sailor boy.

How much I wish I could recollect clearly all that passed in the week I very happily spent in the family, but I cannot do it. I have the vague impression of unbounded hospitality, very kind and companionable young men (of the females I need say no more), a large mansion-like house, very extensive and elegant grounds, plenty of horses and the like accompaniments to wealth, but beyond these, I have lost what I should gladly now relive. When it is considered that at this time I was moving in an entirely new sphere of life, in which almost everything that met my attention was of a different character to what I had hitherto been accustomed, I think it will not appear strange that my memory retains but very imperfect images, and perhaps erroneous ones, of what in a latter day, stripped of the veil of novelty that was then thrown over everything, I should see and remember most clearly. I returned, however, to my ship with great regret, an enthusiastic admirer of Irish character as well as of the Malcolmson family. I returned on an Irish jaunting car,[3] both distance and fare I forget, tho' I do not [forget] an accident that befell a good woman that was one of my fellow travellers to Waterford. As we came over a rather rough piece of ground, the car travelling pretty close to a dry ditch, she was completely jerked off her seat into it, and left behind some few yards . . . [before] the driver pulled up to readjust her in her proper situation. (A [jaunting] car, then drawn by one horse, carries its passengers back to back with their feet upon a board, a little similar to a long coach bow[4] that would hold three).

About this time we made a voyage to London, but I must first dispose of the leak! When the ship had been some days at Waterford, the mud got into . . . [the pump] and stopped it, which is very frequently the case; after this took place, when the vessel was lightened, it [the leak] was believed to be in the upper works, and therefore they were caulked and she was considered afterwards 'as tight as a bottle', but we found our mistake most woefully, one morning on taking off the hatches. We found at 3 heights loads of flour that we had taken in for the great city – one of them was completely under water. We immediately commenced a vigorous search and soon found the water rushing in at the junction of two planks in her bottom, which the shipwright had left open at Swansea and

---

[3] A jaunting car was a light, two-wheeled horse-drawn vehicle used in Ireland in the nineteenth century.

[4] Presumably a bench for passengers situated on the top of a coach.

which had occasioned us much pumping. We immediately saw the ship ashore at the building yard and had it properly secured, and fortunate we thought it that a rapid tide had washed out the mud in time to prevent a repetition of our labours at sea, and then went to sea, proved it still more satisfactory, for we had [as] rough [a] passage up the English channel as ever poor weather-beaten rogues need desire. Then, through neglect, a great expense was gone to that ought not to have been incurred, part of our cargo damaged, and ourselves pestered with hydraulics: and all through the shipwright's carelessness.

Now for the continuation of the London story. We lay wind bound a long time at Passage [the little port in Ireland] in the 11th or 12th month, [the wind] blowing very hard gales from the S.E., which sent into the anchorage a pretty good earnest [i.e. promise] of the sea outside, in the shape of a long, heavy swell. One afternoon, . . . a number of the captains of other vessels similarly circumstanced to ourselves were on board [when] . . . the wind shifted round and no time was lost in getting our boat alongside to put them aboard their own ships, for all were anxious to be off. As we went to the first vessel with her captain, he said 'Go close past her and do not stop, for I can jump onto the side ladder,' which he soon attempted – but as he could but hit or miss, he did the latter, overboard he went, soused, but, with the exception of a good cold bath and a little additional water to the grog he had drunk, he escaped unhurt. As soon as they were all at their respective ships we rowed the boat back and found our good brig with her anchor nearly up, which job [of raising the anchor] over, we stood down towards the entrance of the harbour, first and foremost of the fleet. It fell dark before we reached as far as the lighthouse, and the breeze freshened very fast, the ship pitching very heavily against the strong rolling swell that had arisen with the former wind, and soon the order was given to furl the top gallant[5] sail[s]. I went up, for one, to furl the fore one, and well do I recollect it, I was so seasick that I scarce seemed to care two straws whether I fell overboard or not, but the love of life always stuck to me, and I accomplished my job, glad enough to descend again. I think this was the first time I had noticed the particularly brilliant appearance which the sea at times wears, and which, contrasted with the dark sky above (a contrast the more striking as seen from the masthead of a ship) is certainly a very splendid sight. Often since, when I had got over the terrible seasickness (for terrible it was) that stuck to me in my first onset, have I stopped aloft to look about me. It is a display of Nature's that I am quite sure no description can possibly convey an accurate idea of, it must be seen to be understood.

The furling [of] the top gallant sail knocked me completely up for appetite, and ill prepared me for the coming 'noser' in the Channel, where we soon arrived,

---

[5] The top gallants were the sails immediately above the topmast and topsail.

in time for the foul wind. I think we placed the brig under double-reefed topsails and kept tacking and tacking incessantly for ten days and nights, on one of which latter we were nearly run down by an East Indiaman, who was sailing in stately order before the breeze. It was very dark and rained very heavily, and cold; the watch was just relieved, and we had got below, when there was a loud cry of 'Jump up here on deck, everybody!' Up we jumped in an instant, and saw, to our great delight, our escape from a watery grave. Fancy a little vessel of 217 tons, loaded so deeply that in the smoothest river we could dip a pail of water from alongside, and then imagine a noble, large ship of 1,400 tons, with high and lofty sails, moving majestically, like a huge castle, over the waves, and some idea may be formed of our situation . . . she passed so close to us that we distinctly heard the order to move the helm in the direction that arrested her striking us, which, if she had done ever so slightly, must have sent the *Constantia* instantly to the bottom. As she moved along down channel, we could but make the comparison between her and ourselves which served for a topic of conversation, at which the mate fetched us a glass of whisky apiece, to warm us before we went below again.

Let me here try to give a picture of what a poor seaman endures in the winter months in one of these coasting vessels, for the *Constantia*, I consider, at the time I am alluding to, was a fair specimen. Our beds were all below, at the fore end of the vessel, and the communication to them was down a hole or 'hatchway' as it is called, which at these times is always covered with a weather – and waterproof tarpaulin – for the sea, constantly in a fresh breeze, and much more in half a gale of wind, seas break right over it, preventing any communication with the 'forecastle', as the seamen's berths are termed. The consequence is that, as long as the weather keeps bad, he [the apprentice] has no alternative but that of keeping on his wet clothes and lying down to sleep in them on an old sail that is generally spread out upon the cables or, at extraordinary times, on the cabin floor. The difference of temperature between the air and these confined places is very great, and when called from a broken 4 hours nap on the rough bed that has afforded no repose to the aching bones, to take the watch upon the deck, the feeling is the most miserable one of the kind that I know. The half-warm state gives place to intense shivering – which is never better relieved, . . . [unlikely] as it may appear, than by a sousing spray, wetting you through at once to the skin! At these times, no fire [which] will cook for the ship's company can be kept in, the consequence of which, naturally, is that when poor Jack [Tar] needs it most, he has the least comfort . . . a biscuit and a bit of cheese after the last cold meat is gone, is generally his fare, and he thinks he does well if he can get a little hot tea or coffee, of a quality I do not hesitate to say is most wretched (on shore you would refuse); often, I'm sure, I have jumped at the offer of half a pot of this wretched extraction, for at that time I fared in every respect as the poorest lad in the fleet . . . for which I have never repented. He that has had the deprivations I have done, will always know how to value a good bed and board – a thing one half, nay, . . . one hundredth part, of the youngsters brought up in the East India and foreign trades (that is, general tropics trades), do not know. It may be asked, . . . if this is the case, how is it that men go to sea? Each one can answer it by their own experiences, for few there [be], I imagine, who do not often overcome troubles that they intend shall be the last, and yet afterwards look back upon them without any kind of disgust or dread of their recurring again. It is so with seamen; the present gale is always the hardest, and few of the boys, I believe, that ever went to sea . . . have not resolved [that], on their reaching terra firma, they would bid it adieu – and yet they reach home, but still are ready again for another voyage, and that resolve grows weaker and weaker, till it dies away and they become, in the full sense of the word, seamen. It is then their business, they are beings of a particular class, out of their element when on shore and full of conceit of their own vocation, designating all landsmen by the sweeping terms of 'lubbers' and 'land sharks', and looking with ineffable contempt upon those who, to use their own expression, 'never went out of the smoke of their mothers' chimneys'.

After this long digression, I must resume this twice dropped narrative of our London voyage. We kept at it, beating against the adverse winds, Captain saying, 'If we could only get up to the Isle of Wight, he would go into Spithead and lay for a fair wind,' and much we longed for it, for not one of us that was there (from the Captain to the cook), that was not tired of it. At last we got into sight of the Needles when, tired of it, and the gales still continuing harder than ever, we put the ship before the wind, intending to go into some harbour to the westward. After running over the ground we had worked so hard to obtain, what did he do but say other vessels were at sea and we should keep there too, and to it we went again, hauling to the windward of the Bill of Portland. However, when we had been before the wind we did not neglect to get some dry things on, and the pot boiling – which was soon laid aside, and our clothes as soon wet through, when we again attempted to beat to windward. The brig sailed remarkably well and was very sharp forward, so that when she dived into a sea she would fling the water completely on the gangway; it was therefore quite useless to think of keeping clothes dry. At length the winds, as if tired of persecuting us, shifted off the land, and we soon ran up into the Downs, which we passed through, and anchored in Margate Roads pretty late in the evening. It may easily be imagined how very active we were, after such a bashing, to make up lost time by paying most devoted attention to the eatables that were to be procured – of which, from long abstinence, we had abundance to cook. When each had made a hearty meal, we spread a lot of dry sails out in the steerage and went to sleep [there]; our beds being all wet through, we could not go to them. In the morning, when we were just under way, what was our mortification, to see our [former] companions all on the Road[s] with us! They had been lying comfortably in Falmouth all the time we had been knocking about and, taking advantage of the wind that blew fair lower down Channel than we were, . . . they had slipped through the Downs while we were at anchor, and so were just as far forward as we were. This mortified the Captain very much, but made us laugh heartily about it.

When I got to London I had been away about 15 months, and very glad I was to get home again for a few days. In the time I had been . . . [away], from a deal of it being spent in Ireland, I had acquired quite an Irish accent, so that on my leaving the room at Token House Yard for a short time, a friend that was there, who had known me very well before I went to sea, asked 'Who is that young Irishman?' and was quite amused to make a renewal of acquaintance with one he had taken for a native of the green island.

At this time I began to get tired of the *Constantia*; we were too little at sea, and too much in harbour, and I longed for more active employment. I communicated my views to my friends, and they arranged with Billy [the Captain] that I might leave next time I came to London; in the meanwhile they were to look out for a more congenial berth for me. With this agreement we sailed, after being frozen up in London river for some time. Our day's work was exacted, of picking oakum,[6] after which we might go ashore, some to slide and amuse themselves on Tower Ditch, I to my friends the Coventrys, for at that time I spent 4 evenings a week there; the rest I was generally at Token House Yard or on board the ship. We had as blistering a passage down Channel as we had up, in which we split our sails but were much more comfortable, from her being lightly loaded. Off Dungeness we broke the rope that is put to strengthen the edge of the mainsail, and whilst one of the men [was] gone to get some large twine to sew it on with, I was told to prepare a 'stopper', as it is called, that is, a short piece of rope, to be attached at either end above and below the part broken at the edge of the sail, and thereby taking the strain the broken part had given up. The particular knot I had to make was called a Matthew Walker, and I unfortunately made it wrong at one end, so that when the strain came upon it in a squall, the knot slipped. Of course the assistance to the sail's edge was gone, and the mainsail split right across, to the great mortification [of] Paul Garlick. We immediately unbent the sail and went into the anchorage to repair it, but I

---

[6] Oakum was the loose fibre obtained by picking old ropes to pieces. Afterwards, it was used for caulking.

never lost the credit of it, all the time I belonged to the brig, for if anything miscarried it was sure to be 'like Ned Beck's Matthew Walker', or was the knot to be made, there was a call for me of, 'Here, I say, Ned, we want a Matthew Walker!' till I wished him and his knot to Jericho, or further.

In running round the Land's End this passage down Channel, the wind was so scant we could hardly lay our course, and to make the best of it and not to lose ground, we passed close to the Longships rocks, that stand out some little distance from the land. On these rocks there is a magnificent light shown from a high tower erected upon them, and so close did we go that the light appeared almost over our heads. It was a grand sight; it was pitch dark with the rain and severe gusts of wind which, roaring through the riggings accompanied by the noise of the breakers on the rocks, made the great, broad, bright light above us have a most interesting effect, and we all blessed the good souls that invented and placed there so welcome a beacon for the poor mariners. Well indeed do they deserve blessing.

We slipped across the Irish Channel very comfortably and were soon again in the land of 'praties' [Irish for 'potatoes'], or rather, I should say, the mud, for our good Captain, in piloting us into the anchorage (as we could see nothing of the pilot boat), stuck us ashore on a mud bank, and a rare job we had to get off. After we got up to Waterford I and a boat crew (of which, by the bye, I was only one, not in charge of her, as the said 'I' might imply), was sent to try and get our anchor and ropes that we had left behind us. In going down there [were] a number of weirs, a kind of trap to catch salmon in on the falling tide that projected considerably far from the banks, and we were afraid, as it was quite dark, of running foul of them. 'Oh,' said I, 'Let me steer, I would be bound to keep you clear of them,' to which confident tone the rest acceded, and I took the helm. After this, rowing cautiously as before, they in full confidence of my abilities pulled quite strongly and, to my unspeakable mortification at the time (I was thinking how clever I was), steered the boat into the stakes of a very large one, and nearly upset her – indeed, how we got clear without a somersault I cannot tell, but we did, and we adopted more precaution till we got down to Buttermilk Castle, where the light at Ballyack can be seen . . . by which we soon found our way down to Passage, where we were glad to find a boat with the anchor and ropes all ready for us, as they had weighed the former at a venture. We all went therefore ashore to Mrs Phelan's, to whom I at this time owed 2d [i.e. twopence] for a glass of whisky and water, unless a person paid her to whom I delivered it with interest to do so, tho' I doubt he could never find it convenient.

After we had got some refreshment we went to the custom house officers, who occupied part of a large house inhabited by many families, where we found on the second floor a whole troop of young girls, full of chat and fun as the Irish always are, but they played us . . . most roguish tricks for a while. Some kept chatting over the banisters, another . . . slipped off and fetched a tea kettle full of hot water, with which she saluted us, to the infinite amusement of the rest of them; it was enough for us, we got the custom house officers' clothes which we were commissioned to fetch, and off we started with the flood tide, which had then just begun to make up river.

The way that I got into Mrs Phelan's debt is worth recording, as an act of kindness on the part of a poor Irish woman to an apparently very poor lad. One very cold winter's night I had been left ashore to look after some things the Captain had bought and which the boat was to fetch off to the ship with myself. I had on no jacket, it rained, no boat came and I stood for shelter under a leaky kind of projection over the doorway of the miserable pot house, that called Mrs Phelan 'hostess'. I had not a sliver in my pocket, or I would have purchased a shelter within and a little warmth at a peat turf fire that was smoking there. [While I was] in this plight she came to the door and, seeing me, asked why I did not walk in, and if I would not take anything? I told her I had no money about me, making sure mine hostess of the Dolphin would at that intimation . . . soon retreat, but I was mistaken – she made me some hot whisky and water, saying, 'Oh faith I'll be seeing ye again, and if not, where's the odds of a drop o' whisky?' I know not how I left unpaid this voyage the said two pence, that has escaped my memory, tho' the kind action has not, for the kindness lay far less in the offering than it did in the hospitality of the thing, and I wish she may have been repaid. We must have sailed that night, or something of the kind prevented my discharging the account, and I have never seen Passage and its pigstyes since. I entrusted the commission to one that, as I have said before, I imagine would not take much trouble to clear his conscience of the load I had laid upon it.

It was very late when we got to Waterford (a distance of 20 miles, I think, from where we started) and worst of all, when we did, we found empty platters, at which we all turned into bed in no very good humour. About this time, I had a letter from my uncle, telling me another ship and Captain was found for me to join as soon as I came to London. This made me regret greatly our going to Liverpool first, which we were freighted to do; however, as there was no alternative I soon let that cease to trouble me, and to Liverpool we went, with a freight of corn. Nothing happened out of the usual routine of an old coaster, tho' we had a very stiff breeze as we approached the entrance of the Mersey, which we did in the middle of the night. When reefing the fore topsail I remember being very much struck with the beautiful floating lights that lay off the sands to point out to ships their proximity to danger, an invention for which the late Henry Taylor of Shields well deserved the pension he received from the Trinity House, and for which the mariner has often gratefully repeated his name. How often have I done it when beating about in the North sea of a cold winter's night, that have so many dark hours in them; he was indeed right when he said he should ever have a seaman's blessing for that admirable contrivance.

We got into dock in the morning, and soon began to unload our cargo – which, thanks to the good magistrates of Liverpool, I shall long recollect, for they managed to get out of me twenty-five shillings more than they ever deserved. I have before observed the kind of watch that has to be kept in Liverpool docks. In addition to the necessary one for the tides, there must also be one if there are combustibles on deck. Now to raise the corn off the bottom of the vessel we had taken in at Waterford a great deal of furze (which was put beneath) to prevent any water seepage, as the vessel was still leaky, from getting to the corn and damaging it. As the corn was got out … the furze was in the way and a quantity was taken up on deck, where it was placed till we could get rid of it. Not dreaming of this wet stuff coming under the head[ing] of combustibles, I left the deck in my watch for something – [to] which the watchman, seeing on shore, called a witness and then informed me I should be fined for it; I argued the point a long while to no purpose, and made up my mind for it.

Court day came, and no summons, and I thought I had escaped, but another came, and a man in gold lace yclept [i.e. called] the 'beadle of the court' presented the Captain with an order to appear, and answer the charge of having combustibles on the deck and no watch; he handed it over to me, and to court I went, prepared to try my strength with men armed with a little brief authority; alas, I might as well [have] thrown my words into the dock, for I found afterwards these fines went to the maintenance of sundry dinners upon dock business, something of the kind of a wine feast. After a number of cases were disposed of, the Captain of the *Constantia* was called to answer the aforesaid charge, and when I said I appeared for him, being, if any, the guilty person, immediately a watchman jumped up onto the witness box [and] swore to the particulars I described. He was replaced by his partner, who corroborated his statement, and I was called on for my defence. I pleaded hard that the furze was not inflammable, it was too wet etc. etc., [a] thousand other things, till at last the pursy old presiding magistrate, or whatever he was, growing impatient, exclaimed, 'Bless me, if we do not look after these things we shall have the town burnt about our ears!' On this I told him, 'They had better turn out all the ships at once, for everything about them was inflammable.' He bid me speak respectfully, or he would confine me in the cage or prison that was underneath the court. I told him I meant no disrespect, but it was grossly unfair to take my money in that way, but it was no use, I was ordered to pay the mitigated penalty of twenty-five shillings, which I produced, first asking, in as good a tone as I could muster, 'Now have you the conscience to take that money, that ought to buy me a good warm coat for this cold weather? If you have, take it, and may you all know the want of one!' That they quickly did, and I went out of the court stung to the quick. Just outside stood William [the Captain], waiting to see the upshot of the matter, and he said he came, thinking they might commit me for freely speaking my mind to His Worship. I told him I had been threatened [with this] and I would much rather have gone, as it was, than have paid.

These fines are only recoverable upon the ship, the Captain pays and stops it off the defaulter, and if they are not paid, they will not allow the ship to clear out at the custom house. The same evening, when the informer passed me on the quay, he said to his friend 'Oh, here's our sea lawyer!', but he had caught a tartar, for we so pelted him at night with coals that he never came near our ship after, tho' we were well prepared for him for a considerable time for nights afterwards to salute him. The first edition was enough and he very prudently kept aloof; in fact I think he wished he had never seen the *Constantia*, for we never failed to remind him of her when we met him.

We sailed shortly after this for Waterford again, the last time I was to go there. A letter awaited my arrival, stating that I had a berth waiting for me, when I might reach London, in a vessel employed partly in the coal, and otherwise in the North American timber trade; of this I was very glad, for I grew most heartily tired of the *Constantia* . . . My only fear was, that we should not make the next trip to England, but to Wales for coal – however, I thought if we did the latter, I would get permission to leave at Wales, and to go to London in another vessel that might be sailing. No difficulty occurred, we loaded for the Thames and I thought myself a very happy fellow. I looked with an enthusiastic eye towards the west, as to the land of promise, and longed to follow the route of a Columbus; beside, the very name of a collier spoke the perfection of practical seamanship, it had produced a Cook and I knew the opinion of that great navigator was always in favour of the coal trade as the best nursery for a seaman. It was therefore with pleasure I saw my wishes on the eve of being fulfilled to my heart's content, and I shall always consider that the result proved the change to be most advantageous to me.

I seem to have had but scanty recollections of the *Constantia* and the time I was in her, yet some few things more, then of major tho' now of no importance at all, spring up – one thing in particular. At the time we were frozen up at London we had taken in a quantity of wine, among other things, and one valuable small cask . . . these someone of the crew had broached and, not content with what they had taken, left the holes, from which they had drawn some of the contents, unstopped – in particular the small cork, the consequence was that, with the motion of the ship, the latter one had leaked nearly out, and several of the other[s] partially, but still to a great extent. The plunder was detected at Waterford and the chests searched . . . in that of an Irishman, George we call[ed] him, was found a borer that filled the holes; nothing of course could be brought closer home, for no one had seen him – or if they had, they would not inform. He was discharged and joined another ship, in which he and all the rest perished in the ice of the coast of Labrador. The matter did not end with his dismissal: we were all interrogated and told that if we did not confess we should be discharged also and, worse than all, be had before the [Quaker] Meeting, at least those that were Friends. This made us very indignant, and we counted to be disposed of as the Captain proposed; our earnestness seemed to convince him as to most, but his suspicions were right in one instance, tho' at the time the rest of us were ignorant of the share he had in receiving the stolen wine. An anonymous letter let the whole out, some considerable time afterwards.

In the way of accidents we were thought a lucky ship, never meeting with anything serious while I was in her. Some ships get the name, whether deservedly or not, I will not pretend to say, of being unlucky, and nothing is more common than to hear sailors say of such a vessel that such is the case with her, recounting how and what accidents have befallen the crew. One morning, as we were removing the [landing-] stage that led from the *Constantia* to the shore at Waterford quay, a man walked upon it and, from a sudden jerk given it by lowering it suddenly, he was precipitated overboard and immediately sunk. The drags that are humanely kept at several neighbouring houses were instantly fetched and, after a little time, he was brought to the surface, conveyed to a house ashore, put to bed and, after a good deal of attention and good management, he was restored to consciousness, but certainly I should think it was as hairbreadth an escape as could possibly be. Jem Kekwick one day fell from the deck into the hold where there was not a thing in it; he struck in his descent some planks that broke the force of the fall, or I think he must have been killed on the spot. As it was, on his arrival at the bottom he jumped to his feet and ran up the ladder with quite his usual agility. It had, though, completely turned his head, and he talked quite wildly and incoherently; I got him to go to the doctor's, who bled him and put him a little to rights. He was the first specimen of that aberration of intellect that exists for a time from a temporary cause, of which I have seen so much. As we walked to the surgeon's he kept asking me how he came to fall and, when I had fully explained it to him and I thought he fully understood, from the patience with which he listened, he would undeceive me by abruptly saying, 'But how did I fall?' and he repeated it so often that I thought he must be making fun of me, till the lancet restored his senses.

I have omitted to mention that the last passage from Liverpool was a very tempestuous one. We were driven about a long time by contrary winds within a few hours' run of our port; the squalls were very severe, seeming at times as if they would tear the masts out of the brig. A little while after sunset of the last day we were out, the wind favoured us more by a point or two than it had previously done; it was very cold but beautifully moonlit and clear till midnight, when it clouded over and became as dark as it had previously been bright. The squalls continued very heavy, but the wind did not alter and we hoped, if it did not, by 3 or 4 o'clock to see the Hook lighthouse. Here lay the difference – if it altered half a point, we must keep to the sea – if it did not, we should get into a good harbour. We kept going to the fore top masthead to look out for the lighthouse, but none could we see. At last the watch that was up sung out, 'A light under the lee – steady or revolving?' 'Steady,' was the answer and we were all right – had it been revolving it would have been the Tuskar [light], about 30 miles on the wrong side [of] our port; as it was, [it was] as much as the ship could do to stand towards it, the wind being so very 'narrow' (thus seamen term it), that is, barely fair. We did, however, fetch into the river, and the very first tack we made into it, the fore yard went in halves; shortly afterwards the wind shifted, so that if it had occurred at sea we must have remained there, for the length of time the wind continued, so I think; it was a week beside, the job of refitting it to enable us to carry sail upon it. Had it broke while we were all upon it, reefing the foresail, we should hardly have escaped whole and sound, I think. Happening when it did, it only detained us a tide, we anchored, got the wreck out of the way, and then sent up a spare spar, which lasted us until we got a new one from the dockyard. Our arrival made a deal of talk among the Friends, and I thought we should never hear the last of it; we got however a very capital freight for London . . . which, had there not been a scarcity of vessels, we certainly should not have done; of this I was most heartily glad, and I sailed with a farewell to Waterford for ages.

Wrecks upon this part of the Irish coast are very frequent, tho' not near[ly] so much so as when it was less known and lighted. One of the most painful description occurred about the time I left, accompanied by a great loss of life. It was that of an American packet that was lost in Tranmore Bay, a deep indenture of the coast just to the Southward of Waterford. She had got into it in a thick fog and, when the Captain discovered his situation, he did all that nautical skill could do to avert the melancholy catastrophe – but it proved, as has generally been the case in that bay under such circumstances, quite unavailing. Every tack she made to get out had the reverse effect, and she struck on the fatal rocks (in the afternoon, I think) when nearly all perished; among the rest, two Friends coming from America. It made much noise at the time, if I recollect right, from having among the passengers some of high rank and wealth. Tranmore Bay has often been mistaken for the entrance to Waterford harbour by ships in distress who, running in, have found out their fatal mistake too late to avoid destruction. In one particular spot, where I walked with one of the Davies (who had a house for the watering season at the neat little village of Tranmore), I saw a sample of the terrors that must surround a poor ship under such distressing circumstances. The wind had been blowing in for a considerable time, a fresh gale, and of course brought with it a corresponding sea which, bursting with great force against the black rocks, retreated again in an extensive sheet of white foam, to be again hurried forward by the following swell. Its beautiful whiteness made it, to my nautical eye, a fearful sight; the contrast of breakers and black rocks was so very striking, heightened perhaps by a gloomy, misty day. At one part there was a natural cavern in the rock, through which the water hurried till it was stopped by the end, when it flew up through an opening to a remarkable height, in much the same manner as if ejected from a funnel with considerable force.

The Hook lighthouse, that has been so beneficial in its effects of curtailing so much of 'Ocean's prey', was erected, I believe (such however is the mariner's tale) by a lady who lost her son by shipwreck upon this ironbound coast and who, to prevent the like misfortune to others, devoted a sum of money to the purpose. What a useful monument, how far superior to Chaukey's finest work! If we had many such, with what reverential feelings should we remember the dead!

Smuggling was carried on to a very large extent on the coast during the war; peace, and the now employment otherwise of King's vessels, soon saw them placed hereabout for the prevention of it. Often, when engaged looking for the followers of this illicit traffic, they have fallen in with wrecked or distressed ships and have afforded them most welcome assistance. There happened a case of this kind during the time I was upon the coast that afforded much interest. A small pilot vessel had fallen in with a dismasted brig loaded with timber and taken her in tow but, the wind freshening, she was obliged to let her go and abandon her to her fate, as she could not leave her proper station as a pilot vessel. She was quickly after met with by a lugger in His Majesty's service employed in the preventive service as tender to the Admiral on the Irish station, and again by her also taken in tow. There was not a live creature on board at that time, the log slate was hanging upon or fastened on to the cabin table stating that, as the vessel had been dismasted and was waterlogged, . . . the crew had abandoned her and taken to the boats. In this state she became, to whoever fetched her into port, a fair and legal prize; one moiety [i.e. half] going to the finder, the other to the King. His Majesty's lugger made a successful tow of it as far as to the entrance of Waterford harbour, when it came on to blow so hard that they were obliged (most reluctantly, after all their labours) to let her go for their own safety's sake. They did so and abandoned her, intending to anchor for the night and, if it was prudent, to pick her up again next morning, not doubting they should be able to find her not far off outside the anchorage. What, therefore, was their mortification to find that, by one of those unaccountable accidents that sometimes happen, she had drifted into the harbour and gone ashore on the rocks above high water mark, where she became the legal property of the Lord of the Manor, who of course immediately put in his claim and seized her as his lawful property. She had filled with water from a partial defect only and was a prize worth from 4,000 to 5,000 pounds; the whole of which, I believe, without any reservation for the Crown, went to the latter-mentioned person. This circumstance became the topic of conversation in Waterford as, I believe, the claims of the lugger's captain and crew were advanced, but (I think) without effect.

Part II

The Lady Frances *Trading to Quebec –*
First Voyage

Chapter 1

THE VOYAGE TO SUNDERLAND

5th mo. 8th 1823. Join[ed] the *Lady Frances* (Capt. Robt. Barry) then lying in the Pool of London with a cargo of Sunderland coals, which we discharged after much delay by the 17th, and on the following morning. 1st day [Sunday], sailed with a fair wind which lasted us but a short time. We had Dr Ellerby of Cannon St., his wife, one child, and servants as passengers to the Halfway House between Gravesend and London, where we came to an anchor, when, a steam boat passing, we put Dr E. on board to return to town, his family proceeding to Sunderland for the benefit of the passage. [Mrs] A. Ellerby appeared a very agreeable Friend and was exceedingly pleasant during the passage, though her health appeared to be very delicate, for the sake of which she was flying from the bustle and toil of a London GP . . . to a spot which might afford her a little more repose.

After a fine passage of 5 days during which nothing particular occurred, we arrived in Sunderland and, as soon as we were moored, took our passengers ashore and their baggage; on leaving, A.E. kindly gave me a card and a pressing invitation to call upon her whenever I had leisure, an invitation which I accepted, and was made heartily welcome. The town, on entering the harbour, is not calculated to impress a stranger with very favourable ideas, the houses in the lower part of it and at the riverside being low, dirty and very irregularly built, with a vast quantity of workshops, and as you proceed up, abounding with Carpenters, Yards, Brewers, Wharfs, etc., but it improves upon acquaintance and High Street has quite a respectable appearance, being wide and pretty well built, and though the shops are nothing extraordinary, they are generally very good. It is united to Bishop Wearmouth in the same manner as London and Westminster and, with Monk Wearmouth, which is on the N. side of the river, contains about 50,000 inhabitants. A great proportion are of the lower classes, who are employed partly in the manufactories of glass, pottery and iron etc., but more in the loading [of] ships with coal, in which staple commodity the export is

41

immense, being about 300,000 chaldrons;[7] it is brought from the pits on the side of the River Wear in large flat-bottomed oval-shaped barges called Keels, carrying 21 tons, to the ships, and is thrown into the vessels by men employed for the purpose called casters, whose wages are 2/3 [i.e. two shillings and threepence] per Keel. As there are 5 to each they soon earn their money, but there are so many looking for casts, they never get more than 2 per day and sometimes not one, but generally their earnings are great, which frequently occasions what is called a 'stick' or a cessation of work until their wages are risen – which the merchants are frequently obliged to comply with in order to get their ships to sea, but on the demand slackening, they are immediately reduced.

Shipbuilding is carried out to a great extent; the ships built per annum average about 3 per week, though as many as 50 have frequently been known to be upon the stocks at a time and, as a specimen of the short time in which they can build, one . . . was launched soon after our arrival which had been but 10 weeks building and registered 280 tons. Expectation of a war in which England might be involved had made a stir amongst the Shipwrights and led to the building [of] many ships in hopes of getting them employed in the Transport Service. They are reckoned the finest-modelled ships on the Ocean, as well as the best rigged, though they are generally very slight and last but a short time compared to river-built ones. Most of the Shopkeepers of this town are concerned in ships, and find it the most profitable way of employing their money, carrying coals to London in the winter and going to America or the Baltic in the summer keeps them pretty well employed. The place owes its advancement completely to the spirit of its inhabitants. The harbour was good for nothing until they ran out, at a great expense, 2 piers a great distance into the sea, which makes a fine appearance; they have each a lighthouse, one is a landmark, the other to inform ships the height of the water on the bar – on which, with a gale of wind from the eastward, the sea breaks with a heavy swell at the entrance, which causes vessels frequently to miss it and go to the back of the pier, where they are inevitably lost – and their crews with them, were it not for the admirable invention of the lifeboat, by which many brave fellows' lives are annually saved from a watery grave. There are 2, about 30 feet long, with boxes at the side containing air, which prevents them sinking when filled with water; at the bottom are holes through which it runs until it finds its level, by which method it will empty itself in the space of 2 minutes, and they are so constructed as to be deemed proof to upsetting. They are always kept upon a four-wheeled carriage, on which they are drawn opposite to the ship in distress when, a kind of brewer's pulley being lifted up, they are launched into the sea, manned with volunteers – who are paid

---

[7] A chaldron was about 36 bushels.

according to the risk they run, and who are not permitted to keep on their big jackets or mittens, as they are thought too heavy for a man to exert himself, even to the extent required on these melancholy occasions . . . [The lifeboats] are sharp at both ends and steered by an oar at the bow and stern, and their bottoms are armed with a thick iron keel to prevent their receiving injury from the rocks on which they may come ashore with the crew whom they have rescued; for they are obliged to come ashore at once, and people on the lookout raise them again upon the carriage ready for another start. Their utility has been so fully established that they are adopting them upon many parts of the coast, and it is to be hoped they will soon be found in all places where rocks and sands so often prove the graves of many valuable seamen.

The bridge is deservedly the boast of the county, and the inscription it bears upon the plates of iron in the centre of it struck me as being very appropriate:

Nil Desperandum Auspice Deo.[8]

It was a wonderful undertaking, and is reckoned one of the greatest curiosities of the kind in the world; it consists of small pieces of iron fitting into one another in a curious manner; its span is 247 feet and is sufficiently high to admit laden ships of 400 tons' burthen sailing under it – but, when light, they are obliged to strike their top gallant masts. A gentleman came from Italy for the express purpose of seeing it, and expressed himself well repaid for his journey. When I stood upon its centre, I saw beneath me large vessels taking in their cargoes of coals. I was astonished at the surprising height and elegance of the work and was almost led to consider it as a tale, though it is actually fact, that a sailor got over the railing and seated himself upon the masthead of his ship whilst she was going underneath. As I understand, no painter is willing to paint it, and consequently, whenever that job is required, they find a Jack Tar to do it who, slinging himself with a rope, is lowered down to do his work . . . I cannot say that 24 shillings per week would tempt me to risk my life about it.

In Sunderland harbour no ships cook . . . all the crew get their victuals on shore. I was quartered upon the Capn. and, the hour for being aboard in the evening being 8, after tea I generally took a walk to see what was to be seen about the place; in one of these rambles I met with a young man named Caleb Richardson who kindly offered to show me about, which offer I was glad to accept, and much pleased to find a companion [so] agreeable [in] character. The evening in question we took a ride in rather a novel manner, at least it was so to me; we mounted the hinder wagon of 18 empty ones drawn by a steam engine,

---

[8] There is no need to despair when we are under God's patronage.

and rolled along very pleasantly at the rate of a smart trot for between 2 [and] 3 miles. When they stopped the 'hoise' (as it is called) to fill up the boiler at a pump by the roadside, after they had given him sufficient water they set him off again, and overtook us on our return with another load, at the top of the hill which goes down to the waterside. I confess I did not feel quite safe as he came puffing past us, and I thought it most prudent to descend off the railway until they had passed by. When on the brow of the hill, they unhook the engine and fasten the rest to a rope (the other end of which, being also fast, to as many empty ones at the bottom). The former, being set in motion, bring the latter to the top, with which the 'hoise' starts for another load; it fetches them about 4½ miles and performs the journey in about 1 hour and 21 minutes.

At the bottom of the hill the wagons are drawn over a kind of platform, where the bottoms of them are knocked out and, by means of a large chute, the coals are conveyed to the hold of the vessel loading, but there are engines for lifting them over the hatchway and then letting them drop out . . . these engines are the means of preventing the poor from finding employment and cause a great decrease in manual labour, and frequent attempts are made to injure them and their machinery.

After taking a cursory view of what I have thus poorly described, we went to see the glass bottle houses and pottery . . . I had no idea they could make a set of tea things or blow a dozen bottles so easily; but how many are the articles we are continually using, the art of manufacturing which we know nothing about?

Sunderland contains a good church and chapel of ease, with a number of dissenters' meeting houses, of which the Methodist one is as fine as the Friends' is shabby. It is really a good-for-nothing place for worship and quite warrants them in building the new one in hand which, as far as I am able to judge, will be a very convenient and respectable building. The church at Monk Wearmouth is very antique and is the second that had glass windows in England. I did not examine its inside, time being but short with me when I was on the South side of the river, but some more convenient time (if I ever find one) I intend to look in, as I am told it is well worth seeing.

The country a short distance from the town is very pretty, abounding with fine walks and views. The one in particular, to Squire Ettrick's, is as much so as any I have seen; from the carriage road which runs to the old-fashioned mansion . . . there is a fine prospect of the sea, much of the Yorkshire coast and some fine country, here and there graced with gentlemen's seats which, embosomed among fine woods, make altogether a very rich variety.

The Squire [is] said to be rather an eccentric character, and his plans for keeping the garden free from robbers do not contradict the assertion; the carriage road runs before the house and is a public path, which to him is a great nuisance, and his garden being close to it, he frequently finds his fruit trees lightened of their burthens by the pilfering boys of the neighbourhood; he has therefore some figures, dressed very well, and in natural positions as if they were looking over the wall, whose situation he varies, lest the vagabonds should get aware of the deceit, which I should suspect they are . . . the enormous mantrap hanging up, which is set at night, is the most terrific object. By it is placed the figure of a leg, over which is the warning 'Legs shortened here'; which it would easily do, if any unwary one should get therein.

Altogether I was very much pleased with Sunderland, and as I found in it a very hospitable and agreeable Society of Friends, what leisure time I had passed very happily, and when I bade them adieu, the kind manner in which they parted with me makes me look forward to the time when, if all goes prosperously, I have the pleasure of meeting them again. It is one of the many privileges young persons of our Society enjoy, to be kindly noticed in the way I have been since I first went to sea, and makes me sure no young man, though a complete stranger, need fall into bad company if he is rightly disposed to seek that of Friends – and well he is repaid in this Meeting which, being pretty large, contains some very nice young men, whose company is truly valuable. They seem much of one family, dropping in [with] that sociable, free manner which to me is so very pleasant and agreeable. For other classes I can say nothing, not having it in my power to judge, but I was struck with the great want there is among the servants of that gimp[9] which so highly adorns a woman. I think it is owing to them having to fetch their water from public pumps at the lower end of the town, in the evening when the work is done. To these pumps the sailors regularly repair, and fine romps they have together; oft have I seen . . . [the servants], with their skeels [i.e. buckets] on their heads, stopped by the tars who, knocking it off their heads, make them go back to the pump again, and there are many wives, I have no doubt, who may date their first meeting with their husbands at these places.

Our lading being completed . . . we prepared everything for sea and told our passengers to come on board, [these] consisting of an old man, his wife and one daughter, going in search of a land with no King to oppress them. Next day, the articles being signed by the men, we got our orders and, with a fair wind and three hearty cheers, which were answered by the people on the pierheads, we bade adieu to Sunderland and Old England, which we hope to see in 5 months again, if we are favoured with success. I must confess it seemed [so] like a dream to me to be going to America (having expected to go so often and never gone) that I hardly know how to believe it. We cleared out at the Custom House to go Northward (on account of the expense of lights and harbours incurred by

[9] Lace or other dress trimming.

going by the English Channel), though it is often done without any intention of going . . . [north], by which the said lights are defrauded of their customary tax paid by all ships passing by them, and which is levied at the Custom House at the time the vessel is clearing out. Having thus endeavoured to describe what I have seen in my own country, I shall now begin my daily journal, sincerely wishing all my friends and relations in my native isle health, peace and happiness until and ever after my return.

Farewell to England, fare thee well
For now but faintly can I see
Thy shores where peace and plenty dwell
The lovely land of liberty.

I'm bound across the western sea
And wandering must be my portion
Ere I again revisit thee
Thou sweetest isle of all the Ocean.

But think not, though I leave behind
Thy fruitful vales, thy fertile shore
That vain regret o'erspreads my mind
Or makes me with my fate deplore.

Oh no! To me the billows' roar
Has charms not terrors, there I find
Joy when its waves we scud before
And music in the whistling wind.

But when a sigh escapes my breast
As oftentimes I find it to,
'Tis for those friends whom I love best
From whom some thousand miles I go.

And of whose weal I ne'er can know
As o'er the ocean wide I roam
Until the favouring breeze shall blow
That wafts me to my native home.

And till that time farewell sweet isle
And farewell those whom I most love,

On them may choicest blessings smile,
Those joys which, as through life they move.

On them descend from heaven above
A solace on their way shall be
And in the end a passport prove
To blissful immortality.

Chapter 2

THE PASSAGE TO QUEBEC

Fine breezes from the southward, going about 6 knots per hour, fine clear weather, busily employed stowing things for sea and getting cables bent and anchors unstowed. Passengers quite well, though complaining of a want they feel of sea legs, which we tell them they will soon procure. They find much difference between the green sea and their Yorkshire land, but console themselves at leaving with the thought of an easy life in America. I hope they may not find themselves disappointed in their fond ideas; they are nice, clean, decent, country folks, which makes their company agreeable.

1st day [Sunday]. Still, fine weather with rather less wind. The day observed with great decorum and I find our crew (who are employed reading their bibles and other religious works) to be a very decent set of men, which promises fair for a pleasant voyage. Began with my bible with an intention of reading it through, as it is some time since I read much in the Old Testament. Thought upon absent friends; I wonder, have any thought about me?

2nd day. This morning early saw Peterhead and in the afternoon, at the mouth of the Pentland Firth, we were boarded by an Orkney Pilot and, as the wind was coming from the NW, were taken by him into a harbour called Wide Wall in Ronaldsay, where we anchored in a very nice little snug kind of bay in 3 fathoms water. The *Jane and Margaret* and *Harvest* lightships, who sailed the same tide as us from Sunderland . . . were in here before us by several hours, but as we have got a heavy cargo, we cannot expect to keep company with them. As soon as we were brought up, we hoisted our jolly boat[10] out, went on board our consorts with the Capn., and it was agreed amongst them to take a turn into the island after tea, which they did, and as I was in the boat I took one, also over to

---

[10] A small ship's boat.

the Sth. side, where the scenery was very grand, such as I never saw before. The sandstone cliffs were about 200 or 250 feet high, at whose base lay large stones (for they were not craggy, but quite smooth) and the largest I have met with, over which the sea rolled with a tremendous swell, accompanied with that loud noise which serves to render the scene more striking. One huge rock which projected a considerable distance particularly claimed my attention; the sea, rolling into the angle it formed with the line of the cliff, rushed through a passage it had formed at the bottom into the sea on its other side, with a noise as if the rock itself was going to fall, and then, rolling over a large body of these stones, presented a fine cataract to the eye, which I stopped for some time to admire. As the surge rolled in foaming grandeur towards the shore and dashed at the foot of the cliff, I thought how my ideas would alter, were I in a ship which was unable to keep off at sea in a gale of wind blowing upon these rocky barriers; these reflections, accompanied with the feeling of being in such [a] situation, made me enjoy the scene to its full extent.

The *Lord Stewart* came into the bight [i.e. bay] this evening; as she is a laden ship and bound to Quebec, we have a chance of a companion over the Western Ocean.

3rd. day. Fine weather with some light showers, employed painting the ship, which we accomplished by 8 o'clock. Some people from an island called Hoy came on board with eggs a penny, butter 8d per pound, milk 2d a quart, and mittens 6d a pair, for which they found a ready sale, and went ashore with one of our passengers to procure more. Wind W and N, light breezes and fine weather. Went ashore again this evening, looked into the houses (which are thatched in a curious manner) and took a walk over a barren hill towards the seaside. In one humble abode, hearing the sound of a saw, I was tempted to intrude inside, where a cooper was employed making herring casks . . . of which article he had his shop full; they were all well made . . . he told me all his whole stock would be taken in about a week, as soon as the herrings came . . . which he expected would be shortly. He was very polite and talkative, enquiring particularly after the news and how the Spaniards were getting on; he also wished to know whether England would take part in it [the war] or not; I think he had had a good education, his language being very correct. 9 o'clock returned aboard and went to bed.

4th. day. 11-12, Fine weather with light breezes variable. 2 o'clock went ashore with the Captain, got a drink of milk at one of the houses, which was not very good, though very thick. Their cattle are very small and very low-priced, a steer was 30 shillings and a calf 2 days old two and sixpence . . . fowls of all descriptions one and sixpence a couple, but what amused me more than anything I saw amongst them was their little sheep, not larger than our lambs when fit to kill, and their young by their sides, exactly like little black dogs.

[The people here] are very coarsely clothed, though some worsted stockings I saw were much like silk, being mostly beautifully fine. I observed the people who take snuff convey it to the nose with a small wooden shovel, which they carry in their boxes; the pilot who brought us in used one, which appeared to me a very novel manner altogether. Their accent is not so Scottish as I should have expected from their being so near that coast and having so much intercourse with it, though our pilot was a complete Scot. My hat, being so well covered and waterproof, struck his fancy and he seemed determined to possess it if I would but be moderate in my price, but as I had no other, I declined all his offers, one of which was four shillings, his own 'bonny Scotch bonnet washed weel' . . . and a dozen eggs.

5 o'clock the wind came from the S.E. and we all got under way and, with a little wind, sailed gently among the islands, of which (as it is quite light during the night) I got a full view, but there is nothing different to South Ronaldsay amongst them, except Hoy Island, which is very hilly and, towards the western ocean, very craggy and grand, but the wind falling into a perfect calm, we had enough to do, to get out without damage. The tide runs here (between Hoy and Stroma) at the rate of 6 knots and, meeting another of the same speed, unless a ship has a breeze of wind, she will drive under no command, but cross the stream which, on account of the great swell it raises, becomes very dangerous, making the vessel roll to that degree that her masts are quite endangered; but we got into the Atlantic without any damage, as well as the rest of our company, but having very little wind, we have not made much advancement to the Westward. Wind S and every appearance of a gale which, until we get sea room, will not be very pleasant.

6th. day, 13th. Fresh breezes and foggy weather, reefed the topsails and stowed the top gallant sails. At 4 a.m. double[d] the topsails and stowed the jib; a rich prospect of stiff breezes, but I see I have got a good vessel under my feet and a fine sea boat. Had a great deal of rain, and I think we will soon get white sails, long before we get over the sea to the American coast. The *Lord Stewart* in company.

7th. day, 14th. Strong weather with rain. At 4 a.m. close reefed the topsails, hard gales and squally . . . ship behaving very well, seems determined to be upon the top of every sea. Never had such a dry jacket in a gale of wind! Saw an American ship but did not speak [to] her, we suppose her bound to England . . .

1st. day, 15th. Set the foresail, as it was more moderate, and let one reef out of the topsails; sky looks clear and looks well for a finer night . . . *Lord Stewart* in sight. Passengers all hearty and, I believe, have not felt any inconvenience from the motion of the ship.

3rd. day, 17th. Wind NNW, fresh breezes and cloudy weather. Spoke the *Lord Stewart*; he told us he had split his jib and foresail in the breeze, beside sustaining some other trifling damage to his rigging, so that we had no reason to grumble, having received none, except splitting our jib a little. I think we shall keep company all the way, as we sail much alike. Our male passenger, Robin, seems very anxious for a fair wind, and having learnt the point of the compass which we tell him points to America, he frequently puts his head into the binnacle [i.e. where the compass is kept] to ascertain how she is sailing, but as yet he withdraws it without any comfort; his Yorkshire dialect amuses me much and, as I pay much attention to his tales, we agree very well, excepting in our ideas of American colonization, where we differ widely.

4th. day, 18th. Robin's countenance brightened this morning, when he saw a fair wind and all sail set and immediately went to tell his 'cannie auld wife' and bairn of it, which soon brought them out of their beds. We have now run, in the last 24 hours, 107 miles. I now go regularly every evening into the cabin where the Capn. and Mate teach navigation, and I begin to keep the ship's way, which appears very easy to what I supposed it to have been; I hope to get far enough into the sailings to keep a correct journal by myself upon our return. There are 4 scholars and there is no little emulation excited amongst us; I am the youngest at it and consequently to leeward of [i.e. behind] the rest, but I do not mean [i.e. intend] to be, if application will put me ahead.

5th. day, 19th. Light breezes from the Eastward and cloudy; the *Lord Stewart* in company, and I am sure if she was 300 miles off we should all be glad of it; much as we like company on the ocean, we are continually crowding sail against one another, and we this day sent up a royal mast to see if we can get ahead of him with a main royal sail, but it makes no difference, he sets a sail for every one we do, and I see we will both get to Quebec together, if no accident happens to us on the way.

6th. day, 20th. Very fine weather, wind ENE, all going on very comfortably, and the more I see of my Captain, the more I like him. He is an exceedingly agreeable, kind, man and is much liked by all the crew; he is very desirous of giving me all the instruction in his power, both as to practice and theory, and I think we shall agree very well, because there is a mutual desire of being happy together. I am very well satisfied with the change from coasting to foreign trade, I have more time to myself, excepting when the afternoon watch is upon deck. I have divided it thus: in fine weather, when I have 8 hours upon deck, at night I go to bed from 10 to 12, but when I have had 8 hours below, I stop up from 12 to 4, in which time I write and work at navigation. When the weather is indifferent I go to bed the whole 12 hours, thus providing against a time when I might be upon deck the better part or whole of the 24 hours, but as yet we have not had occasion to be disturbed from our regular time below.

7th. day, 21st. Stiff breezes and cloudy; wind E and N. I think last night I saw one of the finest moonlight scenes imaginable. It was a clock calm, the horizon was obscured with heavy black clouds in every direction of one height, above which all was beautifully clear, the stars shining with the greatest lustre, when the moon rose from amongst the bed of clouds, clothed in splendour and shedding a path of light upon the swelling ocean, in which was seen our consort who, like ourselves all becalmed, merely heaved to the swell that remained of the day's billows. All was quite still, except now and then, when the flapping of the sails and the blowing of the 'finners' [i.e. fin whales] disturbed the breathless silence of the scene. At such a time and in such a situation as this, how does the mind wander back amongst the scenes it lately acted a part in, how does it in fancy take a peep into the circles of those it most loves, and with what pleasure does it look forward to the time when it shall have the delight of meeting them again! How comparatively dull would our path through life be, had we no congenial friend to cheer us on the way! I am sure I should feel miserable indeed, did I not know I held a place in the affections of those I can truly call my friends, and whose friendship I sincerely hope I may never lose.

A vast quantity of . . . 'finners' are going towards the southward, whose blowing very much resembles the noise made by a large puff of steam escaping from an engine; they are called 'finners' on account of a large black fin they carry above the water, very much like a large black anchor stock [i.e. cross-bar]. As yet I have not seen any of the large Greenland whales, though we expect to meet with them very soon; they frequent the seas of Newfoundland in the warmer months of the year.

1st day, 22nd. A troop of porpoises have been gambolling about us the whole of the morning, leaping out of the water in a surprising manner and diving under the bottom of the ship and coming up upon the other side; they seem desirous of displaying their activity in their native element. Our passengers were much pleased with them and Robin exclaimed, 'Ah, ye're the Cannie lads to gae and see your friends!'

I think I observed today the good effects of the Bethel Seaman's Society. Our men read their bibles or prayer books on this day, and behaved with so much propriety that a Sabbath is well known amongst us, and though there is no service of any kind, I think the day is spent according of the command[ment], to keep it holy.

In the evening a number of the men, with the passengers, spent some time in singing hymns, which had a very nice effect; I thought it beautiful, though I suppose the beauty of the evening and our situation rendered it more so than it would otherwise have been. I may be mistaken, but I believe the prayer meetings which are held every evening in most ports have the means of making many a profligate sailor a sincere Christian, and as they are increasing, I hope the time will soon come when sailors will no longer be considered in the same light they have so long been looked upon in; but that from the old school there may arise a generation who shall redeem the character of their forerunners, and as remarkable for their sobriety and virtues as the former were for their dissipation and vices.

2nd. day, 23rd. Light breezes inclinable to calm and no longer fair, but as it is fine weather nobody is concerned about the passengers, who begin to long for a sight of land, but if we get into the gulf this fortnight we shall feel well satisfied. The *Lord Stewart* is still in company, hanging upon our weather and becalming our sails, he has become quite an eyesore to us, but we hope to lose him when we come to tack at night. 12 o'clock, heavy rain and cloudy weather with wet jackets, but having plenty of coals we burn a fire all night in the galley by which, as the nights are light, we sit and 'spin yarns' as sailors term it; that is, tell tales to pass away the watch, and many and marvellous they are.

3rd. day, 24th. . . . Being now one third of our distance over, took stock and found remaining:

    1lb. coffee
    ½ lb. tea
    4½ lb. sugar
    1½ lb. soap

[all in] good condition, which shows half is expended, therefore determine to be moderate in my consumption, as there are no shops upon the road where we can get a supply.

4th. day, 25th. Strong breezes, as expected. At 4 p.m. double reefed the topsail and trysail, raining very heavy. Wind flying about in every quarter.

At 6 tacked ship to the northward, *Lord S.* still in company.

6th. day, 27th. We were frightened last night with what we believe to be a waterspout close to our stern, but it was too dark to distinguish clearly; strong breezes, reefed the topsails and trysails, much rain; no want of soft water, if we [had] a ship's load to wash, but I do not know how they would dry, if this weather continues.

7th. day, 28th. Let out the reefs and set the top gallant sails, finer weather, saw an American ship to windward and a British brig to leeward, spoke neither. We now begin to fall in with ships bound to the eastward, but as yet have not spoken with any. *Lord S.* still in company.

1st. day, 29th. . . . Fine evening and clear weather. I hardly think we shall have so quick a passage as we anticipated, but I am well satisfied, we have aplenty of everything needful and a good ship under foot, which is better than all, and if old England sees us again by 12th month, it will be soon enough.

2nd. day, 30th. . . . This passage has opened a leaf of nature's book to my wandering eyes, and with it I am completely puzzled. At this distance from land we continually see birds, and what puzzles me is how they live, how they breed, and how they can find the land, for if they fly either north or south they will find none; really nature's works are truly wonderful.

3rd. day, 1st. This month has come in in whistling style and given us opportunity of trying our skill at taking in sail quickly; but as bad beginnings often make good endings, we do not trouble ourselves about it. We have been visited by a quantity of small birds exactly like martins (called by sailors Mother Carey's chickens) whose company we never desire, as they prognosticate bad weather; they are seldom seen in fine, but as soon as it begins to look windy, we soon seem them flying about the ship.

4th. day, 2nd. A large black whale was blowing about the ship this morning, but he did not show much of himself above the water. . . .

The passage across the Atlantic to America is very tedious in general, but the passage home is just as short, owing to the prevalence of the Westerly winds, which is about 3 parts of the year. The winds generally come from the N or NE quarter into the southward, when it [sic] goes gradually round till it gets into the NW, where it continues flying about for a long time together. I should not like making 2 voyages a year out to America, the fall [i.e. autumn] voyage must be very bad in general, on account of the heavy gales which ships may expect from about the 9th month, and the sea, when it blows from one point for any considerable time, rises to an astonishing height and obliges vessels to lie to for fear of being 'pooped' (to use the sea phrase), or rather to prevent the huge waves, when scudding before them, from breaking over the vessel's stern.

5th. day, 3rd. Last night fully confirmed me in my opinion that a good judgement is not to be formed of the weather we may expect from the look of the sky in this ocean. I think it was as fine a sunset and moderate-looking horizon as ever I could wish to see and all were expecting a southerly wind, but the sky soon became overcast and we soon turned to, to reef topsails, and this morning the sea became so heavy that we had to hand the mainsail jib and double reef the topsails; a squall came upon us, just as if it had been cut out of a bag, and split the mainsail and top gallant sail, so that we have got a job at mending again; but we soon lose the weather again, it never lasts above 12 hours, though the swell continues for a considerable time.

No observation.[11] Lat. by account 45.50 N. Lon. 42.30 W. At 8 tacked ship to the southward, fine evening but showery; as we are approaching the banks, we must expect rain and thick weather. Saw 2 ships running to the eastward. It would be pleasant to us if their jibs would draw.

6th. day, 4th. Moderate weather and pretty fine, I think we should get a fair wind today as we shall then get a new moon, though as we are situated we might get to the Gulf in about 6 or 7 days with the wind as it is at present, and with a fair wind might be in Quebec in 10 days; we are distant from the banks of Newfoundland about 900 miles and 690 east of Cape Breton. Got an observation today in Lat. 45.54 N. Lon. 43.2 West.

Unbent today our torn topsail and have been busily employed mending it. With a good job repairing, it will last us through the voyage; it is a very useful sail and we should be sorry to lose it but, having seen its best days, it has become very tender [i.e. brittle]. The wind has northerned more this afternoon and we are now sailing our course; what pleasure there is, after tossing to and fro, to be able to move along pleasantly upon our direct road. . . .

7th. day, 5th. I have been having a good deal of conversation this morning with Robin upon the subject of his leaving England for America. I asked him his

---

[11] This probably means no longitude. This depends on sun and/or moon observations, impossible when the skies are clouded.

prospects and expectations, and I really wondered at the man's preposterous ideas; he thinks to get good clean land for 24 shillings an acre and everything in proportion, and told me as a finishing word he hoped soon to be independent. His curious dialect and ideas set one into a hearty laugh, so that he got quite offended with me but, on [my] apologizing for my rudeness, he resumed his usual good temper. Our carpenter asked him his age and, on his answering 55, told him, if he had stopped another 5 years they would have given him some land in England, for nothing. He meant his length and breadth [i.e. in his coffin] but, not comprehending his meaning, he [Robin] said that he never found them willing to give him anything, but rather desirous of taking what little he had away. He is an example of what discontent will bring a person to, that really has been and might now have been doing well, but, letting Will Cobbett's principles and reasoning obtain the sway over sounder judgement, he has turned out of his native country at that advanced age, when a man ought to think most of stopping at home, to seek in a foreign clime a shelter from his . . . [supposed] enemies, the King and the rich, for whom he fancies he is slaving. He is what is called a 'leveller', or one who believes the days are at hand when everything will be equally shared out to the beggars as well as the princes.

Fine weather but quite calm . . . in the evening a fine breeze sprang up from the S and we are holding away from the banks in good style, where we hoped to be becalmed for a day, for the sake of catching some cod fish.

All going on very comfortably, and I think I was never happier on board ship since I first went to sea. The old mainsail being repaired, we have bent it again and it seems likely to last us a considerable time. At 6 o'clock p.m. set topmast studding sails. Fine breezes and clear weather.

1st. day, 6th. This day completes the month since we left Sunderland and 2 since we left London; the time has slipped away almost imperceptibly and, I hope, not unprofitably; I am getting forward in navigation as fast as I can expect, though my undivided attention to it has not let me pay much to Geography – but if I can get enough insight into the former to keep a journal of the passage home, I hope to acquire a pretty good knowledge of one quarter of the globe at least, if not of more. Since last 1st day we have lost our companion *Lord Stewart*, of which we are glad, but whether he is ahead or astern we know not; we conjecture ahead, as he is rather the better sailor of the two in light winds. It was exceedingly foggy this morning or, as sailors term it, the 'Newfoundland boatswain' came on board, but I am told it is generally thick, dull weather within the vicinity of the banks; it is rather disagreeable, being much like a Scotch mist, that soon wets an Englishman to the skin. There is a little black kind of fish that swims about the seas here, which hoists a beautiful sail like a bladder decorated with a fringe; it is called a Portuguese Man of War[12] and I should conceive it to be something of the Nautilus kind, excepting the shell, [of] which I think it has none. We have endeavoured to catch some of them, but as yet have not succeeded; they are said to possess electric powers, but for the truth of the report I cannot speak, none of our people having experienced it. They are of different colours, as blue, yellow, red etc., but most delicately light and look like gauze. On being struck, they furl their sail and descend into their briny abode. I hope I shall be able to get one before long, but as we have nothing but a pail that will answer the purpose, they generally escape, floating off the top of it when drawing it up.

About 5 o'clock this evening the wind came ahead and we are just laying our course, and if I am not mistaken shall be reefing before long, the wind sounding very hollow, which we consider a sign of strong weather. Abundance of whales have been about the ship this afternoon, one in particular came very close to us and gave me a full view of him: and a most huge and clumsy fellow he was. They play in the water much like porpoises, and are in their native element. I had written this when the vessel shipped a bit of sea and the spray, flying over my book, obliges me [to] leave writing till it is again dry.

2nd. day, 7th. It blew very fresh last evening and not only soaked my book but also my back – and my cap, as I was aloft furling the sail, took its departure from the top gallant yard . . . At 8 p.m. reefed the topsails, handed the mainsail and set the mainstay sail; fresh breezes and very foggy.

We have got already to try for soundings, as by our calculation we shall soon be upon the great bank, but as last evening's breeze moderated by 12 o'clock and it . . . [is] now nearly calm, we shall not try till tomorrow. I had but a poor idea of Quebec as a city until last evening, when the Capn gave me quite a long description of it, which has raised my expectations very considerably and I begin to feel a desire to see it, though I am quite agreeable to (as I must be, to be sure) stop at sea a month longer. The weather is very cold and uncomfortable from the mizzling fog we are constantly enveloped in, which imperceptibly wets one through before one would be thinking of it, but plenty of coals and consequently plenty of fire makes us, comparatively, very comfortable; but in winter time it must be dismal indeed, and I do not envy those who stop a season on the fishing ground.

At 6 p.m. hove the deep sea lead but found no bottom with 100 fathoms, though by calculation we are in Lat. 44.44 N, Lon. 48.0 W, and the outer edge of the banks lies in Lat. 50.0 N, Lon. 52 W, so we are but a short distance from it if our calculations are correct, but ships are generally astern of their reckonings,

---

[12] A poisonous type of jellyfish with long tentacles.

which is far better than being ahead of them. 8 o'clock calm, and the

> Sea is like a silvery lake
> And o'er the calm the vessel glides
> Gently as though it feared to wake
> The slumbers of the silent tide.

There is a great mistake in this description of a calm, which we must excuse in a poet that is no sailor; I mean in that line which says, 'And o'er the calm the vessel glides', because it is well known she moves none without wind except in a tide, and then I conceive she only moves with it, and not over it.

3rd. day, 8th. Last evening I was taken very poorly with violent pains in the bowels, but some medicine from the Captain and a night's sleep has restored me to my usual health, excepting a headache, which I hope will not stop long with me; the passengers gave me some oatmeal, which helped me a good deal, when made into water gruel. What an inestimable blessing is good health, and who is there amongst us that would exchange it for the greatest earthly possession, yet how many do we see eagerly pursuing after those ideal riches which, when attained at the expense of so valuable a gift, make their possessor poor indeed; but these reflections strike us not with their full force until we hear the knock of sickness at our door, and then we regret our having ever trifled with what we may never regain.

4th. day, 9th. Fine stiff breezes and foggy weather. Struck soundings in 40 fathoms, large shells at the bottom of the lead; if the breeze continues, we expect to make the land on 6th day. We are going at the rate of 6 and 7 miles an hour with all sails set carrying her on for a landfall which we expect, as we are steering for it, will be Cape Breton; the passengers seem well pleased at the thoughts of land, though for my part I wish it would fall calm, that we might catch some fish for a fish meal. No observation today. Wind SSE and rain at noon. Last night a number of porpoises were sporting about the ship and we could clearly distinguish all their movements in the water, on account of the path of light they left behind them; the water sparkles exceedingly hereabouts and sometimes one bright spot reflects light for a foot around it, but I have not been able to discover from what it arises. I have got the brilliant matter upon my hand but, upon bringing it into the light, I have not been able to discover it, though it again shone when brought into the dark. One of our steady fellows told me the world was destroyed by a flood formerly, but when it is again so, it will be by fire; the rainbow when it rains is the assuring proof that the Lord will no more destroy it with water, but the fire there is in the sea is to remind us that the days are approaching when all the ocean will be one flood of fire and will consume the earth we live upon.

5th. day, 10th. Hove the ship to, to catch some fish, but they, not being quite so hungry as ourselves, would not bite, so we made sail again.

6th. day, 11th. Had a fine breeze all last night, but at noon the wind came from the SW with a thick fog, sounded in 65 fathoms with speckled sand, which gives us reason to suppose we are nearly off the banks, which I am glad of, for I am quite tired of the fogs and calms we have continually had since we have been upon them. The former part of this day was beautifully fine and hot, but whenever it is so it is only a prelude to dirty weather, so that we know what to expect when we have a fine morning and that knowledge often hinders us from getting wet clothes, because we should otherwise wash a few dirty things.

Stock [of provisions] is getting rather low with most of us, and to save my tea have begun to use oatmeal which, with treacle, is pretty good in some people's opinion, but my idea of 'Burgoo' . . . or whatever it is called is not very favourable, though it bears the character of being very wholesome food; but we live very well and generally get a change every day, though the dinners are manufactured out of but few articles, only varied in the cookery; we have puddings, pies, pease, pancakes, potatoes, doughboys, lob scones . . . with a variety of other messes, so that for variety we will not complain; the air and exercise serve for sauce and health finds the appetite, so that we envy not those who live in magnificent style on shore, for, though they may show a good table, we can show against it robust constitutions, which are infinitely more necessary towards the enjoyment of life, than all the luxuries the earth can produce.

I must now begin to write a few letters to England to send home with the first ship I find bound to London, though I have so little variety to tell, I almost think half a dozen will answer for all my western ocean correspondence. How happy I should be, could I but get a line from anyone whilst I may be absent! It seems a long time to be without hearing anything of my friends, but as in most things we can find some consolation, so I do, in the idea that everything will be new to me when I get home, and when sitting by the fireside it will be pleasant to hear of what has passed whilst I have been away. Everything goes on very agreeably amongst us and consequently we are a happy ship's company, I think as much so as anyone sailing on the salt seas.

7th. day, 12th. So very thick that we can hardly see two ships' length and we are rather afraid of the land, which makes it very unpleasant; we much wish to speak [to] some ship but, though we saw one but a little way to leeward of us yesterday, we could not speak to her. It was very mortifying to see her one minute and the next to lose sight of her altogether. We sound every 12 hours but, the wind being foul, we make but little progress toward Quebec, as we carry but very little sail, for fear of falling in with some of the laden ships off the Island of Newfoundland. If the weather would clear up it would be a capital job for us and we should be in the Gulf, but there is no prospect of it until the moon gets near the full, when we anticipate a change for the better; till then, wet jackets must be our portion.

1st. day, 13th. Thick as ever; we had a deal of thunder and lightning last night which we hoped would have cleared it away, and today the thunder has been very loud. At noon it cleared up a little and we tacked ship, but our hopes of clear weather are but small; we are by calculations but about 40 miles from Cape Ray, though we have plenty of room to the westward towards Cape Breton. Wind about WSW and very light breezes; we keep a reef in each topsail and the square main sail furled to provide against the worst.

I think it is a great pity that in a ship like this there is no time for religious worship on this day when the weather permits. I think it would be very agreeable to the people's feelings if there was prayers read amongst them; but the day is observed with great propriety and decorum and not unprofitably spent.

2nd. day, 14th. This weather still continues and makes about 70 or 75 hours since we could see 2 ships' length; it looked rather better this morning, but it soon came thick as ever. It may, to be sure, clear up at noon, which I wish it may, for it is some time since we had an observation we could depend upon; we keep a tight lookout and keep sounding every 2 and 4 hours, by which we suppose ourselves, by the quality of those soundings, to be upon the southernmost end of the Green Bank, but it is hard to say, as we are very likely to be a degree or two out of our reckoning. It was nearly calm last night, but not quite enough so this morning to try for some fish, a meal of which we should all enjoy. Our passenger Robin has almost become torpid, spending almost all his time in sleep, just rising to eat a little, then down again upon his beam ends before the fire, and nothing but talk about politics seems to have any effect upon his torpor; at the mention of the King he becomes half awake, but as soon as the topic is dropped he again relaxes in his usual posture. I am thinking he will get so lazy that he will not relish clearing land upon the banks of Lake Erie. At 6 p.m. hove the ship to and tried again to catch some fish and great success we had, considering the bad qualities of our lines; in about half an hour the Captain hooked . . . a fine large halibut, but he soon broke the line on seeing his situation. In the same manner we lost 3 repeatedly, but in the end succeeded in catching 2 fine fellows of about 40 or 50 lb. each, which was pretty good fortune, though with the loss of a good part of our hooks and snoods.[13] We immediately got on the pots and put some to bake and sat down to sup upon what would, I daresay, in London have been most highly prized as a great luxury. They are the finest fish I think I ever tasted, and are so fat and rich that they need nothing with them; merely put them into the oven dry and a little salt, and they are dressed for the table in about half an hour; I think the pair will last all hands 3 days. Very thick and rainy tonight, sounded in 40 fathoms.

3rd. day, 15th. Clear at last, but no land in sight, or ships; it is an agreeable change [from] the thick weather we have lately had. We are now carrying as much sail as possible, with the hope of soon seeing the Isle of St Paul, from which we are distant 140 miles by our calculations. At 6 p.m. every appearance of becoming thick, which makes but a dull prospect; when this weather will be over I cannot guess; I mind not a foul wind but I am no friend to these 'Newfoundland boatswains'. 'Tis thick as ever, for wet jackets a rich prospect.

4th. day, 16th. At 10 a.m. spoke [to] a ship at last, the *Crown* of Whitby 15 days from Quebec; [they] saw Cape North today and observed in the same latitude as ourselves at noon. Our reckoning agreed with his to within 20 miles of Longitude, which is a capital job, as it is quite clear and the wind from the eastward, because we shall now run 80 miles (the dist[ance] to St Paul's) without any fear. At 4 breezy going, 6 knots, but the wind draws more ahead, which is rather mortifying, as it is the third time we have had a fair wind which lasted but 12 hours, but we must be content. I saw a butterfly and moth but I could catch neither; they were small and seemed desirous of taking a passage with us to the land. At 6 very thick, but we are carrying on, in hopes of making the entrance of the Gulf tomorrow morning; much rain towards midnight.

5th. day, 17th. This morning at half [past] three made the northern end of the little isle of Cape Breton, and soon after spoke the *Harvest* of Sunderland, one of the ships that sailed in ballast from the Orkneys when we did, so we have made better progress than we could expect, though to be sure we might have been lying to, all the thick weather whilst we were running. The island is inhabited and is covered with wood down to the water's edge. It is very uneven and high; the tops of some of the hills look very comfortless, on account of being continually enveloped in fog, which hangs sometimes upon the sides and at others covers

---

[13] A short line fastening the hook to the main fishing line.

their summits, though I should think, from the look of the woods, the island is not by any means barren. Our passengers were pleased enough with the sight of terra firma; though, the wind being at NNW, there is little chance of our beating into the Gulf, as there is always a current setting in the direction the wind does. At 7 we were close into the land and, as it blew fresh, reefed the topsails, the trysail and stowed the mainsails; strong breezes and foggy with rain, which we hope will bring the wind into the Southward.

6th. [day], 18th. Last night the wind came from the SE, shook out the reefs and made all sail, set studding sails and we hope, if the breeze continues, to see the island of Anticosti this evening.

We just saw St Paul's as the weather cleared a little, but Cape Flyaway still attends us which will oblige us, if it comes thicker, to heave to, as we dare not run, which will be exceedingly mortifying when the wind is so fair, but we are making the best use of it whilst it is not so thick, and are going about 5 knots per hour.

6 o'clock. Keeping as much to windward as possible, because we have to haul as soon as we are near the island of Anticosti, between which and the Gaspé Land our passage lies, but it is so very thick we can see nothing ahead and I expect we shall have to shorten sail before night, which will be very unpleasant, though being better than being run foul of or getting ashore by far. There is one thing [that] reconciles [us to] the thick weather . . . we expect the wind will come more from the westward if it should clear up, and until we get to Green Island we shall have no tide, there being none here, and a vessel can gain no ground unless the weather be very fine, on account of the lee current setting always the way the wind blows. We have a stiff breeze and a heavy sea running, which we feel not, because we are going before it at present.

7th. day, 19th. Fine breeze from the SE, no land in sight, though we are between the island of Anticosti and the main[land]; spoke the *Royal Edward* of and bound to Liverpool, a barque that I would not venture across the western ocean in, without [being] required [to do so] by something very extraordinary; although she had but very little sail upon her at the time, her gunwale was in the water. I really wonder how men will sail in such vessels; there is far more likelihood of their going to England upon their beam ends, than upon their bottoms.

Sea stock quite expended, so it is high time we made our port on that account.

1st. day, 20th. Very rainy and unpleasant weather . . . and though we could just make out the land from the fog, we could distinguish nothing but the headlands which, being somewhat lofty, were not capped with mist; but this afternoon it has cleared up finely and the sides of the river are very clearly to be seen. The hills appear to be one immense forest of large trees . . . finely diversified with valleys, up which we see for a considerable distance. At the foot of one of the highest hills near Cape Chateau [there are] some small huts of a whitish appearance, but we are too far distant to distinguish clearly much about them. There are a great number of ships in the river, bound home – and who see with pleasure, I have no doubt, our yards braced up and the wind fair for them. It seems a pity it favours us not for a day or two longer, for then we might get to our port of destination, but for my part I am well content if it holds fine weather, because tacking will let me see more of the river than if we had a fair wind.

2nd. day, 21st. Fine, sunny, warm weather, and I feel the moisture my body has inhaled for the last rainy days beginning to evaporate in the same manner it does from the mountains, of which we now have a very fine view, and really I think it is the most romantic scenery I have ever beheld; the hills which form the banks of the river, and which are a considerable height and entirely covered with large trees, are overtopped by the mountains, down whose sides rush beautiful falls of water which, I suppose, must spring up upon the tops of them, as there is no higher land at their backs. It seems as if Nature had here delighted in confusion; the mountains rise some in peaks, others quite round, and others again exactly like a sugar loaf.

The north side is inhabited by the Eskimos and is barren in appearance excepting close to the waterside, but we have not seen either canoes or inhabitants, though if we could get another slant of wind for a couple of days, we should soon see plenty. It strikes me our passengers' courage begins to fail now they see their desired land, though they say but little; indeed I cannot wonder at it. It is like beginning the world afresh to them, and at their years they cannot have the energies and spirits of youth to help them in what I consider an arduous undertaking. Wind quite against us and making but very little progress towards Quebec, but we hope to get there by the latter end of the week (which will be plenty soon enough) if it lasts fine weather.

3rd. day, 22nd. This morning about 9 o'clock saw a pilot boat on the south side of the river. We, being on the North side, backed the main yard and waited for him; when he got alongside and had handed all his stores out of his boat, we again proceeded. He came, attended by an apprentice, in a fine large boat like a ship's long boat with 3 sprit sails, in which were accommodations for sleeping, cooking etc., they living entirely in it, from the time they leave Quebec till they meet with a ship. It is a long way for them to come down, though they frequently go as far as Anticosti, which is 200 and some odd miles from where we are now, which makes 420 miles from home, but as they are paid according to their work, it makes them more vigilant and [ad]venturous than they otherwise would be. They are both Canadians, speaking French to one another, but their English is rather broken. The pilot himself has a fine countenance and, I think, [is] completely Indian. He is very civil, as well as his apprentice, who is a large man-grown full-faced boy. Wind west and beautiful weather, but getting most desperately hot, the further we proceed; I do not feel at present much inconvenienced from it. The river is about 25 miles broad at this part and the scenery is very grand. On the North side I saw a small village called Mitary inhabited by Indian farmers; the houses were small and quite white, surrounded with large trees.

4th. day, 23rd. Quite calm and hot, but hazy over the land; we are now losing ground, dropping down again with the current. I think it is the most perfect calm I have ever witnessed, not the least breeze of wind, not a sound to be heard either of man, beast or bird, except what is made on board our own ship. Vast quantities of butterflies are continually coming on board, of which there is a rich variety, as well as moths, but none larger than our own, or more beautiful; a collector would have a good show in about a couple of hours or so, in the early part of the day.

5th. day, 24th. Still solemnly calm, and has been, all last night; we are yet losing ground rather than gaining any, everything is so calm and quiet that one does not like to disturb the universal stillness by talking loud. Nothing to be heard but a waterfall which, by our distance from it, must be rather a grand one; it sounds much like distant thunder. We are now off the mouth of the river Columbia and but a short distance from Point Neuf, which is rather a fine object, but rather barren of trees compared to the rest of the country.

6th. day, 25th. Light breezes eastward and clear in the morning; towards evening it freshened and we made Green Island, but we could scarcely stem the tide, which we first found here. About 12 o'clock p.m. we were all taken aback by a squall from the westward which set all the fine weather sails flying about in fine style, but we quickly got them all in, braced up sharp and went to bed, though I suppose we shall soon be called up again to tack ship. Put 4 letters on board the *Harrier* barque bound for London, 1 for Hitchin, 1 Uncle Joseph, 1 Brother John, and 1 JFC, which I hope will reach England shortly.

7th. day, 26th. This day finishes our passage, I believe; we had a stiff breeze all night and are decreasing our distance very fast, the banks of the river are now all cultivated and houses are in plenty, and I think of all the scenery I ever saw, this is the crown of it. The islands are very numerous and some of them appear to be well cultivated, one in particular, Crane Island, is a charming spot. It belongs to a person named MacPherson, a Scotchman, one who possesses, I can see, a very good taste. He has left some of the finest trees about the house (which is upon the end of the island) which throw a venerable shade over his little white mansion and give it the appearance . . . [of being] built in the old style of those old-fashioned buildings so frequently met with in the vicinity of London. At 8 p.m. past the falls of Miranca, which I should think are rather a fine object, but it was too dark to see anything clearly. 9 o'clock, we are now anchored under Quebec and they are getting the boat ready to go ashore. I shall go for one, I know, so I must be getting ready – though, as I am not known, I need be by no means particular. 12 o'clock. Just returned, the Master has finished his business, which here requires great promptness, as the timber is rising [in value] very fast.

1st. day, 27th. Dark, gloomy, rainy weather, but from what I can see of the town it is a very noble place, but we cannot get on shore until tomorrow, when we shall haul into the wharf to discharge the coals and glass.

2nd. day, 28th. Fine, clear weather but uncommonly hot, more so than ever I experienced before, but I think I shall be able to bear it as well as other people; got our orders to go to the wharf tomorrow. After dinner went on shore with the passengers, who are going by the steamboat to Montreal, and in the evening went up into the cove on board the *Victory* of Whitby, and returned in the evening after a fatiguing row against strong wind and tide.

3rd. day, 29th. Very close, with heavy rain; started to heave up the anchor, but could not weigh it for about 3 hours and a half, when we brought up with it a new anchor, and about 40 fathoms of cable, which are owned by a brig, the *Hazard Sheldon*, and which we hope will pay for our trouble; we did not get to the wharf till about 2 o'clock, when we got comfortably moored, cleared up the decks and got all in order and readiness for discharging, then had to move our ship again about 9 o'clock to another part of the wharf, which we did not accomplish until midnight, having been much impeded by another vessel.

5th. day 1st.[14]   Afternoon began to discharge.

---

[14] Beck has forgotten that there are 31 days in July, so that his dates from 1 August to 10 August are all incorrect, and should read 31, 2, 7, 8 and 9 to make sense.

7th. day 3rd.   Landed the glass.

5th. day 8th.   Discharged all the coals, cleared the hold.

6th. day 9th.   Took in at the wharf 120 deals [timber], in the afternoon moved the ship up into the Wolf's Cove.

7th. day 10th.   Went into Sillery Cove for timber and got all ready for beginning to load ship on 2nd. day.

7th. day 23rd.   Finished loading the lower hold.

6th. day 29th.   Finished loading the twixt decks.

7th. day 30th. of 8th. mo[nth]. Got the deck timber on and announced the glad tidings to the rest of the ships in the cove with three loud hurrahs, which were all answered. Wind East and ESE, which will prevent our leaving for some time.

Quebec has an exceedingly striking appearance from the river, and one that cannot fail of impressing the stranger with very favourable ideas; the heights, the churches, wharfs, stores and the city altogether, present a view which I wonder never to have heard spoken of or to have seen engraved – but upon seeing it, one feels disappointed. The houses [of] wood, irregularly and awkwardly built, the narrow streets without anything in the way of shops to enliven them, and the unpleasant ascent the city is built upon, make it appear rather an indifferent place to what one would have expected. But of all the scenery I ever beheld, none ever equalled that which extends as far as the eye can reach, from the heights up and down the river; it is beautiful beyond description, no sameness, but one wide field of infinite variety, on which the eye can gaze without feeling satiated in the least – but, on the contrary, can dwell with increasing pleasure. On the left, the island of Orleans presents a very interesting view; it is the finest of the islands in the St Lawrence, its shores are lined with small white houses with apparently well-cultivated land about them, backed by fine thick woods, amongst which they look exceedingly pretty. On the right, Wolf's cove with the shipping in it, the river winding for a considerable distance, the boats and bateaux passing up and down and the lofty hills in the background claim the notice of every admirer of scenery, whilst the town below, with its tin-covered roofs which dazzle the eye if the sun is shining upon them, makes it altogether the finest panoramic view I ever beheld.

I sat gazing beneath me some hours delighted, yet not without regretting that those present in thought and memory, though widely separated, could not enjoy with me the beauty of the scene; it was 1st day afternoon, the after part of a beautiful day, and I was led into a train of reflections which I love to indulge in, because they flow from a source I love. That source is home, and those that render home endearing to everyone. Is there, thought I, one that now thinks upon me? Is there one that wishes me present with them? Could I but know it, how delightful it would be! But, widely separated, 'tis impossible to convey our thoughts to one another with that rapidity the heart could wish, else should I quickly know what has transpired in what already seems to be a long separation. Distance makes it appear much longer than it really is. Actually, it is but short; but 3 weeks and a fair wind, and I expect, with swelling sails and a flying ensign, we shall bid adieu to America, for that island I prefer infinitely before it.

On the side of the river, the tribe of New Brunswick Indians have pitched their abodes; I have been over to see them, and was much amused with all I saw. They were exceedingly civil, some spoke good English, others French, and invited me into their wigwams, the most simple abode man has ever dwelt under; a forked stick in the centre, on which rested a number of poles and covered with large pieces of bark, composed the habitations of these people, in which a family of 5 . . . [or] 6 were huddled together. After being among them for a short time, they began to assemble in the chief's wigwam, and divine service soon after began. Their singing was very agreeable and they appeared to be very attentive; by the crucifixes hanging to their necks, I suppose them to be Catholics. When it was over, men came out, lit their pipes, and were very conversant; they spoke capital English and French, and one of them sang some English songs, out of a book a gentleman present offered him, in good style. The men were the finest figures I ever saw, without exception, but the squaws were very dirty, disagreeable women. Both men and women tie up their hair behind and adorn themselves with trinkets, of which they seem very fond; some of them are tin, cut into stars and suns and a variety of shapes. The youths were amusing themselves with bows and arrows, shooting at small birds or halfpence, stuck up in a split stick at a considerable distance from them, which they struck with admirable dexterity. They make an annual visit to Quebec, and receive from the Governor a present of a musket and blanket – for the purpose, I suppose, of keeping them in alliance with the English, of whom at present they seem very fond, and call them by the familiar name of 'brother'. They are ardently fond of rum, and have often been known to commit serious mischief (when in a state of intoxication) upon the persons of the Canadians, which has occasioned a law to be passed that no person should allow them to drink in their houses, but that they should carry out whatever spirits they shall purchase. I have often regretted to see them, men, women and children, drinking rum with a ruin[ous] avidity, and destroying in a short time the fruits of the winter's chase, as well as the money their small baskets and canoes, which they sell in the market, produce. They are exceedingly dextrous in managing their canoes; these are made of bark and are capable of conveying 4, 5 . . . [or] 6 very conveniently at the same time; they are so light that, as soon as they are landed, one of the men shoulders it with his head within it, and lies it out of reach of the tide, bottom upwards that the sun may not hurt it, till they return, when it is carried into the water. But I must say, from what observations I have been able to make, I am disappointed; I expected to find a dignified race of men, endowed with superior abilities . . . [to] most uncivilised people – instead of which, they are a drunken set of beings and as great beggars as our gypsies, of whom they often reminded me. But there are exceptions, and I met with a few whose behaviour was very different; . . . it is to be regretted that there are not means adopted for their civilisation.

Point Levi, where they remain in the summer, is a pretty spot and the woods abound with fruits of different sorts, of which I have gathered great quantities, but the quality is not equal to our English garden produce. Filberts, raspberries, currants and a small but very sweet fruit called by the Canadians 'sugar plums' are very abundant, but the filberts are covered with a kind of prickly husk, the small darts of which, getting between the fingers, cause an intolerable kind of itching, but as they ripen they lose this property, and a hatfull may be obtained in a short time when the bushes are found, which is by no means a difficult job. The rocks are a rotten kind of slatestone which, crumbling off, forms a rich top soil, and it is surprising to see trees growing upon the steep banks of the river where there appears nothing to forward vegetation but the bare rocks, which notwithstanding, [the trees] are some of them of a great size and throw a fine covering over what would otherwise appear desolate and barren.

The market is well supplied with vegetables and fruit, but not at a cheaper rate than in England; it is held every day of the week, but it is larger on 7th. than on any other day of the week. On that day the country people for a considerable distance round come to the city, and it is a curious sight to see the [Indian] women coming down the river in large canoes made of the trunks of trees hollowed out, singing as they row along. Generally it is a kind of humdrum tune which, though agreeable to their own ears, must be considered by Europeans as very discordant. The anchorage is not good in the river . . . and takes a deal of time and patience. Wolf Cove is the place where almost all the ships load, but a few load at the town, for what reason I cannot tell, for they are obliged to come into the Cove for their timber, which must necessarily cause them a deal of trouble and time, that in the timber trade could be better employed. There are wharfs built, running out from the shore a considerable distance into the river, from which stretch along great pieces of timber called booms; the space[s] they enclose are called ponds, and contain immense quantities of timber, which the purchaser or captain chooses from. It is then rafted, shoved out of the booms and towed on board by the ships' boats which, when the tides are rapid, is very unpleasant work. A person in the timber trade ought to possess as much patience as Job; there is as much to cross his temper, such as delay for timber, rafting it, getting it off the ship and then stowing it, beside the anxiety when a large raft is alongside and it blows a fresh off wind. I must confess [that] when the ship was loaded, I joined in three as hearty cheers as ever were uttered by a British seaman. It is the custom here, when a ship has completed her loading, to hoist her ensign and give three cheers, which are answered by other ships.

I must not forget to mention the steam boats, which are very large and commodious. They are not so handsome as the English ones, the cabins being built upon their decks as the hold is entirely applied to stowage. They go regularly twice a week to Montreal and carry an immense number of the lower classes, who are continually pouring into Quebec, to that degree that it is quite astonishing.

I have often had to lament at the sight of a family in a strange country with but a few shillings, the father unable to procure work and often some of the children too ill to allow them to proceed up the country, begging of the ships to allow them to cook at their fires, and requesting a few biscuits to lengthen out their little store. They come out (I mean great numbers of them) under the idea of getting plenty of work and no wages less than a dollar a day, when actually the hardest work is done for three shillings, and some as low as two and sixpence, per day. Finding themselves quite disappointed in their golden dreams, they proceed up the country with a heavy heart and sincerely wish they had never left home, where they were sure of a meal of potatoes.

1st. day, 31st. Stiff easterly breezes accompanied with rain, but last night it blew very hard and the ships in the Cove seemed to have much loss of timber.

2nd. day, 1st. 9th. mo[nth]. Went to town for sea stock, but it rained too heavy to bring it up. Fetched up 6 spars for studding sail booms.

3rd. day, 2nd. A passenger came on board who had come out with the ship 2 years ago. He appears a pleasant and agreeable man, and wants to go to England to see after some property he wisely left at home to go to, if his Canadian visit did not answer.

4th. day, 3rd. Fetched up all from the town and got up one anchor ready for sea.

For my sea stock:
1lb. tea   1 Indian box
6lb. sugar   1 canoe
1lb. soap   1 pincushion.

This finishes our stay at Quebec and Wolf Cove, so farewell to them; I have passed some very agreeable days in America, but I gladly turn my face eastward, when I hope to meet those who make Old England the dearest isle of all the earth to me.

5th. day, 4th. At half past 5 got under way, wind WNW, stiff breezes with showers of rain, and ran down to the town under the foresail. At 8 o'clock brought up opposite [?] Gondie's wharf, the Captain having some business ashore. Great numbers of ships proceeding down the river; it gives me pleasure to see us again upon the move to Old England. 12 o'clock weighed anchor again and in a short time were out of Quebec; the falls of Macanza appeared to great advantage, being much swollen with the late heavy rains, and I greatly regretted we soon lost sight of them. About 4, encountered a tremendous squall with very heavy rain, in which we lost our main top gallant mast, broke the yard in two, and were in great danger of losing our top masts. If this is a specimen of our passage, welcome the conclusion of it.

6th. day, 5th. At half past 2 got under way, with a stiff breeze in the same quarter with rainy showers. 10 o'clock saw a specimen of the effects of yesterday's squall, the sight of which made our loss a mere trifle; it was a small schooner upon her beam ends. We hove the ship to, and the Captain, 3 others and myself, went in the pilot's boat to the wreck; she was loaded and, had we been bound up, most likely we should have endeavoured to get her upright and towed her ashore. The pilot knew her and told us she had passengers aboard, and he thought [they] were about 8 in number. They must all have perished, the boat being alongside fast to her quarter, though we saw no bodies or clothes by which we could be certain. It was a melancholy sight, the contemplation of which gave rise to feelings of gratitude for a preservation from a similar fate; from the sails all being set, I should suppose it was from want of care in not taking them in before it came on, though very likely they apprehended (like ourselves) it would not be so heavy. We stopped about half an hour with her, but as there was no chance of getting her ashore we abandoned her, and went aboard our own ship again. At midnight strong breezes, all sails set.

7th. day, 6th. Employed securing the deck timber, stowing anchors and lashing boats the whole day, and we are now ready for encountering the strong western ocean. At 3 o'clock our good-natured old pilot left us; he spoke very bad English, though he had been conducting ships up and down 33 years. He lives at Matan, and when he shoved off in his boat he gave three cheers and wished us a pleasant passage. It was done in so good-humoured and jocose a manner that he set the whole ship's crew in a laugh; the old man was such a pleasant body I quite regretted parting with him.

10 o'clock p.m. The aurora borealis is shining in great splendour and [this] is the first time I have seen it to such advantage; sometimes it shoots up in a vast number of pillars of light and then illumines the heavens with a column of fire, by which one could almost see to read. But when they are seen so bright they are a sure sign of strong weather, and we are now scudding before a freshening N. Wester that I am afraid will compel us to heave to, but I hope not before we get well clear of the land.

1st. day, 7th. Stowed the square mainsail topsail, and fore top gallant sail, a heavy sea running and a strong westerly wind; we expect to get clear of the Gulf tomorrow. Saw a lightship under close-reefed topsails, and think by her appearance she has had a rough time of it. I hope by this day 5 weeks to be among my friends in Sunderland, if we are at all favoured by the winds. If we do get to England by that time it will be good work, as we shall have been away but 4 months. At midnight less wind, set top mast and lower studding sails, the northern lights very beautiful.

2nd. day, 8th. Fine clear weather and stiff breeze at NW. The *Harrisons* of London (the largest ship trading to Quebec) upon our starboard quarter, she sails far better than we do, and I suppose we shall soon lose sight of her; all sail set and all going on very agreeably.

4 p.m. Breeze freshening and, by the appearance of the sky, we shall soon have as much as we can show top gallant to, but we carry sail as long as possible, making hay while the sun shines, so that we may take it easy when the wind is unfavourable. The *Harrisons* [is] hull down, if she goes at that rate she will soon see the English shore. Hope tomorrow to take our departure from Cape Race.

3rd. day, 9th. This morning at 6 o'clock took our departure from St Paul's . . . the Captain says it is the finest run he ever had from Quebec; should it continue, we shall soon be upon the banks of Newfoundland. We have beautiful fine days and clear starlight nights, which makes it very agreeable, but we must soon expect fogs and rainy weather as we approach the banks. It is very singular that it should be so continually thick – 2 fine days together are a great rarity, and it is either calm upon them, or blowing a gale of wind. I should rejoice if this wind would carry us over them [i.e the banks].

8 o'clock p.m. Strong breezes and clear weather.

4th. day, 10th. Last night our fair wind left us and it fell entirely calm about 2 this morning, but I am glad to say it has returned and we have again spread all our fair weather sails. I have had a good deal of conversation today with our passenger, he is a steady, dry, pleasant young man and, having seen a great part of Upper Canada, is an agreeable addition to our little number. He tells me he possesses about 30 acres of clear land near Port St George which produce enough and to spare, and that he has 176 more in a state of forwardness. I think he is coming home for a wife, as well as to see after his English property, as he seems to wish for a change from a single state ... from his dislike to the Canadian women, I expect he intends killing two birds with one stone. He says there is a good living to be got in Canada for a man who with a little money joins sobriety and industry, but that anyone coming out with the idea of an easy life must starve, as the work for himself, or manual labour [for others], is of the most laborious kind. Wages for labouring men in the summer months are as high as 14 and 15 dollars a month and their food, but in the winter they are as low as 6 and 7. Now as they have but 5 summer months, these wages are [rather] low than otherwise, and but a poor sum for a family of 4 and 5 to subsist upon. One thing to be sure, there is always plenty to do, winter and summer, for those that seek it, therefore a man need not stand idle. Deer, rabbits, pigeons and partridges are in the greatest abundance, also those less agreeable neighbours, bears and serpents; of the latter species they have a great variety. He says he prefers England far before America, if he could do as well in the former as he does in the latter, it being a more agreeable climate and more society, the loss of which he tells me he feels most. He has seen all the lakes, as well as the falls of Niagara (of which he gave me a long description), 'For,' said he, 'I found I could not settle until I had seen all I had read or heard talked of.'

5th. day, 11th. Fine, clear, beautiful weather and a moderate westerly breeze; should it continue, we shall soon be upon the banks. Last night a fine sparrowhawk boarded us and took up his quarters upon our fore yard; he had picked up in his flight from the land a Mother Carey's chicken, which he then began to pick at his leisure. We let him finish his meal in peace, but as soon as it was dusk we went aloft to catch him, but coming upon him too precipitately, he flew away ... we saw him return about half past 5 with another chicken, which he took upon the main yard and began to devour, making the feathers fly about him in fine style; thinking it a good opportunity to entrap him, one of the men went up and succeeded in catching him; we then cut one of his wings and turned him upon deck but, preferring death to slavery, he jumped overboard and was soon freed from all the troubles of this life – at the same time freeing the seas of a tyrant, for had he continued with us at large, the poor little Careys would often have shared the same fate as the 2 he caught whilst with us.

6th. day, 12th. We are favoured with extraordinary weather, such as no one in the ship, tho' often this road, ever before experienced; the days are fine and sunny and are very much like our summer ones in England. It is a pleasure to be at sea, though it would be very hot if we had not the fine, steady NW breeze we are running before. 5 o'clock: a strong southerly swell has visited us since noon and most likely it will be followed by a southerly wind; we are now off the Green Bank and expect soon to be upon the great one of Newfoundland. We have all our fishing tackle ready; if it would fall calm, I think a mess [i.e. a meal] of fish would be very agreeable.

7th. day, 13th. This morning it fell quite calm and about noon we got out the 'jollyboat' and sent one hand in it, fishing; he found bottom at 50 fathoms, but neither had a bite nor caught a fish. We again tried at 6 o'clock, but without success, so returned on board. 7 o'clock a fine, light breeze sprung up from the SE.

1st. day, 14th. Fine, stiff breeze and fair going, rather more than 6 knots an hour, brave sailing for us; rather foggy at noon, but it soon cleared up again. This makes 15 weeks since we left England, 4 more and I hope to attend a Friends' Meeting. It seems a long time since I had that pleasure, it will indeed be pleasant to attend a place of worship. All continues to go on comfortably . . . to me it would be a miserable thing, to be in a ship where there was a quarrelsome crew. To me it is a matter of astonishment, how a number of men who cannot choose other companions, but must continue together, can ever give way to quarrelling and dissatisfaction; there is something in it so contrary to commonsense, that it is wonderful men should ever yield to such ridiculous practices. Yet it is a lamentable fact that sailors are more given that way than any other class, or at least were so, though, as I remarked on the passage out, I believe . . . [them] to . . . [be improving] fast, and it was with sincere pleasure I noticed the [Christian] standard under which they are enlisting, and under which I believe them to be improving, flying at different mastheads both at the town and [at] Wolf's Cove, Quebec. I mean the Bethel Union Seamen's Society: that those engaged in so desirable a work may meet their just reward is, I believe, not only my wish, but also that of numbers of worthy characters who are rising up, an ornament to their profession.

8 o'clock, in fore top mast studding sail . . . blowing strong and running 7 knots. Midnight, stowed the top gallant sails.

2nd. day, 15th. Very foggy and windy, at 8 o'clock a.m. took one reef in each topsail, and stowed the jib and trysail; she will be off the great bank by 12 o'clock today, by our calculation. At this rate she will quickly be half seas over.

The sea is running very high and the ship steering but badly makes this stiff wind rather unpleasant, but we must take it as it comes, and be content . . . all I am fearful of is that the sea, not the wind, will not allow us to scud. At noon took another reef in each topsail and stowed the square mainsail, the wind going . . . round, but gradually. At midnight the wind came to the SE quarter; the swell, being very heavy, makes her roll very heavy. Set the main sail.

3rd. day, 16th. Noon: a fine, stiff breeze is wafting us to the Southward, where we shall find it warmer, I expect; we are so lumbered up with the timber, that we cannot keep up a fire, as we did upon the passage out. This makes it rather uncomfortable but, as we have had dry weather this far, the inconvenience has not been very forcibly felt. At the time we were reefing the fore topsail yesterday, the sea was covered with foam as far as the eye could reach, all round us, more so than I have ever noticed before. It was a grand sight from the yard, to see our ship scudding through it and leaving behind her a wake of light for a considerable distance, and I was sorry to see the wind come ahead; it is so much more agreeable to be scudding, than knocking about with a foul breeze. 6 o'clock p.m. The wind increases and is more against us. The ship, being deeply loaded, begins to throw the green seas over her bows and wet the poor sailors' feet, whilst the rain, which has just commenced its career, wets their backs; but it is all a trifle to those who are used to it.

4th. day, 17th. Fair winds again and fine, clear weather, which are both quite welcome to us, but the heavy northerly swell still continues without any abatement, which causes the ship to labour much and makes it necessary to pump her now and then, but at present it is quite trifling, and long may it continue so, for a leaky ship in the western ocean is not an agreeable companion. I expect we shall have a quick passage, a few weeks more and, if all goes well, we shall be in Sunderland, I expect; the thought is very agreeable, and I look forward with pleasure to the time that will give me some news of home and friends. 10 o'clock, supped on pork and potatoes and went to bed.

5th. day, 16th. Alas, alas, this morning, carrying a press of canvas against a heavy swell, we lost one of our number [a fowl]: a heavy sea broke in at the gangway and washed the poor fellow overboard. He strove with all his force and powers to reach the ship but, not being able, soon disappeared. By his friends he is much lamented, but not by me, as he required far more of my attention than I could well spare. In fact I am glad, as it will cause the death of his partners tomorrow, to prevent them cheating the cook and the cabin gentry

74

of a dinner of fowls. Also a 'duck',[15] whether tired of life or not, entangled himself in a coil of rope, and hung by his neck in a gibbet's tassel until he was dead. An inquest was held over him respecting the disposal of the body when, after some little consultation, it was agreed upon that, having committed suicide, he was not worthy of the honour of lying in state, as is customary with his caste, but that he should be committed to the deep, a sentence immediately executed.

12 o'clock, fine NW breeze and clear weather. A difference arose last night among the petty officers, but due care was taken speedily to end it.

6th. day, 19th. Fine, stiff breeze from the westward, all sail set, a fine ship to windward, apparently American, going towards that country. 10 o'clock, turn into 'Blanket Bay' [i.e. bed], having been up 9 hours last night.

6 o'clock p.m., a gale of wind fast approaching, the sea rising prodigiously high and threatening to run over us every moment; I heartily wish we were but safely hove to, but the Captain is determined to scud as long as possible. Took in a deal of sail at noon; one thing pleases me, we have fine moonlight nights.

8 o'clock. Thanks to time, 8 o'clock has relieved me from the wheel, where I have spent two as anxious hours as I ever recollect to have done; the safety of the ship and crew depend entirely on the helmsman – a mistake would very likely prove fatal to [all], so that the utmost care and vigilance is requisite for their preservation; we have not been much washed at present, except by one enormous sea which, breaking in by the main rigging, compelled us to take to it [i.e. the rigging] to get out of its way.

7th. day, 26th. Rather less wind last night, but as much this morning; obliged to set more sail, to make her run clear of the sea, which has a wicked appearance. Noon, in top gallant sails and took two reefs in the top sails, thick weather and much wind; I should not be surprised if this breeze continues till we make the Scotch land. We are now nearly half way home.

1st. day, 21st. About 1 o'clock a.m. the breeze died gently away, and it became as beautiful and clear a morning as ever shone out of the heavens; we immediately spread all our canvasses to keep her steady in the swell, for really it makes her roll to that degree that, to use a seafaring term, it is enough to roll the bones through our skin. At noon a light breeze from the northward, with a very heavy swell; a few porpoises playing about the ship, I suppose they take her for a monster of the finny kind.

8 p.m. A fine, fresh breeze sprung up from the SW, but veered into the old

---

[15] A 'duck' was a seaman.

quarter with a Scotch mist attendant upon it; we immediately set all sail to catch the favouring breeze, which is now sending her along about five and a half miles an hour. Midnight, a dark lowering threatening scud flying over the moon with great rapidity; stowed the fore top gallant sail, it being split very much. Since this day week we have run towards home nearly 1,000 miles; rare good work for the old coal wagon.

2nd. day, 22nd. Fine breezes from the NW and very thick; our passenger seems in a great hurry to see his native land, continually asking the Captain to set some more sail, and to please him we set two top gallant scudding sails at 8 o'clock; whereupon, the yard rigging out the booms, I heartily wished the good fellow at York, if he is to bother us this way. He does not consider we are [paid] by the month, and not in such a hurry as himself. I pity much the ship bound to Quebec, the wind is right against them and I am sure, by the time they get there and are loaded, it will be high time to start [home] if they wish to keep clear of the ice; it was getting very cold when we were there, and by this time the morning and evening must be rather severe.

3rd. day, 23rd. This is my birthday, 20 years I have been a sojourner upon earth, and I am afraid, to but little purpose; another year has gone, with but little improvement, I am afraid, another is commenced, what it may produce time only will tell, but I hope, if I remain in this world, it will bring forth more abundantly than the preceding ones have done. When I look back, even as far as I can remember, I find cause to regret that much precious time has passed away, without my making what use of it I should have done . . . and at last time has found me, at the age of 20, with as few qualifications for getting through the world as many have possessed at half that age. But as the recollection of the past can only now serve as a spur to the future, it were pity to mourn over hours that are fled and to neglect the present, so here [I] enter another year with a determination to:

> Defer not till tomorrow, to be wise,
> As tomorrow's sun to me may never rise.

10 a.m. Strong breezes and very foggy, going at the rate of 6 knots per hour, obliged to take in all our scudding [?] sails and furl the big sail, keeping a good lookout for lightships bound to the westward. 4 p.m., took 2 reefs in topsails and stowed the top gallant sails, strong gales and foggy weather. Midnight, more moderate, let out one reef of the topsails, wind drawing ahead.

4th. day, 24th. Quite moderate, all sail set again, wind about NNE, but every appearance of it westering again; fog all gone, but in its stead cloudy and much rain, sometimes attended with heavy squalls. It is surprising the swell the breeze has left; were it not for the wind we have to keep her steady, she would almost roll her bulwarks under water.

Meridian. Wind favouring us again, and I expect we shall soon have to set our scudding sails; a small bird of a curious description is among the rigging, but I have not been able to catch him; I may perhaps tonight, when he goes to sleep.

I think a great number of the birds of passage must fall a prey to the fish, upon their flight over the sea; I saw a small one yesterday fall into the water, apparently exhausted with fatigue, it looked much like a sparrow, or some such small bird.

6 o'clock p.m. Strong breezes and cloudy weather; the sky bears a very angry appearance, but we have yet got a reef in our topsails against the worst, which I think is a very prudent measure, as it frequently comes upon us with very little warning, and seems almost ready to tear away the masts and the rigging. 8 o'clock, winds favouring us more and more, but she is diving into the sea in high style.

5th. day, 25th. Strong gale from the northward and a heavy beam sea, at times very squally, with rain and hail; it is as bitterly cold as ever I felt in my life, I am sure it has come from Greenland and, for my part, I wish it were there again. The further we go northward, the more unsettled we find the weather; it is, to be sure, what we can only expect, as it is generally so here at all times of the year. Our passenger is obliged to keep [in] his cabin, the ship's motion being too great for him to bear upon the deck; I believe he seriously wishes himself in York. 8 p.m., in second reef of the topsails and stowed the top gallant sails; whilst I was furling the main one I fell off the yard, but happily caught the top gallant shrouds and foot rope of the yard, or I should never have stowed another.

6th. day, 26th. A strong gale, which I believe must compel us to heave to. At 8 turned the hands up and reefed the foresail, stowed the trysail and jib; very squally, with much rain and hail. When I sometimes look back at the heavy sea and it seems ready to break over us every moment, it seems surprising how man's courage can lead him over such a vast extent of water, in a ship not near as large as the waves that roll around him, but well knowing how to act with her in every situation and confident of her ability, aided by his management, of conveying him safely, he ventures over an extent of some thousands of miles without seeing any land, devoid of the least dread of failure in his intended run.

Now very bad weather, one ship to windward hove to and, I will engage, not one in a hundred would be scudding with the heavy seas under her broadsides that we now have. It is wonderful how she rises upon the top of the seas in the manner she does; if one were to break over us, it would inevitably sweep the decks of the boats, galley, timber and, in short, everything upon them, which I hope will not be the case.

4 o'clock. I am happy to say, more moderate and less sea than before, heavy squalls at times, with much rain north. Midnight. Much finer weather, let the reef out of the fore sail and one out of the fore topsail; saw (for the first time, if I remember right) a beautiful rainbow; it being in a dark sky, appeared to great advantage. Much better night than the preceding. Wind rather to the eastward.

7th. day, 27th. A beautiful fine morning . . . from the appearance of the sky, I expect a southerly will bring us to the land, from which we are distant about 600 miles, a distance easily run in 5 days and then, with a northerly I think, we could bring Sunderland pier to bear west in two days more. I hope we may get there in nine days, because unless we arrive when the tides are good, we must lay in the roads for some time, which will not be very agreeable, though if we were to go to Shields, I should like it very well; but it is hard to say how we may get on; only, as there is such a prevalence of westerly winds in this quarter, one speaks with a little more assurance than one would otherwise. The track we come is so little frequented, except by ships bound for Scotland and the east coast of England, that we very seldom see any. Indeed, I think the southerly way about must be far more agreeable than this, the weather in general must be finer and more settled, though on account of the lights and pilotage it must be far more expensive. At noon, shook out all the reefs and set all sail, a light breeze. There is a heavy swell meeting us . . . which, not being very agreeable with the heavy northerly one the gale has left, between . . . [them], our poor ship rolls so much, that it is enough to do, to hold fast.

8 p.m. A clock calm, the clouds all hanging in threatening heaviness, waiting for a breeze to disperse them over the bright blue concave overhead.

1st. day, 28th. A day of calm and silence, a noon of heat, and an evening of beautiful weather and light breezes, fair with all. What an agreeable change from the weather we lately experienced, but, like the crosses of life which serve to give a later relish to its enjoyment, so the late gale has served to prepare us for the greater delights the present yields. It has seemed a sabbath with all nature, the porpoises gambolling about the ship, and the birds reposing upon the bosom of the ocean, seemed to rejoice in the day as well as ourselves, who, lately tempest-tossed, now yield to the repose such beautiful weather affords. Every sabbath brings us nearer home, one more, and I hope we shall get to our desired haven. I begin to feel rather eager, I must confess, once more to meet my friends; blow, ye breezes, and waft her to her port of destination.

8 o'clock p.m. The breeze freshens very fast and I am rather doubtful of 'Blanket Bay' having much of my company tonight, as I feel confident we must take some of the sail in.

2nd day, 29th. 4 a.m. How true that old saying is, 'After a calm comes a storm,' we are able this day to judge; it came upon us so suddenly that I really thought we must have lost some of our canvas, with very heavy storms of rain. We were obliged to keep taking in reef after reef, until we got her under the 2 double-reefed topsails; all the other sails we were obliged to furl. At 7 were 'pooped' by a heavy sea which did much damage, washing away the roundhouse, paint locker, floating part of the deck boarding – it was a mercy the poor fellow at the helm was not washed over the quarter. He most certainly would have been, had he not held on by the wheel. The sea broke all the panes in the skylight and washed . . . all away from the breakfast table in the cabin, and filled the passenger's bed and chest with water. It would not have hurt us, but it fell calm, or rather lulled a little, when, as the sea had more run than the ship, she could not . . . [outrun] it, consequently the unwelcome visitors came on board.

Noon, better weather again . . . the rigging is full of wet clothes from the cabin, hanging up to dry.

4 o'clock. Saw a ship reaching to the Southward under her three topsails, expect she is a whaler from Greenland.

8 p.m. Steady breezes from the NW with much swell, set the studding sails and shook out all the reefs, the northern lights very splendid.

3rd. day, 30th. Fine weather, all sails set, wind NW and SW, stiff breeze. We begin now to see great numbers of birds, a sure indication of our being very near the land; we shall be looking for it the day after tomorrow, if the breeze continues.

Noon. Much rain, weather very unsettled, and the wind unsteady, I more afraid of its coming to the southward and bringing thick weather than anything else. If it does, we must go Northward of all the Orkney Islands, as we dare not make the land whilst it continues.

6 p.m. The sky looks very unpromising for fine weather. Took in the steering sails and stowed the jib, prepared everything for a breeze; well, let it come, we are now all ready. I think next 1st day will see us very near Sunderland.

4th. day, 10th. mo[nth], 1st. This morning at 6 o'clock saw the land; we suppose it [to] be the Butts of the Lewis Islands, but cannot say positively. Should it prove so, it is a very fair landfall. Unfortunately the wind is against us and looks but very unpromising weather, being very squally, with much rain. Should we get a good observation at noon, we can be confident of what land it is, and should it prove to be the Butt and the wind favour us a little, we shall soon see Cape Wrath, the entrance of the Pentland Firth. The land proved eventually to be the Flannen Isles, but from the masthead we can discern the Butt of the Lewis, which we shall soon be to the eastward of. A large Greenland ship and a brig, both to leeward, are making for the Pentland Firth.

5th. day, 2nd. For fear of getting to leeward, we carried sail last night to that degree that the ship completely dived under every sea that met her. We were obliged to lower our topsails every squall, and as soon as it was over, hoist them up again; this made our deck timber work exceedingly, and gave more employment for our pumps than was at all agreeable. At daybreak, finding ourselves well to windward, took in sail and eased her off her canvas, all hands upon deck, ready for making the Orkney Islands – for it is so thick, we might be almost ashore before we should be aware of it.

4 p.m. Got well through the Firth into the North Sea, it happily cleared up at noon and continued so, till we were in a fair way for going clear of all dangers; as soon as the tide favoured us, she was through in about half an hour, till then it had been against us. We are now in a fair way for home in 48 hours; if the breeze continues, it will see us in Sund. [i.e. Sunderland] roads; the idea is pleasant to us all, and we please ourselves with the idea of spending next First Day on shore and amongst our friends. Thus far we have had a fine run, I think we have not had 12 hours' foul wind at a time since we left Quebec, and as the sky bears every appearance of a fair wind continuing, we shall, I think, have made as quick a voyage as any ship out of Sunderland has done this year.

6th. day, 2nd. Last night hope told a flattering tale. I had scarcely done writing before the yards had to be braced up, and by morning the wind was right ahead and began to blow fresh . . . at 10 p.m. stowed the foresail, strong gales and much rain. Now all hopes of getting home this week are over, for this wind may last for the next quarter of the moon and is as likely to as not, as we have had a deal of northerly winds lately; when so near, it is rather mortifying thus to be baffled, but all we can do is to bear it patiently. I really cannot write, the pitches so very heavy, so I believe I shall take 40 winks, as it is my watch upon deck at midnight.

7th. day, 4th. A hard-hearted South Wester which, if it continues, will soon run up the shortness of the passage to a long one, although I suppose we have not farther to go than 180 miles – less, I should think, [rather] than more; we are now somewhere about Aberdeen, but we cannot say positively, not having seen the land today. The weather is much finer than it was yesterday, which makes the foul wind less irksome than it would otherwise be, but I know not that it matters much whether we are here or on the passage to London.

3rd. day, 7th. Since I wrote the above we have had a series of very tempestuous weather, in which we have lost much ground, and if the wind continues, I suppose we shall still keep losing, until we fetch at last the Orkneys again.

On the 1st day we had a very heavy gale from the southward, which obliged us to take in all our sails excepting our close-reefed topsails. It frequently rained very heavy and, there being a very heavy sea running at the time, she shipped a great deal of water, so that we spent but a poor first day and night. In the morning it became rather more moderate, but returned with all its vigour at noon and lasted till midnight, when it cleared up a little.

4th. day, 8th. Still from the southward and blowing very fresh at times. At noon, tacked in Aberdeen Bay; I wish we were in some snug roadstead instead of knocking about upon this Scotch coast! Although we keep close in to the land to take advantage of the tides, it is so misty that one cannot tell much of the appearance of the coast, which I much regret. 8 p.m., another gale in the old quarter fast coming on, to me now it is a matter of perfect indifference, because I am confident we shall have no change without some disagreeable weather preceding it.

5th. day, 9th. More moderate, made sail again, with the wind rather more westerly than yesterday and I hope, from the appearance of the sky, it will be more northerly as the day comes on. The late weather has completely baffled all our weatherwise gentlemen. 2 p.m., saw the Cheviot Hills; if the wind continues, we hope to complete our voyage tomorrow night. If we do not, we must keep the seas for another week, because there will not be water over Sunderland bar.

6th. day, 10th. All hopes are now gone of getting to port for another week. It is a bad job, as all our tea and sugar is gone, all our beef spoilt, and our water growing short; the rigging also is getting bad and needs much repair, and all this within 30 miles of our harbour, it is truly mortifying, but as it cannot be helped we must bear it patiently, remembering the old proverb, 'It is an ill wind that blows no one any good.'

A coble[16] belonging to Holy Island came alongside this morning, with whom

---

[16] A coble is a flat-bottomed fishing-boat.

we exchanged a bottle of rum for a bucket of small codfish, a very welcome supply of fresh food for the present.

7th. day, 11th. 'Hope long deferred maketh the heart sick.' I am sure I am sick of looking for a fair wind or even expecting one ... nothing but gales ... seem to be our portion. The whole of this day and the preceding night, it has blown a complete hurricane from the SW, with much rain.

1st. day, [12th.] More moderate, set more sail, and stood close into the land, which is here very pretty; some well-cultivated ground with neat dwellings upon it yields a delightful prospect, compared to the one yesterday presented. The ruins of Dunstanbro Castle have a very venerable appearance and add much to the beauty of the coast scenery. There are many fine ruins on this part of the English coast.

2nd. day, 13th. Now it is too late to get into the harbour we have got a fair wind, but murmur we cannot. At 10 a.m. a Sunderland coble came aboard and at 12 we got into the roads, after an absence of 4 mo[nth]s and 7 days. I must say it was with feelings of pleasure I saw our wished-for port again.

The Captain went ashore immediately, whilst we stood out to sea, where we must stop till next day, as till then there will not be water over the bar for our ship. Should the wind come into the NW, we may anchor in the roads, but as it is at present, we must keep a good distance off[?] the shore ... we could go into Shields very well, but the owner will not consent. I hope he will send us off some stores, for we are all at a pause for tea and sugar, as well as beef.

In taking a review of the voyage we cannot complain as to time, but though it has been moderately quick, it has, at the same time, been a very tempestuous one. We have had, from the banks of Newfoundland, a constant succession of heavy gales of wind, and the last 10 days especially we have experienced some tremendous weather, such as was not fit to keep [to] the sea in, whilst there was a good harbour under our lee. However, we seem to have been well where we were, several fine ships having suffered, during our absence, upon this part of the coast during the heavy gales from the southward.

3rd. day, 14th. Last night the wind northened and we came to an anchor in the roads, very much to the satisfaction of all us. At 8 a.m. the Keelman ... came aboard with the Captain and we got out all the deck timber and towed it into the harbour. I cannot say as yet 'on dry ground', [as] although I have been upon the land, ... it was knee deep in water, through which I had to wade to make the timber fast to the anchors in the timber yard, but I hope tomorrow we shall get into the harbour. This evening the *Hunter* of Sunderland came into the roads; she sailed a week before us from Quebec and appears to have suffered much in the gales, altho' she has been in some harbour in Scotland.

4th. day, 15th. The wind having kept in the north and west quarter, the tides have so much improved, as to enable us to get in this tide. 10 a.m., the pilot came on board and we weighed anchor. 11, got safe in but, owing to a great number of ships coming out, we got aground upon the Canch and, although we used all our exertions to get her off, they were unavailing – so, making all safe, we took our bags and went ashore, happy enough to get once more upon terra firma.

I found all my Sunderland friends well, and was received with their usual kindness. Thus our American voyage concluded, a voyage which has afforded me much pleasure and instruction, and next year I shall feel quite ready to accompany my worthy Captain to any part of this world [to which] our interest may lead us.

Part III

The Lady Frances *Trading to Quebec* –

Second Voyage

Sunderland, 4th. mo[nth] 22nd. 1824. We are now busily employed preparing for the reception of our passengers, who are all in town and in a great hurry to get on board, which is not to be wondered at, as their lodging and board ashore must necessar[il]y decrease the sum they have provided for the prosecution of their enterprise, and which some amongst them can but badly spare. They are all country farmers or labourers from the County of Yorkshire, bent upon improving their condition by emigrating to America; that several of them should [bother] surprises me, as in all probability they have but a few years to live, being about the age of 55, and one but a few months short of 60; an odd time of life to think about leaving the land of their forefathers for a settlement in a strange land and amongst a strange people. They all assign different reasons for it, but I cannot find one that warrants, in my opinion, such a scheme. Beside these, there are an officer of the 94th and his lady, going with us as cabin passengers.

I quite expect she [i.e. the *Lady Frances*] will prove very leaky when we get to sea and, if I am not deceived, we shall have some sickness amongst the passengers, unless they refuse to take a family that has the smallpox amongst the children, one of whom they expect will not live. The whole amount of passengers will be about 47, so that we shall be a brave company. In addition, a Scotch man is going to work his passage out, a noted performer upon that sweet-toned instrument, the Highland bagpipe, with which as his sole companion he intends, like the celebrated Goldsmith, to push his way into the settlements of his countrymen and delight their ears with those melodious sounds which erst proceeded from it in their native country.

25th. This day our ship floated and we took her into the 5 berth tier to take in her cargo . . . consisting of 9 Keels of coals, 1 Keel of glass bottles, and 1 of earthen pots. The coal dust made much work for the poor passengers, as it flew over their bedding and amongst their baggage, and of it they complained justly.

28th. Took aboard about a wagonload of Captain Read's baggage, as well as 2 sheep belonging to him and 2 lambs of another passenger, also a jenny ass[17] and 2 dozen old fowls, so that altogether I think for livestock we shall be well off.

30th. Got our water and finished taking in our stores, intending to sail tomorrow if the wind be out. Spent the evening with a party of the young Friends [i.e. Quakers] of this town, who kindly met on my account. We passed the time very agreeably, and with considerable regret I bade them adieu, not expecting to see them again in less than 5 mo[nth]s.

5th. mo., 1st., 1824. This morning bade all my friends farewell and went aboard. 12 p.m., cast off from the pier and, with many ships in company bound to the southward, proceeded down the river, the Scotch piper . . . playing 'Farewell to ye agin I ne'er cum back agen'. 5, hove to off the pier, for the Captain to come aboard, half past he came off in a coble, gave three cheers, which were answered by the Company's Friends, and set all sail, a light breeze from the NNW.
 4 o'clock, all being set, secured the water casks, anchors etc. and got tea; many a heavy heart aboard, I believe. 6, watched the town till it was hid . . . bade it adieu and went below; five mo[nth]s and I hope to see its spires again.

1st. day, 2nd. Being a fine morning, the passengers assembled in the twixt decks for divine worship; after reading a portion of scripture and singing some hymns, a young man (who has officiated as a preacher, I understand) knelt down and petitioned for as speedy and prosperous voyage as the Lord might think fit to grant, to bless all their honest endeavours, and to grant that, if they should meet their friends no more on earth, . . . they might in a far better world. He appears to be a very pious young man and I think there are many amongst them who seem to be very religious characters, tho' of what denomination of Christians I cannot tell.
 Noon, the wind became unfavourable . . . should it continue, we shall most likely go south about. I am sorry to say, the passengers who had the smallpox in their family have been taken on board, and that their youngest child is at this time very ill with that disorder; it must make the other passengers feel very uncomfortable, I think. However, I hope, as they have provided some medicine, their child will improve with . . . plenty of fresh air. 6 p.m., as there appeared a likelihood of a smart breeze, turned the skiff bottom upwards over the sheep and

---

[17] A jenny ass was the name for a female of the species.

ass, to prevent their suffering from the weather.

Midnight, took a reef in the topsails, passengers getting sickly.

2nd. day, 3rd. At 4 a.m. bore away to go south about, the wind seeming to continue and to blow hard. Stowed the top gallant sails and double reefed the topsails; squally, with thick weather and rain, passengers all abed.

3 p.m., Flambro [i.e. Flamborough] Head, bore SW 6 N, dis. 12 miles.

Midnight, heavy weather, ship rolling very heavily to windward, passengers battened down, to prevent the water going down the hatchway, all very sickly and repenting ever coming on board. Saw the Dodgeon light in a short clear wind, NNW and very rainy, unpleasant weather; the ship, and indeed all the livestock, suffering much from it.

3rd. day, 4th. This morning, with a heavy sea lifting our stern boat, she broke the belt the davits hooked on to, but by being handy with the cat block and fall, we hoisted her up and secured her again; I should not wonder if we lose her in the Western ocean.

Two of our passengers very ill, one of them showing signs of the smallpox. The child seems to be very near death. 10 o'clock, a fleet of light Colliers bound to the southward passed thro' the roads, who will most likely tell the owners of our being here.

4th. day, 5th. Beautiful weather the early part of the day, hoisted out our skiff and put two empty water casks into her to get filled at the jetty; the 'jolly boat' with Captain Read and his wife were to follow us in about half an hour, which to me appeared plenty of time to see a bit of the town [of Yarmouth] and quay, so took French leave and deserted the watering place.

I first went towards the marketplace, which I soon found, and a fine, open, clean part of the town it is; the persons who attended the stalls, which were mostly open, had each a watchbox with his or her own name upon it, in which they sit and employ themselves between the times of waiting upon customers. Having satisfied myself in that part, I walked towards the quay, which by the by has but one street . . . the rest are all narrow passages, which admit of no other carriage but a Yarmouth cart or a wheelbarrow, and then not more than one at a time. I should think the inhabitants must find them a serious inconvenience, as a cart must necessar[il]y stop until another, that entered first, has got to the top or bottom. The quay is a very pleasant and agreeable one, more so than any one I ever saw, being of a good width and rendered very agreeable by a double row of trees planted the whole length of it, between which is a very pleasant walk and, at the time I was there, had a number of genteelly dressed persons walking upon it.

There were a number of vessels discharging on the quay and one ship on the stocks, which gave a bit [more] life to the place, else it looked rather more like a promenade than otherwise. There are some fine old-fashioned houses in the town and, looking at the generality of them, I should expect it was rather an ancient place; the streets were well paved and remarkably clean, and the shops were, many of them, handsome and apparently well supplied.

5th. [day], 6th. Sent the 'jolly boat' ashore to fill two casks, by way of keeping up our stock [of water]; when she returned, hoisted her up and got up the anchor, wind right ahead of us, turned her into Corton [?] Roads and brought up. I rather suspected this to have been done to keep Captain Read on board as, when we . . . [lay] abreast Yarmouth, he was continually wanting the boat and 4 hands, to row him about for his pleasure. Wind SSW and fine, clear weather, great numbers of lightships passing thro'. Our passengers are still very sickly, one of them, a good-natured man, though deformed, being without a neck, has almost assuredly the smallpox, but as it seems likely to come out, I hope he will do well. Another young man, who has his cousin in company, a young lass about 17, is very ill and seems to get worse. Tomorrow we shall go ashore for a doctor; if there be one to get either in Lowestoft or Yarmouth, come he must.

6th. day, 7th. Directly after breakfast put the small casks into the 'jolly boat' and went ashore for a doctor to Lowestoft, the passengers still getting worse. About 11 a.m. returned, with a fine, stout man named Smith, formerly of Deal, who recollected my Father and Friends at Dover very well. On examining the invalids, he commenced operations and bled three of the worst; the young man of whom I spoke [above] he declared to be in a very dangerous state, and entertained little hopes of his recovery, which has so much affected his poor cousin that she is continually in tears, although we use all methods to dispel her fears. Ralph, the deformed [man], is now covered with the smallpox, which the doctor says is a good sign of his doing well, and the child he thinks out of danger. He sent back by the boat medicine for the sick, powders etc., and an invitation to breakfast with him if we stop till tomorrow.

7th. day, 8th. Ed[war]d was so much worse that we again went for the Dr., but he thought him better than yesterday, so determined, the wind being from the NW, to get underway.

10, set sail and bade a long adieu to Lowestoft and the Stamford light, that have been our friends this past winter many a time. [At] noon the wind easter'd and it came thick all at once, light breezes inclinable to calm. 4 p.m., Ed[war]d grows still worse and I think an inflammation has taken place, as he is so very quiet and free from pain, and yet evidently going towards his long home. Poor fellow, he talks of his home and parents, wishes to write but is too weak, looks on his cousin . . . and weeps, whilst she, poor girl, sits and watches by his side and weeps as if her head was breaking. Their affection has excited my curiosity to know more of them, and on enquiry I find they are second cousins, both going to their friends in America, and that when they had arrived there they were to be married; they are both of families in the lower classes, but bearing an excellent character.

Midnight, Edward is evidently going, tho' he says nothing; I suppose him incapable, but he moans most piteously, but even that grows more faint, and ere long he will be gone whence no traveller returns.

Half past 12, all is over with him; a deep-fetched sigh and a convulsive struggle declared him no longer an inhabitant of the world. I hope and, from what I have observed of his conduct previously and during his illness, I believe . . . [he will] enjoy a better inheritance than this state could afford. He was a thin, slender, delicate-looking young man [of] between 22 . . . [and 23], of a quiet disposition and very diffident, and one that had made a very favourable impression upon my mind. The poor lass has not been made acquainted with the circumstance but, ere we commit the body to the deep, for which every preparation is being made, she will be informed of it, though I greatly fear it will add another invalid to the list.

1st. day, 9th. 2 a.m., quite dark, the body, sewed up in a blanket and rug with a great weight at the feet, was brought upon deck and laid upon one of the main hatches, which was rested upon the bulwark, the inner ends held by two men. At the main mast stood the Captain and the crew, with a few of the male passengers, a lanthorn [i.e. lantern] in one of their hands, by whose glimmering light the service for the dead was read in a manner that did credit to the Captain's feelings; when he came to the part 'ashes to ashes' etc., the inner end of the hatch was raised and the body, sliding off, was deposited in its watery grave, I think not without the tribute of many a tear. When the service was concluded and all put in order, sail was again set and we proceeded again upon our way.

When I look back on the past it seems like a dream, but this day week Edw[ar]d was a living body like myself and, at that time, likely in all human probability to live as long. This morning has seen him launched into the deep, a dead, inanimate, lifeless body; true indeed is the part of the scripture which saith, 'In the midst of life we are in death.' May we, the survivors, profit by the lesson that this week hath read. Poor Ann, who was informed of his decease previous to his interment, weeps and cries in a most mournful manner, taking no nourishment and listening to nothing in the shape of consolation; altogether it is a mournful scene, one in which I have felt much, no doubt in common with others. Evening. The day has passed in a mournful manner; we went by Dover at 11 a.m., but the sight gave me but a melancholy pleasure, former recollections and our present situation marred the pleasure I should otherwise have enjoyed. We intend putting into Plymouth, our state being too bad to proceed; there, I suppose, we shall get the sick on shore into a hospital if we can . . ., [then] proceed to sea.

2nd. day, 10th. 2 a.m. . . . hauled in for Portsmouth, and Ralph gets worse and worse; last night he sent for the mate at 11 o'clock and told him, he believed he should not live till the morning, but about midnight he grew rather better and took a little coffee. I believe, had he not kept up his heart in the way he was, he would have been dead before this, but I think it yet very doubtful whether he will live or not.

8, a pilot boarded us and we shortly after anchored at Spithead, about a mile from the town.

10, went ashore with the Captain to get a doctor and to do something about lodging for the sick, as there is no hospital where they can be admitted; returned and dined, then put the water casks into the boat and again went ashore with Captain Read and wife, who are to go to Cowes until we proceed to sea. After filling our water [casks], I took a walk about the town and fortifications, which latter are here stronger and, I should think, [it] might be called the first fortified place in England; it has an imposing effect from the sea, and I should think would make a very stout resistance in case of attack. The inhabitants complain of business being very dull, and as their trade arises from war alone, I hope their complaints may not cease. There are but few men-of-war in it, except what are laid up; one arrived from the East with us and saluted the Admiral with 11 guns, which in the distance, as it was beautiful weather, sounded very pleasing; the Admiral answered when he was abreast the castle. 4 p.m. Hoisted out the skiff and put on the sick with their baggage for taking them ashore; before we went, their companions bade them goodbye. Poor Ralph seemed much depressed, and I am sure no one in the ship saw him go without regretting it; he was a nice, sterling, honest man, one that would lend a hand to the ship at any time and was continually doing one or another a good office. We took them and their chattels to their lodgings, where I think they will be comfortably provided for. Whilst we were away, those on board whitewashed all the berths and aired the bedding, so that I hope we shall now be again clear of disorder and be able to proceed to sea; several are still poorly, but the doctor declared them free from anything infectious. 10, returned, properly fagged out and went to bed.

3rd. day, 11th. 6 a.m., put all our empty water casks into the boat and rowed her ashore, filled them, and after walking about for 1 hour and a half, returned on board. We had a very bad passage back, as the wind and sea were very heavy, and having a strong tide to cope with, we just reached the ship and no more; had we missed her, we must have gone alongside one of the men-of-war who were lying astern of us, and there have waited till the flood made to windward. Got dinner and weighed anchor, proceeding along the Isle of Wight under bare poles, unpleasant rainy weather.

3 p.m. Brought up in Cowes roads and, to my great joy, got orders to go ashore; I have longed to go into the island many a time, but never had an opportunity before. We landed at the Wine Inn, and I immediately started through the town and up the hill. Although it was wet and raining, I thought it delightful country and the prospect charming – indeed, I have not enjoyed anything for a long time so much, as our sail between the island and the main[land], and my walk at Cowes. I looked round me with feelings of regret that it was likely to be the last time of being on English ground for a considerable time. Every foot I trod, I conceive to have been passed over before by those who, altho' now no more amongst us on earth, still live in the memory of those by whom they were beloved; everyone must feel a pleasure, when thus a stranger in a strange land, in the recollection that the scenes it presents were once frequented by those we love – at least it is so with me, and it was so at Cowes. 8 o'clock, after getting a supply of fresh meat, milk etc. etc. went on board, Captain Read to follow us in the morning. This being the last port we are to touch at, completed my supplies and took stock, acting in this instance up to what the . . . [General] Meeting [of Quakers] advises annually, to inspect the state of our affairs. The following was the statement:

2¼ lb. tea
1¼ do. coffee
10½ do. moist sugar
7 do. lump [sugar]
1 lb. figs
1 do. raisins
4½ do. soap   ALL IN GOOD CONDITION

One consolation – if I fail, [i.e. run out of anything] I alone shall be the sufferer.

4th. day, 12th. 3 a.m., got under way, Captain Read on board, rainy, unpleasant weather, but a prospect of a fine day . . . 7, the Pilot left us, just through the

Needles. The scene here is very fine, the passage being very narrow gives you a view of both sides of the channel, but I think the most striking part is the Needle Point and rocks. We found [the] tide very strong and, it being in opposition to the wind, there was no want of swell. Set our fine weather sails and got breakfast. Passengers growing very sick with the motion of the ship. At present I have hardly looked at my thermometer; the passengers have served my purpose, being pestered with them when the quicksilver stands high, and the reverse when it is low. They do not like the exposed deck when it feels cool. 8 p.m., saw the Start Point; hope to take our departure from the Lizard tomorrow morning, if the breeze stands.

5th. day, 13th. Half past 8, the Lizard bore by compass NE by N, distant 12 miles, from which we have dated our departure, in the expectation of its being the last land we shall see this side of the Atlantic; strong breezes, with slight showers of rain. The passengers came up on the deck to take a farewell look at their native land; as it faded from their sight, they went below. Poor Ann watched it till, it becoming more misty, she could discern it no more, then burst into tears, no longer capable of containing her feelings. I think she seems to be recovering by degrees, but 'tis slowly indeed; she meets with attentions from everyone, indeed, any would do anything for her, but her grief must have way, and then I think she will come aboard again. She has carefully mended, washed and put by all Edward's things, and in so doing she seems to be more easy than when idle. I hope someone will see her to her brothers in America, or she will feel his loss more than ever. Evening. More wind, took in the steering sails and furled the top gal[lan]t sails; a large circle round the moon promises us a breeze, a strong sea running.

6th. day, 14th. At 4 p.m. double-reefed the top sails and stowed the jib, strong gales and very heavy squalls, accompanied by rain; duty just now comes very heavy upon me, as both my partners in the watch are unable to take their . . . [turn] at the helm, one from having a fester in his finger, the other from the multitude of his engagements, being cook. It is not very agreeable work, standing at the helm 4 hours in such weather as this. Last night, orders were issued to put all upon an allowance of water, the quantity to be 5 pints per man or woman per diem, children 3, . . . but the weather has been so bad, that none have ventured out of their beds. I went with a light to see how they were getting on, but I returned far quicker; many were leaning over their bedsides, casting their accounts [i.e. vomiting] upon the floor, whilst the children crying added to the sickening scene. To tell the truth, although it was dinner time, I felt no appetite after the sight, but went to bed. 4 p.m. Got up and got my tea, rather better weather, but a prospect of but a poor night. Wind N and by E, very squally.

7th. day, 14th. We had but a poor night and, to make matters worse, the smallpox has again made its appearance, upon a young man about 25; it is truly very disheartening, [and] beside him 2 elderly women are very ill – of what, I cannot tell. I earnestly hope we may get a quick passage out, I am sure no one can be easy under present circumstances; this evening makes our second week from Sunderland. Noon, it fell less wind, and the swell (continuing very great, as it always does for a considerable time after a breeze) causes the passengers to complain greatly of her rolling. One of them, an extraordinary-sized man (being 6 feet 7 inches, but bowed by reason of weakness and age), from her taking a heavy lurch, rolled to leeward, and but for the boards of the bed cabin giving way, would most likely have received a severe contusion upon his head – which, acting like a battering ram of old, stove in the berth and, frightening children lying in it, created no small disturbance, mixed with some fun at the oddity of the event. It amuses a good deal to observe the little children running about the decks, they use much caution, but notwithstanding they get many a fall, but in a short time they will no doubt get their sea legs.

1st. day, 15th. Fine clear morning, turned the . . . [between] decks folks up to clean their berth, womenfolk employed making cakes etc. for breakfast; a very good sign of a plentiful supply for our mess, as they always make some for us when so employed. Indeed, there are but few mornings when we get no cakes for breakfast and tea, so far so good and, what is better still, I believe a dog will die today. I wish I could say so of all of them [i.e. the animals], I hope to be able to in time; when we get into 29 degrees of West longitude, we are to kill a sheep. Blow, my gentle North Easter, to the westward let's go.

Now mustered all hands to prayers in the twixt [i.e. between] decks and, the evening tea over, they met again to sing hymns, which as the weather was fine and had a very pleasing effect, though they met with a grievous interruption from the swell being still very heavy.

2nd. day, 10th. This being the day one of the [apprentice] lads is out of his time,[18] we kept holiday, and as usual, 'buried his wife' with the accustomed honours; all got double allowance of ale and spice cakes and, in the evening, the piper played in the twixt decks, a number of the favourite tunes of Auld Caledonia, and it finished with a step amongst the tars, altogether we spent a pleasant hour or two. I thought Ann seemed rather pleased, and better than she has been for

---

[18] Has finished serving his apprenticeship.

some time. The old folks are still very poorly, but I hope nothing serious is to be apprehended. The dog I hoped would die, has recovered and seems likely to annoy us all the passage. The sheep and lambs, with the ass, thrive exceedingly well, though there is talk of putting them on an allowance, lest their provision should not last out; on the same account they begin to kill off the fowls, which prove all . . . the better for keeping a week, being nothing but a pack of tough old hens, although purchased for young birds.

3rd. day, 17th. I have just got up; the incessant noise, with squalling children and scolding mothers, quite forbids the hope of getting a little sleep, after spending 8 hours upon deck last night; I have now a little better idea of the disturbed nights fathers of young children so frequently complain of than I had before; I have wished them in America, or anywhere else, a score of times within the last hour, but finding all of no use, I put on the covering of patience, and am set down to write a few lines about wind and weather, by way of employing myself until the breeze in the twixt decks is over – then I will make another essay at rest. We had a beautiful night and a fine, fair breeze, which latter good companion still continues with us. About 6 a.m. I roused the womenfolk up to prepare their breakfasts and get their paste for cakes ready for me, as I had volunteered to stand baker every other morning. I believe I cooked this morning about 3 score cakes of different sorts, and my tribute [i.e. commission] amounted to about 10 beside; I find if it continues, it will be a profitable employment. I had to employ a mate to see they did not burn, whilst I carried them backwards and forwards; so much for my baking, fine employ[ment] enough in good weather, but [not] in bad. 10 o'clock, quietness again being restored, I will again go into 'Blanket Bay'.

I managed to get 2 hours sleep, then went up on deck. After dinner I was employed bottling ale and porter, of which I managed two casks and had nearly concluded without any loss when, from boasting to the Captain of my dexterity, I unfortunately turned round too quick and kicked 5 bott[le]s into the lee scuppers, thereby overthrowing all I had just advanced, and ruining my character as a tapster.

3, a sail we had seen some time . . . fired a gun, hoisted his ensign and bore down upon us before the wind; thinking him a man-of-war, we immediately took in all studding sails and back the main yard to wait for him; as he drew nearer, we made him out to be an East Indiaman, apparently a free trader. 4, he was nearly alongside when he hailed us, and as it is a fair specimen of what passes between ships thus meeting, I shall give verbatim what passed:

Stranger: 'Brig ahoy!'
Us: 'Hallo!'

Sr.:	'Where are you from, pray?'
Anr.:	'From Portsmouth last. When did you leave?'
Sr.:	'On the 12th we sailed from Cowes roads.'

His question answered, we began:

| [Us]: | 'Pray, where are you from?' |
| [Sr.]: | 'From Calcutta, out 5 mo[nth]s.' |

A flourish with the speaking trumpet bespoke our Captain satisfied. He then asked, could we spare a few potatoes? On our replying 'yes', he said he should send his boat aboard. In about ¼ of an hour he was alongside, with two boxes of cigars in the boat, accompanied by an officer in the company's troops. I then could but observe the difference between the little feeling one comparatively rich man had for another, when contrasted with the conduct of the sailors; for although Captain Read abounded with all sorts of provisions, fowls' eggs, butter etc., which would have been so highly acceptable to the cabin gentry of the other ship, they obtained nothing, whilst the sailors mustered up every individual thing they could, for their poor fellows who came in the boat and who were 3 out of 4 afflicted with the scurvy; there was everyone contributing some tea, coffee, a little spirits, pipes, in short everything they could muster that would benefit them. But there was nothing pleased them more than the pipes, of which they were quite out, and although our men were short, I believe they gave them nearly all, reserving but a few for themselves, and those the short ones; in return they gave a few cigars, though as they expected to come again, there seemed a prospect of my getting something, so begged them to bring a few shells, of which one said he had a number; unfortunately they would not let them go aboard, but to return with 5 boxes more cigars for the cabin. Our Captain gave them 2 sacks of potatoes, a crock of butter, a quantity of eggs, a cwt of cabin biscuits, for which the Captain seemed very thankful. I gave him a few hastily written lines for I.F. Cover, through whom I hope my friends in England will hear we are now quite well. When their boat left us, we set sail again and bade them adieu, wished them as fine a passage as a fair wind for us will allow them. Thus, although they much need a fair wind, we cannot wish them one, so much selfishness is mixed up in our nature.

The stranger's name was the *Earl Bathurst* of Liverpool, which place he left 11 mo[nth]s and 9 days since.

4th. day, 18th. Saw several ships but, although we were very near, did not speak one; I think two or three of them were West Indiamen, from their size and their deeply-laden appearance. The long continuance of this easterly wind, so favourable to us, must be rather irksome to them; however, they have nothing to do but to bear with it patiently, as it has quite the appearance of lasting another week. If it should, I hope we shall not be far off the shores of Nova Scotia. I say hope, altho' if it were to continue so fine as it has for the last week, it would be a pleasure to have another two or three weeks, which may yet be our lot, for all I can tell. The passengers complain greatly about the water; as long as they grumble and go [on about it], it does not signify, but if they steal, which they can do without a possibility of our hindering it, I should not wonder to be ... [down to] a pint [a day] before we get to the far end of our journey, which will be very dry work.

5th. day, 19th. This morning light airs easterly, got up our royal mast and yard; I wish I could have said it had blown away all together, we had so much trouble with it last year, that I hate the sight of it, except when it is upon deck. Passed under a large ship's stern about 3 o'clock and, for the sake of knowing his nation, hoisted our ensign, which was answered by their displaying over their stern the white clout of France; I should think she came from one of their West India islands and appeared well stocked with passengers like ourselves, I wish them joy of them. We have now a fair prospect of fruit, as a large box of young trees, belonging to one of our emigrating squad, are all out in blossom; they look exceedingly pretty upon the quarter deck and, as he has planted between the fruit trees a number of sweet-scented shrubs, they yield a very grateful perfume, especially after a sunny shower. At tea time our wandering Willie, the Scotch minstrel, was ordered up on the quarter deck at the lady's request – whether to pipe her into an appetite or to keep up the good custom of having music at meals (which is the fashion in the army, I believe), I cannot tell, however there he piped, till a tumbler half full of rum told him he might descend from the exalted regions of music to finish the job he had previously in hand, of putting a patch into a pair of canvas trousers. I will not say the rum had the effect, but I observed his fingers moving exceedingly quick after he again commenced operations upon his old breeks. 8 o'clock, went to bed; any attempt at reading or improvement of any kind is rendered abortive by the incessant noise of scolding mothers and unruly bairns who, not wishing to go thus early to bed are, I suppose, in a state of mutiny.

6th. day, 20th. Wind southerly, light breezes and clear weather in the morning. We have had a most delightful run ... [since departure from the Lizard on the 13th] and if we have, what must the *Essex* and the other ships that passed us so quickly, have had? Why, I expect they are very near the banks, if not quite; a fair wind to them, that we may follow. About 4 p.m. one of our men told me to expect a gale of wind, as he had dreamt greatly about womenfolks, relations of his, lately. I laughed at him, but he bid me take notice, and mark if it were not a true sign. 5, took in the top mast studding sail, rather hazy with squall, great numbers of Mother Careys and other birds about the ship; I particularly noticed the Newfoundland boatswain[19] with his marlin spike tail, and the sea swallow. If it should fall less wind I will try to catch some of them, in which I shall have the assistance of an able sportsman in that way who, having been compelled to it from a state of starvation when shipwrecked, understands the best methods of snaring them. About this time the deck was swarming with children at play about the main hatchway when, from the carelessness of the man at the helm, the ship yawed to windward and the top of a stout sea broke among the children, from whom burst forth such a cry of terror that all hands came running up on deck, mothers, fathers, sailors and all wondering what could be the matter, but upon seeing the cause, their fears turned into loud laughter at the expense of the children who, wet through, were stripped and put to bed.

7th. day, 21st. George's dream has come true about 8 p.m. After a stiff breeze all the morning, we got her under the two close-reefed topsails, foresail, stowed jib and trysail split . . . bad weather and every appearance of its continuing, in my opinion, though the Captain thinks . . . [there was] less wind at midnight. We have been obliged to batten all the passengers down under hatches, as the water breaking over the ship would drown them all in their beds. The long-continued easterly wind having raised a heavy sea, and the wind being now from the westward and consequently bringing a sea from that quarter, makes it very laboursome work for the ship, causing her to pitch and roll as if t'would be her last, but I hope before long the sea will run true and she will make better weather of it. The cabin passengers are very sick and the two old women who were ill before complain more than ever; I went down to get a look at them about an hour since, but I could make nothing of them. 10 o'clock, got some mulled ale and am going to bed thoroughly wet and weary; blowing a gale of wind and a very awkward cross sea running. Our bowsprit too we have found sprung . . . but we hope it is not much the worse.

1st. day, 22nd. It fell calm about 2 o'clock this morning, one of those deceitful smiles beneath which lurk nothing but mischief. At daylight shook out the reefs and set the top gallant sails, light airs from the WNW, glass at 51. 8 a.m., were just going to breakfast when we were taken aback by a tremendous squall;

---

[19] The name given to a seabird, e.g. a gannet.

clewed up all the sails and kept the ship before it. Before the squall came, the sea was very high, but during the height of it was as smooth as a mill pond and of a frothy white, I never saw such a one before. When it was over, double-reefed the topsails, stowed the jib, square mainsail and trysail; blowing as hard as ever, and as heavy a sea. The passengers who were up on deck were ordered into 'Bull Bay' (as we call their twixt decks [place]) and then battened down; if they get their fortune in America they will have earned it. 6, close-reefed the topsails and stowed the foresail and trysail; blowing desperately hard and a mountainous sea. 7, eased in the jib boom to ease the bowsprit, the children and passengers in a pretty pickle, Captain Read (from taking a lee lurch) with a black eye. She pitches, so I can write no more, so I will put my pen away.

2nd. day, 23rd. Rather better weather . . . 6 o'clock, got one of the sheep out of the long boat; bad weather as it is, they were determined to kill it, although the passenger that has volunteered to do the part of the butcher declared himself incapable of officiating. However, after much entreaty and after being well laughed at and his abilities doubted, he prepared for the business by pulling off his jacket, tying round him a large piece of canvas as an apron, and sharpening his knife. He then tied the animal's legs together and, laying it upon the windlass, quickly dispatched it; the worst of the job was the skinning it, as he could hardly stand, rolling into the side whenever the ship lurched. For my part I gave him a wide berth, being rather afraid he might roll against me with his deadly weapon and accidentally serve me as he had (intentionally) the sheep. Before he had concluded his job I went to bed, not doubting but that, when called to get dinner, I should find a fresh one for me, but at half past twelve I rather think, of the dinner and me, I look the more sheepish, for all had so faithfully herded past, that they did not leave even a little fat wherewith I might grease my shoes – but that I will have, in spite of them and their care, whether by fair or foul means; it is but my due for taking the care I have of them, and have it I will.

6 p.m., a large ship was seen to windward, apparently wishing to speak. At 8 we met; she proved to be the *Hercules* of New York; as we were not very near each other, he chalked his longitude upon a board, 39 degrees West, which differs from our reckoning two degrees, we being in W 37 degrees; I should think, from her appearance, she was a packet. The sun set in beautiful style last night and rose as well this morning, promising at both times fine weather, but from appearances since, I guess we shall be deceived in them, the wind moans very much . . . and to the southward there hangs a deal of wet and dirt. I hope not to have rain, but I never was more deceived if we do not get a heavy and severe beating before 24 hours are over our heads. The women and children are all up on deck this afternoon, and as usual making between them a notorious noise; we

want a few sprays to clear them out of the way.

6 o'clock, it is fast coming on; we have already double-reefed the topsails, trysail and stowed the jib, but little rain at present. Scouted all the passengers below and battened down the main hatchway, after lighting all their [lanterns]. They grumble a good deal about it, but we cannot leave such things to be done at night, when perhaps we may have to take in sail. We have made a passage for the men to come up on deck if they like, but I think they will go to bed.

4th. day, 25th. It blew most desperately hard last night, with a very great deal of rain, the wind about SSW. At 10 o'clock called up all hands to close-reef the topsails, and stow the trysail and foresail, the sea running very high and seeming all on fire [i.e. with phosphorus], every moment looking as if it would have broken on board. Indeed we shipped one sea that stove in the water cask that Captain Read had made into a dog kennel and set the poor dogs floating into the lee scuppers; one of them I quite thought would have gone overboard, but he managed somehow to get up on the quarter deck, where he sent up a most lamentable howling. 11, spliced the main brace, raining most terribly, and so warm that one could hardly bear the oppressive weight of a thick jacket and trousers, glass as high as 62, which made me expect the wind would souther – but I was deceived, as it came from the NW and fell quite calm about 12. Then the rolling game began, and I felt glad I could go below and turn into my hammock, though even there I made very bad weather of it. I was very much pleased with a novel sight that presented itself in the height of the gale last night, a very heavy spray, flying all over the foresail previously to our furling it, gave it the appearance of a large sheet of fire, from the great quantity of that luminous matter the water contained; it glowed for about 7 minutes before the phosphoric appearance subsided, then merely shone bright at certain spots, which ceased shortly altogether.

5th. day, 26th. The weather much better; all hands employed repairing damage sustained in the breezes, though from the rolling of the ship it is very unpleasant work being aloft; the sick passengers complain of being worse from the excessive disturbance they are in from the same cause.

6th. day, 27th. Better weather, but every appearance of a return of the gale, the sky looking very windy and the wind moaning very hollow, which I now begin to take as a sure indication of approaching bad times (I mean only in clear weather, for in foggy, it sounds hollow at all times). Glass at 54.

6 p.m. On it comes, the strong swell continuing made me conclude we should either have a stiff breeze shortly, or that there had been wind hereabouts lately; the former now looks the more likely. I observed about noon a number of

Portuguese men-of-war, but could not catch one, although I tried with a net. I feel, however, perfectly satisfied that they have no shell. 8, a strong breeze from the NNW, topsails double-reefed, mainsail and jib furled; passengers battened down. Midnight, close-reefed the topsails, a very heavy sea running from the beam, and breaking greatly. Captain Read up on deck declared he had rather lie upon the cold ground rolled up in a blanket than be exposed such nights as these upon the Atlantic; he declares the ship is full of misfortunes; his wife bears it much better than he does, and rails a good deal at him.

7th. day, 28th. Rather less wind; reefed the foresail and close-reefed the trysail . . . much rain with thick weather, furled the foresail and topsail again, worse and worse sea breaking, very heavy at times.

2 p.m. Split the fore topmast staysail, unbent it and bent another, eased in the jib boom, struck top gallant yards and mast and secured the boats afresh; one comfort, she does not roll so heav[il]y as she did last breeze. 6, about half an hour since, when taking a trip into 'Bull Bay' to see if there was any kind of better provision to be had than cold salt beef and bread, I fell in with a [soft] loaf . . . and a jar of butter. 'A fine prize!' cried I and, without waiting to lay the cloth, sat down upon a[n] empty water cask and began to employ myself most comfortably, when a heavy breeze sent me and my seat to the lee side . . . and worst of all, I lost my forage underneath one of the bed cabins, from a plank having been taken away to get to the cargo. However, I was not [prepared] to lose my supper so quickly, so got up another plank and searched amongst the crockery ware for it. After some time I found the remnants of the loaf, but the butter was gone for good; however, I managed to finish my meal, using instead of butter the old proverb, 'Better is a dry crust with quickness' etc. I am just returned from my foraging expedition and going into 'Blanket Bay'.

1st. day, 29th. This makes the third 1st. day we have had a bleaching instead of a sabbath; the weather is as bad as ever but, I think, at its height. From the wind veering about as it does, we have a very awkward cross sea to deal with, which washes over us in a very unpleasant manner, but we are compelled to put up with it, and bear it patiently. 12 o'clock, the gale broke and it became much better weather, shook out one reef and set the foresail, square mainsail and trysail. I was glad to see it, for I am quite wearied of this weather.

2nd. day, 30th. This morning we have had fine weather, I hope it may continue for a time, the wind is foul but I am well contented if it holds fair weather. I am inclined to think that a succession of bad weather, like what we have had lately, tends much towards making sailors superstitious, as I could not help noting one or two of our crew rebuking persons for whistling.

3rd. day, 6th. mo[nth], 1st. Tried all the methods I and my partner could invent to snare some sea fowl, of which there are now a great variety about us, but all proved ineffectual. They are so well fed that they will not take the bait. Had I a gun, I could get some, as, the weather being quite fine and very little wind, we could pick them without trouble with the 'jolly boat', but as I had not one, I must be content, I suppose, to look at them and long.

4th. day, 2nd. Struck sounding this morning at 4 a.m. 38 fathoms, small shells and sand; got the fishing lines in order for trying to gain a mess of fish. I am afraid I shall get but little with mine, from having brought but a very poor set of gear. However, I can but try, with the rest. Our passengers are all in thoroughly good spirits and anxiously looking for a fair wind. I believe some of their provisions grow short, especially flour; I think they flattered themselves, from our having had a fair wind and a fine run so long, that it would continue with us ... [throughout the voyage], but they have found out their mistake. Evening, we saw a shoal of small birds flying about the ship, and as it became dusk they began to seek for lodging; two of them coming upon deck I secured, and took them into the cabin; I put them upon the stern locker and watched them. The poor things from having flown so long were so weary, that they immediately tucked their little heads under their wings and fell asleep. I looked at them and thought I should like their skins to take home, yet how could I kill them, when they had suffered so much and had such a claim upon our hospitality? It would seem very cruel, so I determined on the morrow to give them their liberty, though I cannot help wishing they may die [meanwhile].

5th. day, 3rd. Rather breezy, double-reefed topsails at 3 a.m. At daylight, as I could not find any more of the birds about the rigging, I suppose they must have ... [fallen] overboard and have got drowned. The two I caught both died, and at the first opportunity I shall skin them, though now I have them, I am afraid, from them being so small and tender, I shall make a bad job of it. Wind NW and very cold, I quite expect to see some ice before long, I should like to if it be clear weather, but if thick and foggy I should rather be excused, for fear of falling foul of it and getting damage.

6th. day, 4th. The glass before breakfast this morning was 2 degrees below freezing, the wind NNW and a fresh breeze; it continued as cold till noon, when the power of the sun seemed to conquer the sharpness of the air. We were obliged to get one of the fires into 'Bull Bay' for the passengers, as they declared it to be so cold they could endure it no longer, and that their bairns were nearly dead with it; after making a large roasting one for them, they expressed themselves more comfortable, though from having no funnel they find some inconvenience from the smoke; there is a vast quantity of combustibles under them, which makes us keep a good look after them, for fear of setting the *Lady* on fire. I could but laugh heartily at seeing the tall 6 ft 7 man with his four stout children between his long legs, sitting upon the floor warming himself, whilst by his side sat his wife, a middle-sized woman whose father is 10 years younger than her husband, with her baby upon her knee, whilst strumming in his ears the songs of the cradle . . . at his age, such an infant and such a wife, I cannot avoid thinking, [are] mere nuisances. 8 p.m., skinned my birds and, I think, succeeded tolerably well; none of the country folks ever saw . . . [such] like before, though I am told they are much like jacky blue caps [jackdaws?]. I [had] thought them cock and hen of the same species, but I believe I found eggs in both of them. Evening, set more sail, after sounding in 45 fathoms coarse sand and shells; tomorrow we try for fish.

7th. day, 5th. Hove to and put out our lines, but nothing could we catch, so again proceeded upon our way with a fine breeze from the SW. Beautiful clear weather and immense quantity of sea fowl of all the descriptions that frequent the banks swimming or flying about us. Some flocks upon the water would contain, I have no doubt, 2 or 3 hundred; I have tried again with a baited hook, but cannot catch any of them, though they would immediately take a piece of the bait if it remained stationary, but as it goes through the water with the same speed as ourselves, I do not think they can pick it up; I must try therefore the first calm day. Evening, quite calm, caught one large codfish but no birds, so I must now give up all hopes of taking them that way; we lost with a line a fine halibut, apparently weighing about 1 cwt or nearly; his struggles for freedom broke the line like pack thread, when he was on top of the water. The cabin gentry took the tail of the cod and then gave the rest to the passengers, who liked it vastly, although I am sure it was a diseased fish and greatly pestered with a little insect called the cod louse.

1st. day, 6th. Thick, foggy, unpleasant weather . . . I shall feel very glad to get off the banks again, being quite tired of fogs and wet jackets, which are not even rendered passable by catching a few fish. It being the Sabbath, we have not of course tried today, but tomorrow I have no doubt we shall; success attend us, is my hearty wish. 10 a.m., all hands assembled to hear prayers read in 'Bull Bay', the service concluded with a few hymns sung by those passengers who profess Primitive Methodism, alias 'ranters', of which denomination we have a great number on board. I was at the helm during the time they were engaged, and as the sound of the voices rose upon my ear, then fell until I could scarcely hear it at all, I was most forcibly reminded of the days of my childhood, when I remember I used to sit at the window of the house at Dover whilst the family were at Meeting, and listen with rapture to the people singing in the Calvinist Meeting opposite; there was something so sweet in the recollection of that happy part of my life, that I could but indulge myself by lingering . . . amongst scenes, the recollection of which, although . . . they are fled, still affords the mind a sort of agreeable, melancholy pleasure and yields a joy in living them over again. About 5, another flight of small birds visited us, of which I caught one which, from a heavy blow I unintentionally gave it, soon died. Another, of a different species, fell overboard, a prey to the fish. Midnight, moderate breeze and clear weather, got soundings upon the Green bank, upon the lead were a number of green shells, which I quite expected to get, but my lady Read monopolised the whole of them.

2nd. day, 7th. A fine morning, but it afforded me but little pleasure, from having foolishly given way to discontent – but, having occasion to refer to my commonplace book, I found something I had written in it last time I was in Canada, which corrected me for my folly, and restored me again to a happier state. It was this! I had been hard at work from about half past 3 in the morning, taking timber into the ship, a very laborious employment, and at that time rendered more so from being shorthanded; the bell had rung 12 and I was just seated at dinner, when I was ordered to go immediately to Alley [?] Cove to procure a culler, whose business it is to examine and raft etc. timber previously to its going alongside the ship. I hastily finished my meal and, dissatisfied with myself [and] dissatisfied with all around me, went ashore. It was exceedingly sultry; the sun was darting his fiercest rays upon me and extracting copious draughts of perspiration from every pore; in a fit of ill temper I threw myself down upon a large piece of pine timber, which had, ere that time, flourished amongst the loftiest trees of the forest, but which now was lying across a small pond of crystal water the ebbing tide had left in a recess amongst the rocks which composed the bed of the St Lawrence at this part. Here, stretched at my length, my attention was soon attracted by a number of beautiful little fish, who were apparently enjoying life to its full extent, sometimes swimming upon the surface, then diving to the bottom and secreting themselves along the tangles of the rock! Happy little beings! I exclaimed to myself, how little do you know of the toils and troubles man undergoes to struggle thro' this life; you have no care, no anxiety, your meal is provided, your wants are all supplied. I know not how far I should have gone with my soliloquy, had it not been suddenly interrupted by the appearance of a black daemon-like fish which, rushing from underneath the piece of timber upon which I reclined, and where hitherto he had been concealed, made several of the poor little beings his prey; here there was a downfall of all I had been building, their gambols now proved to be nothing but the excitements of terror which the enemy inspired, and whom they had seen, unknown to me! It was enough; I shouldered my tomahawk and proceeded upon my journey, ruminating upon the error of my short-sighted judgement.

4th. day, 9th. Still cold, raw weather with a foul wind, but I am inclined to think we shall soon have a fair one. About 3 o'clock, there being but little wind and a great number of birds about, Captain Read thought he would shoot some in their flight over the ship; accordingly, the gun was handed up and he fired at one which, falling overboard, we lowered the boat down to pick him up. Captain Read came with us with the gun and ammunition, whilst those on board got the lines overboard and began to fish in 48 fathoms. We were glad to hear when we returned that they had caught a fine halibut; I especially, as I had a line to use which I immediately commenced with, and in a short time caught 2, one weighing about 70 lbs, the other 25, very acceptable sights to all hands. When we opened the largest, I examined very particularly his crop, to know what he lived upon, and I was never more astonished than to find it contained a codfish measuring 2 feet 5 inches half digested, 3 crabs, 11 small eels . . . and a quantity of broken shells; I should have supposed it was provisions enough for him for a month, and little should I have expected him to have taken a bait of salt Irish pork. We cut him, as well as another, into lumps and served it out to the passengers, with which they seemed well pleased. Another singular thing was, our catching one of the 2 by the tail; it must have been done in hauling up the line – however, tail or head equals all one with us. I obtained fine birds that I must skin tomorrow, but I am afraid they are so very fat, I shall not be able to save them, if we get warm weather; we could not get one of Mother Carey's chickens, altho' we much wished.

5th. day, 10th. Very wet, uncomfortable weather . . . caught a small codling about 2 feet long, whose stomach was a complete cabinet containing curious mussel shells, small uncommon starfish, and a species of seaweed very hard and not unlike bladderwrack [?], none of which I obtained, altho' caught with my line; Captain Read's wife took the whole, with which she appeared much pleased.

6th. day, 11th. Having had a fine breeze, all last night as well as today, from the southward, we expected to see the land but were disappointed, tho' none more so than the passenger who owns the livestock; whose provision grows so small, that the poor animals have but just sufficient to keep nature alive. I wish heartily some provision could be obtained, but it is useless wishing, that will never help fill their empty stomachs.

7th. day, 12th. This morning at daybreak, it being pretty clear, made the land 30 miles to the southward of Cape North; having the wind from the SSE, we immediately shaped our course for the bird islands in the Gulf of St Lawrence. Noon, saw several ships homeward bound, but spoke none. The two boxes of trees and shrubs have nearly all been killed by the late sharp weather and thick fogs; considering how well they were thriving until we got upon the banks, it seems a great pity to lose them, when there seems a fair prospect of our soon getting to the far end of our passage; some pots of hothouse plants belonging to C[apt] Read are also dead.

1st. day, 13th. After a very thick, foggy night and morning, it cleared up a little and gave us a view of the bird islands and 2 ships, apparently from Quebec; were it to fall calm and hold clear, the Captain would most likely go ashore in the boat to obtain some eggs, of which there are immense quantities upon the largest island. Noon, spoke the southernmost ship; she proved to be the *Sally* of So'Shields, from Quebec bound to Cork, out 13 days . . . we gave him the bearing and distance of the islands as, from the fog coming on, he had not seen them; we asked him to report[20] us but, from misunderstanding what the Captain asked, he said he would not.

2nd. day, 14th. Being quite calm, we got the lines over, and before 3 this afternoon had caught no less than 83 codlings from 2 to 4 feet in length; unfortunately we have no salt on board, I am therefore afraid we shall not be able to eat them all before they are spoilt. We found several curious things in their insides but, as before, I obtained none, the lady had the preference. We caught no less than 11 out of them by various parts of the body, which proves how very abundant they must have been. 5 p.m., a fine breeze sprung up and, its becoming clear, we saw the island of Bon Adventure dist. three and a half miles, also the continent.

3rd. day, 15th. The wind has become quite foul and I should not wonder if it lasts for some time; for the poor animals it will prove a great misfortune, as they are perishing by inches, indeed the owner is already obliged to feed them with thick oatmeal gruel; soaked biscuit, and peas, they have quite refused. We have

---

[20] Report in this context means report to the owners, or to friends in Sunderland, on the safety and whereabouts of the *Lady Frances*.

seen a great number of ships since last evening, bound up for Quebec, which makes us suppose they brought up a fair wind with them, the circumstance by no means uncommon at this time of the year and in this part of the world. That part of our crew and passengers who use tobacco most earnestly desire a fair wind, as their stock is quite expended, and some have been thus early obliged to smoke herbs, which they had intended to use for tea.

5th. day, 17th. About 8 a.m. this morning, being the time we always serve out the fresh water to the passengers, there sprung up amongst them a most terrible breeze, in which the female oratory was notoriously conspicuous. The cause of it was this: one of the casks which was abroach only contained sufficient for half the number, and as it was a rum puncheon[21] it was very bad water; the one half was served out of this cask, and then we broached a fresh one, which contained excellent sweet water. The first customers, who got the bad, declared they would have some of this sweet, and that others might share with them, to which the 'sweet' ones would not accede; the 'foul' ones, to be revenged, began to upset the good water and then began the rumpus, men shoved, women scratched and screamed, children cried, etc. etc., altogether presenting a most ludicrous scene. However, when the 'sweet' was nearly all spilt, they settled matters by sharing the 'foul' and, instead of drinking 3 [cups], contented themselves with one cup of tea for breakfast, and like proportion through the day. I think their salt provisions and the thirst they occasion will prevent the like misdeeds for the future; they have known this day what it is like to be upon half a pint.

7th. day, 19th. This day completes our 49th day, the time we were upon our passage out last year, consequently we shall be a greater time this voyage. I give yet another week to go the remaining 240 miles. Noon, spoke the *Friends of Aberdeen*, from Quebec 4 days, begged him to report us, which he promised to do. I hope he will keep his word, for at present there seems no hopes of my friends knowing thro' any other channel of our arrival, writing letters being quite out of the question. Ere I got here last year, I had 11 ready to send per first ship, this year I have not one; it is the same with the Captain.

1st. day, 20th. We have caught a light breeze from the NE; that it may freshen I sincerely hope, for alas all my sugar is used, as well as all the potatoes and flour, so that we now get but beef and bread one day, and split peas and beef another, for a change, and the best of the joke is, that it is the same in the cabin,

---

[21] A puncheon was a name for a large cask. Presumably a 'rum puncheon' had previously held rum, and the stale remains of this had had a bad effect on the water.

all their white biscuits are used, all the fowls are killed, and in fact they are quite poverty-struck; a foul wind, salt beef and bad bread will soon make them draw long faces.

6 p.m., the passengers assembled in 'Bull Bay' and spent the evening till 9 singing hymns and reading the scriptures. I have noticed before they are mostly Ranters, and I may . . . remark that all their tunes to the hymns were what they call 'lively', being similar to those applied to common songs, such as 'Begone dull Care' etc. etc., a plan I cannot approve, as it appears to deprive their singing of that solemnity which I consider to be so particularly attended to in our [Quaker] religion's gatherings for worship.

2nd. day, 21st. This morning, 4 o'clock, was born unto the jenny ass a son, who is named after the owner, Robin. He appears to be doing well, although coming into the world at a most unfortunate scarce time. 8, sent up a Union Jack fast to an oar, being nearly abreast Matan, a place where many of them live, and in about 1 hour had the pleasure of seeing one alongside, but oh!, what looks of disappointment followed the answer of the questions, 'Have you any tobacco, sugar, rum?' etc. and, when the negative sounded in their ears, all wished him ashore again, and a richer one aboard.

3rd. day, 22nd. Got all ready for anchoring ship, as we expect we must this night, if the fine breeze we have continues; we are carrying all the sail we can crowd, but notwithstanding all that, we have seen [others] have gone past us with ease. 5 o'clock, took in all the steering sails, though much against the pilot's inclination, who was for carrying them as long as possible; I do not think he has got common prudence about him, when it is to be remembered we have got a dangerous narrow to go thro', called the Traverses, he having determined to run all night. I hope he may with safety, tho' for my part I feel loath to trust him. 7 p.m., beginning to rain and, from appearances astern, we may expect a deal of it; all hands ordered up on deck, in case anything should happen.

4th. day, 23rd. The stupid fellow, after taking the ship into the narrows, all at once, from the water shoaling, declared he was lost; the next minute, the man at the lead sung out, '¼ less 3!'. 'Stand by the anchor!' cried our Captain . . . All was clear and in 10 minutes she was at anchor, whilst the pilot stood like one amazed; this was 10 o'clock, stowed the sails and laid down till half past 2, then again got under way, daylight enabling the pilot to tell where he was, in as fair a way as could be; what would such fellows do in a collier, of dark winter nights upon the east coast of England? . . .

Noon, the spire of Quebec church was seen peeping over Point Levi; the falls of Monmorenci (which were greatly swelled with the rain), the finely cultivated island of St Orleans and the novelty of the scenery had attracted much of the attention of the passengers, but [when they heard] of Quebec being seen, [this] fetched them all up, to gaze at that object which has so long been the summit of their wishes. As the town opened to their view, they expressed their several opinions, all of which were very favourable.

2 p.m. After clearing the ship, went ashore with some of the passengers and the Captain when, after procuring a supply of fresh provisions and stopping awhile, we returned on board. To me, Quebec offers nothing particularly pleasing and our arrival at it, although being a long time at sea, does not afford that gratification a coasting passage does, for here I find none to welcome us, no friend to shake hands with, none that care a copper about me except those who expect to profit by me, and that latter is too selfish to be in any way pleasing, so that, on the whole, I would freely board the ship again tomorrow and steer for some other port.

We find there has been desperate losses this year amongst the ships that left England in the spring. Many regular traders find ships are missing, whilst many others are known to be entirely wrecked; we have therefore to be thankful we escaped with the small proportion of bad weather we had.

5th. day, 24. Hauled into Atkinson's wharf.

6 – 26.   Set off all our passengers, excepting 1 family, in the steam boat for Montreal.

7 – 27.   Began to discharge . . .

29.   Sent two letters per Quebec packet for Mother and Richard.

7 mo[nth] 10. Clear ship.

          11. Began to load.

          23. Finished lower hold.

          30. Finished twixt decks.

8 mo[nth] 4. Got on all the deck timber.

8 mo[nth] 5th. Got on board all the water casks and the spare spars, expecting to sail on 7th. day.

Thus we have been here nearly 6 weeks, and greatly have we been troubled to get loaded, having as far as 9 miles to go for our timber aggregate, [and] trouble to get it in when we get it to the ship, from strong tides and heavy winds; we are notwithstanding loaded, and I feel glad of it, though I cannot help thinking that we are very deep[ly laden] to cross the western ocean: but we will not be frightened, it being a very fine time of year. There have been but very few Indians in Quebec this year until within the last few days, when 3 camps arrived of the Mic Mac[?], Cherokee and New Brunswick tribes. Since they have been here, articles have . . . [fallen] much in price, but from my having procured all I can take, I lose the advantage of their arrival.

I spent a pleasant evening with Macksman, an Indian chief who was a clever, engaging man, very open and communicative, a father of the finest family I ever saw; amongst many other things, he showed me two small beavers, quite tame, and a beautiful black squirrel, upon which his wife sets so much store, that she replied, in answer to a question I put as to the price, 'Not all Quebec!'; a tame fox I could have had for 1 paistre, but greatly preferred my dollar for half a doz[en] of them. I bought of him, before I left, his tobacco pouch ornamented with beads, tho' I quite forgot the name of the skin it was made of.

I have noted with feelings of great regret the excessively bad manner in which the English sailors spend their sabbath ashore in this city. There is scarcely a first day night but they are to be seen fighting and making disturbances in the street, swearing and behaving in the most disorderly manner, so that I have at times wondered the inhabitants do not use some decisive method of suppressing such disgraceful work. The cheapness of liquor is a temptation few amongst them are able to resist; I do not mean to say they all get intoxicated, but I can, I think with safety, say that out of 100, that came here, not 20 can say they have not been tipsy during their stay; it is indeed the poor sailors' besetting sin. Great numbers have been drowned this year, as many as 9 were washed off the rafts in one day, from the strong swell running in the river; with a fresh of wind from the east or west, it is very difficult to keep upon the timber.

7th. day. Hauled the ship off from the wharf and anchored off the marketplace, took on board 5 passengers and a young lad with a broken arm (left by a Shields [i.e. South Shields] ship), going to England with us, also all our stores; intend to start tomorrow if the wind shifts, at present it being from the eastward. In the evening were visited by the heaviest thunderstorm I ever recollect, the peals and flashes of lightning were exceedingly awful, and the rain fell in torrents.

1st. day, morning. Went ashore at 7 a.m., the ship got under way, wind westerly and with her sails loosed dropped down, got our little business done and followed her; at 9 overtook her, about 9 miles below the town, half the length of Orleans [Island]. Without the least regret I saw the town disappearing as we rounded Point Line, but with pleasure I felt the soft west wind blowing its gentle breeze and filling our extended sails, wafting us down the St Lawrence, whose banks clothed with trees looked exceedingly delightful. We have in company the *Mint* of London, *Merchant* of Bermuda, and *Stockton* of Liverpool, all bound to the several ports from which they hail.

Evening. Came to an anchor under Goose Island, not being able to get thro' the traverses – our old pilot not willing, at least, to risk it.

2nd. day, 8. At daylight got under way, fresh breeze from the WNW. *Mint* only in company, set all steering sails and sent up a main royal. Noon, light winds with a few light showers, got the booms over the side and began to paint the ship, standing knee deep in the water. 4 o'clock, got just below Brandy Pot Island, where we were taken aback with the wind from the eastward; as there seemed a prospect of it continuing in that quarter, bore away and anchored in 10 fathoms. 6 p.m., the pilot boat with the Captain and some more went to the island to gather blueberries, but returned without finding any. They fired at a hare and a pigeon, but missed both.

3rd. Wind easterly all day accompanied with much rain, and some thunder, but about 5 it cleared up and the wind veered into the WSW, tho' very little of it; hove apeak[22] and got tea, after tea it freshened, weighed [anchor] and set all sail; the *Mint* in company.

10 p.m., got the length of Green Island, breeze increasing but looking as if it had a desire to be easterly, with much swell from that quarter occasioning the passengers to cast up their accounts [i.e. be seasick] previously to their leaving America for the Old World.

Midnight, a desperate fray commenced between some Canadians who accompanied us in the pilot's boat as his passengers; the fact was, they had been making rather too free with the rum cask, but upon calling Monsieur Magneash . . . [the] pilot, he soon settled the business with kicking a couple of them in a masterly style – the one his apprentice, the other another man's.

4th. day, 10. 4 a.m., being as far as Father Point, the pilot left us, without the least regret upon our part, for he was a fidgety, lubberly [i.e. clumsy] old fellow, always complaining about the steering altho', when he happened to take the helm himself, he steered as wild as anyone. The reason she steers so badly is, she is quite as deep[ly laden] as ever she was in the coal trade, and when deeply loaded she certainly is as bad a ship to steer as ever yet spread canvas. Noon, Cape St Ann . . . fresh breezes and cloudy weather, secured our timber and spars, water casks, anchors and kedges.[23]

---

[22] Apeak is a technical term for when the anchor is nearly straight down and not angled.

[23] A kedge is a hawser (i.e. rope or small cable) attached to a small anchor.

5th. day, 12. Morning rainy, with a strong westerly and much sea which, from us being so deeply loaded, washes us rather too much; however, the voyage we must go, so we must make ourselves content. 6 p.m., got the lines overboard and caught 4 mackerel; I for my part took a large dogfish, after which we caught no more mackerel.

Midnight, the northern lights appeared most beautiful, being of a light greenish colour, tinged at times with dark red streaks. I have heard it remarked that to see them so bright in these parts is a sign of wind, but the sky at this time looks like very fine weather.

6th. day, 13. A very delightful morning, with a fine breeze from the NW. Expecting to see the Bird Islands shortly, tried for fish but caught nothing, except another large dog[fish], which we stripped of his jacket for the use of the carpenter. I am afraid we shall catch no more mackerel whilst we take the dogfish, as they are seldom in better company than themselves. Our poor female passenger has not left her bed since we left Brandy Pot [Island]; she is a very delicate woman and looks, I think, very consumptive. Noon, the Bird Islands bore S and SE dist. 24 miles, light breezes and clear weather; tomorrow, I hope, we shall bid adieu to the American land.

7th. day, 14. From having had but very light breezes last night we have made but little progress, but we cannot help being satisfied, there being delightful weather. At noon the breeze freshened and we soon saw the Island of St Paul at the entrance of the Gulf, as well as many vessels turning to windwards.

A number of small birds visited us this morning, of the flycatcher description, but they soon flew off again for the land. 6 p.m., saw a number of large finners [i.e. fin whales] steering to the northward, making a great noise with their blowing.

1st. day, 15. At 4 a.m. the Island of St Paul's bore by compass WSW 1/2, from which I take my departure, it being in 47.11 N Lat. and in 50.0 Lon., distant 14 miles.

Farewell, Gulf and river of St Lawrence, and farewell, Canada and Nova Scotia and Newfoundland; twice I have visited your shores, but without a particle of regret I view you receding from my view as our vessel, swiftly ploughing thro' the Atlantic waves, hastens towards my native land. This day 6 weeks and I hope to spend this day in a different manner amongst those I esteem, and once more to enter a place of worship, a privilege I have not enjoyed for many months; there is a pleasure indeed in the very anticipation of again reaching the shores of Old England.

Star of God in safety guide us
To the shore we ask of thee,
Long tempestuous winds have tried us
Star, at sea.

2nd. day, 16. This morning, from the wind being at SW, it veered into the ENE quarter and, increasing rapidly, soon compelled us to take 2 reefs in our topsails, and to stow the mainsail, trysail and jib. At noon it blew a gale of wind and we were about to furl the foresail and close-reef the topsails when the wind, again getting into the west, saved us the trouble, in a manner very pleasing to us all. 4 p.m., from the heavy head sea we have to cope with and from our being deeply loaded, the green seas come in over the bows in a fair body and, washing against the ends of the timber, give it the appearance of broken water upon a sand; boots we cannot put on, as the timber is very slippery, and we prefer a wet foot to the risk of going overboard.

3rd. day, 17. Better weather, with a true sea and less wind, saw the *Mint* in our wake, hull down from the top masthead, as well as another three-masted ship.

10 a.m. As they seemed to be overtaking us, and not liking to be beaten by a worse than ourselves, shook out the last reef and set the top gallant sails and a top mast studding sail.

Our female passenger has not yet left her bed and her husband does not seem to wish she should, so I expect she will keep it until we reach smooth water again; their three children are all very hearty, and if they could, would run about, but the height of the timber makes us forbid them, lest we lose them.

4th. day, 18. As we now begin to near the banks of Newfoundland we begin to experience the customary foggy weather, though from the wind being from the southward, it is not so raw and uncomfortable as we frequently find it; the glass stands at 45 but, altho' warm, it is very damp. Captain Barry is at present very unwell and has been ever since Quebec. I sincerely hope he may not be laid up; some of the men also have been but poorly for the last few days, but as medicine has been served out, they appear to be recovering. It will be cold comfort to get a ship's company on the passage home, after having had so much of it on coming out.

5th. day, 19. Very thick, foggy weather . . . Our livestock, consisting of 9 fowls, 2 squirrels, cats and dogs, appear to dislike the fog, as they look very mopish. One hen we lost overboard, being shaken off the foresheet, upon which she was sitting; not wishing to lose more, we have secured the rest in the skiff. We unfortunately, when about to leave Quebec, had stolen from us our 'jolly boat', worth about eleven pounds; altho' we searched the river nine miles east and west, we could get no intelligence of her. We feel her loss much, as she afforded shelter to us, when turned over upon the skiff.

6th. day, 20. This morning the fog broke and we spied ahead of us a large red-bottomed ship who, hoisting his ensign, backed his main yard to speak with us. He asked our longitude and where we came from, and to report the *Lord Sidmouth* of Blyth, which our Captain promised to do; the latter is, I am happy to say, much better than he was and will, I hope, continue to improve.

7th. day, 21. This day the wind has been from the northward, with a fresh breeze obliging us to take one reef in our topsail and to stow the top gallant sails and jib with rather a heavy sea; saw several ships to windward but spoke none, much to our satisfaction, for there is too much trouble attends it. Our female passenger is still very ill, but I hope nothing serious is to be apprehended . . . being of a delicate constitution, seasickness has much effect upon her.

1st. day, 22. This makes the second week since we left Quebec, in which time we have had much fine weather and a good proportion of fair winds. I hope they may continue, for of all sailing [weather], fair winds are what we like. Finished a second reading of T. Chalkley's journal; the more I read of him, the more I admire the character of the man, and pity it is there are not more of his profession following in his footsteps. Our ancient Friends seem to have felt a lively interest in the welfare of the rising generations, looking forward with anxiety to their conduct as the basis upon which the welfare of the Society [of Friends] greatly depended, tho' I am afraid, were they to see the present state of things amongst us, they would have cause for sorrow in the degeneracy of their sons.

2nd. day, 23. Wind WSW, one of those lovely mornings which, even upon the wide ocean, are truly delightful. The sun rose in all his glory, shedding his bright beams all over the heavens and dispersing the fog that lay upon the water; our vessel with all her sails set and filled by a fine, steady breeze, was ploughing her way thro' the fine sky blue sea. The young finners were sporting around us, apparently enjoying life to its full extent; when, delighted, I seated myself upon the bow, and indulged myself in thinking upon those I love, tho' far away. Sail on, my gallant ship! exclaimed I to myself, four weeks more and I hope we shall both be in Old England; we have travelled together about 10 or 11 thousand miles and I hope, with a blessing, we shall yet reach our destined ports.

3rd. day, 24th. It is not the finest appearances that always are followed up with the success they had given reason to expect; instance yesterday morning, when everything promised a fine day . . . which deceived us completely, as about 5 in the evening it freshened from a fine steady breeze to a complete gale, the hardest we have experienced since we left Sunderland. We were soon obliged to put the *Lady* under close-reefed topsails and a stowed foresail. About dusk, a fine Mother Carey flew against the main rigging and apparently fell into the boat; if it did, I may get it tomorrow.

4th. day, 25. Rather more moderate, set the reefed foresail at 6 a.m. after splicing the mainbrace – all hands wet through above and below from the ship straining – bedding and all alike; unfortunately for me, I have lost my bunch of keys in the breeze and cannot open my chest, unless by main force, which I am determined not to do, unless compelled by dire necessity. I am also deprived of all my stock of tea, sugar etc., all being locked up, but as my credit is pretty good, I must borrow for awhile. Found poor Mother Carey with a damaged foot in the stern of the boat; it is a fine specimen and I hope to get it home to England. Evening, the bird died; better weather, tho' squally at times.

5th. day, 26. Shook out all the reefs and set the top gallant sails, wind N and SW, light breeze and clear weather. Set to work and skinned the petrel, but did not succeed very well with it; a professor in the Upper Town, Quebec, who had a fine collection of Canadian birds, told me I did not act properly with them, but as he expected rather a large perquisite for his instruction, I declined.

6th. day, 27. Last night the wind eastered, braced the yards up, set the tacks down and made up our minds to a foul wind; considering the long spell of westerly breezes we have enjoyed, we have every reason to be well satisfied. We have had great numbers of sea fowl around us all the way across, principally sea swallows[24] and hawks; indeed, the Captain says he never recollects seeing so many before.

7th. day, 28. Saw a number of ships bound outward, though none near enough to tell much of them, one of them under a jury foremast, a sign of her having had a rough time of it. From the difference there has been, every time we have had an observation, between it and our lat. by account, we have every reason [to think] there is a current sitting to the northward. We tried to determine by an azimouth[25]

---

[24] Probably skuas or tern.

[25] An azimuth is an arc of the horizon.

today, but the ship was not steady enough to allow it.

1st. day, 29th. The beginning of this week sees us within 16 days' sail of England, but we cannot flatter ourselves with a prospect of so soon getting home. The female has not yet been seen upon deck, her sickness still continuing as great as ever; how miserable must be her situation, but as it is but the effects of the ship's motion, she has but little sympathy expressed for her. Even her dear husband speaks of it as being likely to be of great service to her in the end.

2nd. day, 30th. Wind SE, with a strong breeze and a promising look of plenty of rain and wind. I have got so care-hardened that I can look at these signs of the times without feeling any trouble about them. Noon, reduced the topsails, two reefs, and furled the mainsail, trysail and jib. Midnight, stowed the foresail, strong gales with heavy rain, which perhaps may make the wind wester. At 11 there was a light settled upon the bowsprit, about the size of a candle flame,[26] where it rested about 20 or 25 minutes; said to be a sign of heavy weather.

3rd. day, 31st. A mountainous sea with a heavy gale from the SE of E, hove to under the close-reefed main topsail, very heavy rain continuing all the time, and has done since yesterday; the ship, altho' behaving very well, is sorely washed and becoming very leaky. Noon, bad weather but the wind more southerly, it no doubt will soon fly into the nor'west, that famous wind on the western ocean. It would be well if it did, for the sake of getting one's things dried again.

4th. day, 9 mo[nth], 1st. 4 a.m. Set the fore topsail, wind about NE and E and blowing very hard. 10 a.m., part of the deck loading was washed overboard, though nothing very material, consisting only of a few handspikes and some lath wood. Noon, opened out clear weather which made us look out for a north wester . . . but it soon . . . came on again with a good heart again, accompanied with much rain.

5th. day, 2nd. 5 a.m., better weather, but a very heavy sea; got something cooked for the first time in the gale, which proved very acceptable, as heavy weather and little to eat are by no means pleasant companions. 8, bore away with a gale of wind and a heavy sea behind us, which renders scudding in our deeply loaded vessel rather dangerous, but we become so used and naturalised to these stormy climes that they serve to harden us against fear.

---

[26] This would be St Elmo's fire, a luminous electrical discharge sometimes seen on a ship during a storm.

6th. day, 3rd. Less wind, but plenty yet for the two close-reefed topsails and reefed foresail, but as it is driving us home at the rate of 3½ degrees a day it is not any trouble, excepting that she still strains and rolls, much water on board. We begin now to get very far north, being as high as 57 degrees, and we see occasionally great numbers of fish and sea birds; many of the latter, on account of the wind, have at times taken shelter on board our ship.

4 p.m., now moderate, set more sail, sky quite clear.

7th. day, 4th. Now, *Lady*, do thy best, there remains but now 20 deg. to the land and 48 hours' sail afterwards, ere thou shalt be at home. If thou get there in 10 days, well; if not, thou must stop out for 20, for the tides will not flow sufficiently for thee to go in after 2d. day week. Step forth, old friend, then, and let us close the voyage, a fair wind is behind thee, a safe port before thee, where thou mayst rest thy old weary bones and I my young ones.

Midnight, squally, with much rain and a stiff breeze yet, notwithstanding all these favours . . . the old wagon will not go faster than 5 knots an hour. If she was the more sure for being slow it would be a consolation, but being still leaky, I doubt she is not.

1st. day, 5th. Fine, clear, beautiful weather; the ocean, as if tired of persecuting us, now rests tranquil and serene, the winds that apparently before were trying to rob us of our sails, now scarcely fill them, and the sky that before seemed to threaten us with evil and frowned upon us, now smiles and promises good, but the experienced seaman, whom they have tricked so often, sees thro' it all and prepares for a S. easterly wind and dirty weather.

2nd. day, 6th. I find myself becoming quite weatherwise for, as I foretold, so we have got it, a return of the gale from the SE by E. We began at midnight to take in sail, and kept at it until we had her again under the two double-reefed topsails. At 8 a.m. a fine, large, hawk boarded us and settled upon the main boom, but not liking the situation he soon left us, to seek a better. 6 p.m., hove to again, under the close-reefed main topsail, making bad weather and continually at the pumps. Passengers very ill.

3rd. day, 7th. Bad weather and apparently likely to continue; unable to cook anything, as the sea puts out the fires. Looked over our stock of beef and pork and found but enough for 10 days at the present rate of living, which is plenty without waste; if we get no fairer wind in 2 or 3 days, we shall be put upon short allowance. 4 p.m., shipped a heavy sea amidships which washed away the better half of the cook's coals; still, there remains plenty to cook all the provisions we have left. Midnight, set the main stay sail, wind at NE and cold.

4th. day, 8th. More moderate, sea reefed foresail, fore topmast, stay sail and trysail, wind NNE. 6, quite calm, but a heavy swell from the quarter the wind has been in makes our ship very uneasy. Midnight, the wind westered, set all sail to catch the favouring breeze.

5th. day, 9th. Being a fine morning, got the boat cleared out and painted her fit for harbour service, also bent the best bower cable and put fresh puddings on both rings. 6, thought we saw the land, but it entirely disappeared whilst we were at tea.

6th. day, 10th. After a fine run all night, at daybreak we discovered a sail upon the wind right ahead, apparently outward bound; the sight of her gave us great satisfaction, as we felt sure of knowing where we were. 11 p.m., we spoke [to] her, she proved to be the *Prince of Orange* of Sunderland, from Archangel bound to Chepstow, Captain Cooke the Captain's brother-in-law; as it fell less wind just as we met, we had plenty of time to know of each other what cheer. They had experienced all fine westerly weather for a long time, and had not had any of the easterly gales which we have. A relation of the Captain, of a fine brig called the *Robsons* which sailed on 4th month 1st. for Quebec, and which is no doubt entirely lost, learnt the melancholy tidings from us; he hopes, he says, to hear in time of the crew being saved. They saw the island of St Kilda at 3 this morning.

4 p.m. Still quite calm, the brig in sight at times, one wind will suit us both, and for it we are waiting; sailors say a calm is half a fair wind, but from appearances we shall have an easterly one, a S. easter perhaps. An immense number of large whale porpoises[27] have been with us all day; their gambols have afforded much amusement. They blow exactly like a whale, but are not so active as the bottle-nosed species; I think one of the largest would yield a very large quantity of oil.

7th. day, 11th. At half past 7 last evening caught a fine breeze from the SW, which lasted to 12, when it became showery and more southerly. Half past 1, whilst at dinner, the fore topmast stay sail gave way and blew to ribands; unbent it and got another set. 4 p.m., blowing harder and harder, clewed up[28] and stowed the fore topsail, hove the ship to. Half past 6, the wind flew suddenly into the

---

[27] These were probably pilot whales.

[28] To clew up is to draw the lower ends of the sail to the upper mast ready for furling.

NNW and fell nearly calm . . . bore away ES to sight the Butt of Lewis if possible; before we made sail, got a cast of the deep sea lead and found bottom with 80 fathoms, speckled sand and small pebbles. 8, fine, clear, weather, tomorrow I hope we shall get thro' the Pentland Firth and jog towards home down the Scotch coast. In the future time, if ever I hear any person excusing the loading [of] a ship in the way we are by saying ''tis a fine time of year', I will not fail to mention this midsummer passage, in which we have had nothing but gales of wind and have been continually washed over head and ears; 'tis too far north for fine weather.

1st. day, 12th. At daylight made all sail, wind SSW and a fine breeze. 4 a.m., the island of Barra bore by compass NE dist. 9 miles, hauled to the wind. 6, Rona, another rocky barren island, was seen when the mist cleared away; it appeared quite white from the immense quantity of sea fowl upon it, most likely set there to breed. Noon, fine clear weather with the wind southerly, saw the Highlands of Caithness; it is at this part exceeding high and mountainous, rising in lofty peaks, with their tops covered with mist. I cannot say I envy the inhabitants their land, it looks too dreary and comfortless for me, I prefer the fertile-looking shores of England far before these Caledonian mountains. Not even the sight of land, that great stimulus to exertion in the seasick traveller of the main, has had the effect of getting our female passenger out of bed. I think it high time she got an airing!

2nd. day, 13th. At daylight entered the Pentland Firth with a prospect of a fine wind, but it soon came from the southward. 4 a.m. got the tide and turned there; about midway a boat boarded us, wanting to pilot us into the Orkneys, gave them some tobacco, rum, and boiled beef and set them . . . off about their business; their looks, I believe, got the supply, as they bore the appearance of being half starved. 8, tacked ship to the western wind SSW, a complete 'noser' for us; I hope we may not be detained here for the same length of time, and encounter similar weather, to that we did last year; it would be far from agreeable. Noon, tacked ship to the northward.

3rd. day, 14th. 2 a.m., this southerly wind freshened upon us, took in the m[ain] top gallant sail. The boy that helped the man stow it was very nearly lost, being pulled over the yard by the sail blowing over his head, but he held fast and the other man helped him into safety. 4, another gale of wind came on; close-reefed the topsail, it blew into tatters, and an unfortunate job for us, as the one we have to bend is not worth the trouble of it.

4 p.m., better weather, shook out our reef in the topsails and set the fore

topmast stay sails, topsail and main stay sail.

4th. day, 15th. We had a beautiful clear night but a return of the breeze this morning, which lasted till noon, when the wind came from the westward and we immediately made more sail; I hope it may last us home, for many reasons – one of them is, I have a very bad finger and it grows worse and worse, so that it is with much difficulty and pain I do my duty. We have caught several mackerel these last 2 days, which as a fresh mess have proved very acceptable to all; I did not expect there were any hereabouts, thinking it too far north. Midnight, answered a Revenue cutter's questions about when from, where to, etc. They are a set of inquisitive fellows, I think.

5th. day, 16. Being a fine morning, commenced mending our tattered foresail ... soon passed Buchan Ness and Peterhead, for the 3rd. time since I have been in the *Lady Frances*. 4, tacked in shore and fetched into Girdle Ness, hove about, lying SE and E right on end. When will this weary wind cease to blow and let us get home! I feel more impatient because I am becoming useless, having but one hand.

6th. day, 17. Fine weather, but still this old wind of which all . . . [are] tired, as we have now in hand but 27 pieces of meat and 1 stone of flour. What makes the case more aggravating to our captain is that, thinking from what we had consumed on the passage out, we should have more than sufficient for home consumption, he spared two casks to one or two ships in Quebec who were in want. Should it come on to blow westerly and we get off the land we shall be pitifully off, as some unfortunate leaks our ship has sprung in the heavy gales encountered give an additional appetite, from the exercise of pumping. That is the dark side of the case; on the other hand, if we should get to the roads in a couple of days, it will be a good job.

Noon, tacked and fetched Aberdeen Bay; the land here is very bald and apparently but ill-cultivated, the corn that is cut is not yet carried, altho' we have heard the harvest is over in England and that it has been a very abundant one. Such news is very agreeable, for who is there that feels no interest in the welfare of his native land? Evening, caught a mass of mackerel, but a dogfish spoiled our sport by carrying away the hook of my line. Saw, a short distance from us, a large 'finner' [i.e. fin whale], a fish I did not expect to find upon these coasts. I think he must have missed his road.

8 o'clock, wind SSE, I hope it will not become more easterly still, a lee and an iron-bound coast being but poor comforters.

7th. day, 18th. The appearance of the sky has looked rather like a S east wind this morning and I should not be surprised if it became more easterly. At night it will not hurt us much if it keeps fine weather but, should it blow hard, it will be but poor comfort to think, we have an iron-bound shore under our lee. Noon, caught a number of mackerel and gurnet [i.e. gurnards], a very acceptable supply and affording an agreeable change from salt provisions; now there remains but a cask of salt herrings and what we may chance to catch with the lines – for I suppose, with the wind easterly, we shall not venture ashore for a fresh supply.

4 p.m. The wind veered from SE to W, from that to NW, and from there to the NNE, with rain and much thunder and lightning. I have no cause to grumble, but it would have been far more agreeable had it been from the NW; we could then have stopped in Lund. roads. It is not very pleasant, after coming off a long passage and landing the Captain, to have to stand off to sea and thrash out a week before we can get into the harbour.

Midnight, fresh wind and much rain and lightning very vivid to the southward; split the fore top gallant sail or, rather, shook it to pieces. It was so very dark that we could not see it until it was discovered by the lightning.

1st. day, 19. Daylight, saw the Bell Rock in a short, clear, light breeze and much rain; to windward are a great number of Dutch fishermen, who are most likely catching herrings; they bear a very droll appearance when contrasted with the vessels of our own country. This I expect will be the last day for us at sea for some time. I feel pleasure in the prospect of soon being again amongst my friends. 10 p.m., fresh breeze and cloudy, expect to see Tynemouth light by daybreak if it keeps clear; much rain throughout the night.

2nd. day, 20th. At 9 a.m. saw Tynemouth castle bearing WSW dist. 8 miles, and in about half an hour were boarded by a Sunderland coble [i.e. fishing-boat], which brought the welcome intelligence of there being sufficient water for us to go over the bar. Quarter past 10, the town of Sunderland opened in sight, the pleasantest prospect I have enjoyed for many a day; hove to, and sent the Captain away in the coble. 11, made sail to keep to windward of the harbour, kept tacking until the running fitter came aboard, then with light hearts made sail and at half past 1 p.m. were moored in safety, after an absence of 4 months and 20 days, in which time we have experienced a round [i.e. ample] share of trouble in sickness and storms.

Part IV

First Voyage to India

Journal of a Voyage in the Ship Woodford

Capn. Alfred Chapman	–	Commander
Edward Chapman	–	Chief Mate
Duncan Lard	–	Second Mate
Edward Beck	–	Third Mate
Ino Anderson	–	Fourth Mate

To Madras via Bengal

BEGUN 4th month 21st 1825

PASSENGERS:

Capn. Smart
Mrs Smart
Mr Dougal
Miss E. Ray
Miss C. Ray
Miss Dale
Mr de Grange
Mr Littlejohn
Mr Jeffreys
Mr C. Marshall
Mr Brown, surgeon
Mr Purton, 3rd officer, passenger

Mrs Cheek
Miss Cheek
Mr Ray
Mrs Ray
Mr Beynon
Miss Pefford
Mr Pefford
Mr Connolly
Mr Gillashall
Mrs Beynon

From Madras to Calcutta:

Mr Brown
Miss Connolly

Mr Connolly
Mr Dalrymple

1825, 5th month, 23rd. First day, washed down the decks and sent the young gentlemen to church; for my part, having bid all my relations and friends farewell, I felt no desire to go thro' that painful ordeal any more, so quietly sat down on board my ship and spent the day all alone in peace and quietness; spirits at a low ebb at leaving Old England and all it contains so dear to me. I feel at this moment no fear of [not] meeting them again, and altho' the voyage is longer than any I have heretofore been, yet I cannot even let in a doubt but that I shall again tread my native shores and rejoice in the company of my relations and friends. My hopes of a pleasant, instructive, and happy voyage will not, I hope, be disappointed, for from the character of our captain, I think it would be his study to see all happy around him. After tea wrote to Thos. [i.e. Thomas], to bed, then adieu. . . .

24th. Employed taking in and stowing away stores and cargo as fast as possible; shipped all our sailors, which I am much pleased at, as with Irish labourers I am quite tired. They are, generally speaking, stupid, lazy fellows. At noon Capn. C. came on board, mustered our crew, and signed the articles for the voyage. Wages for seaman two pounds five shillings; I have been agreeably disappointed in them, as I had quite expected to see a vile, drunken set of fellows, but our men have to this time behaved with the greatest propriety, altho' they have had part of their advance.

2.00 p.m. The pilot came on board, cast off from the buoy and made sail; all around looking most delightful and raising those feelings of regret we are all subject to at such times. I observed it, at least, in all around me this day except the pilot, whose greatest care is to get us off to the Downs, where he will be paid and leave us, I expect.

10.00 p.m. Brought up with the small bower[29] at Gravesend, wind WNW. The ship, from this day's work I can plainly see, is a heavy ship to handle, for which I am sorry, . . . of pulling and hauling, I will freely give my share to anybody! Midnight, the pilot went ashore and another took charge. This does at last appear like a start, but I have had quite plenty of it for a year or two, and to be saying we sail tomorrow or next week without fail and still not to go, is to me completely miserable. I feel quite tired with my day's work and shall feel happy when the watch which I command will be out, that I may pay another visit to my swinging cot, the first for more than 5 months; but I must say I feel very happy at my promotion, tho' in the slightest degree regretting the way I followed to obtain it.

---

[29] The bower is one of two small anchors carried at the ship's bow.

5th. month, 25. Busily engaged setting up (tightening) the rigging fore and aft; at 12.00 Capn. Smart with his lady, Mr Ray, a missionary, and two children, all passengers, came aboard, and about an hour after, Abel Chapman, the owner, with the Captain's sisters, came to pay the last visit to his ship and son previous to our departure, which we quite expect tomorrow. I am exceedingly pleased and gratified by the kind attentions of A.C. to me, enquiring of me after our mutual friends and giving me his good, sound, wholesome advice.

3 p.m. Sat down to dinner, about 14, many visitors, friends and relations of the Captain's on board.

7. After bidding us all goodbye and wishing us all a safe, speedy and prosperous voyage and a happy meeting of our friends, the owner and his party were lowered over the side, the Boatswain and all the crew manning the side and giving them three hearty cheers, which were returned by them. Got ho[ve?] and retired to rest. Wind SSW, fresh breezes and cloudy weather.

5th month, 26. This morning, just as the Boatswain piped to breakfast, came down the last lighter[30] for us; as soon as the hands were turned up [we] began to clear her. I was pleased to see in her all my stores for my messmates, . . . [had begun] to be afraid they should get nothing but salt junk [i.e. hard dried meat] for the voyage, and as I have been in the habit of generally writing for your amusement [of] my stock of stores, I shall at this time do the same, because I wish to give you an intimate acquaintance with the life I had on board the *Woodford*:

25 jars of pickles
12 lb. mustard, 2 of curry powder
½ do. cayenne, 12 bottles ketchups, sauces
2 do. pepper, 2 do. celery seed
3 kegs of neats' tongues   and one large
3 do. pickled tripes   Cheshire [cheese] for
3 Westphalian hams   extra occasions
25 Berkley cheeses
7 jars – 125 lb. butter

You must allow that with fresh meat twice a week, plenty of flour and biscuit, with ale for drink etc., we shall be to blame if we suffer want.

7 p.m. The custom house officers, after clearing the ship, left us, and we immediately hove short; 2 o'clock, up anchor, and made sail. After a pleasant

---

[30] A lighter is a boat used for loading and unloading ships not at the wharf.

run we fetched into the North Foreland but, having the wind from SSW, we were unable to get into the Downs, and after tacking and tacking and tacking after that until I was tired of tacking, we were obliged to come to an anchor, having worked till 7 o'clock on the morning of the 27th without having accomplished our aim. . . .

Turned in quite wearied. Quite calm, but looking very much like an easterly wind.

I have had to remark this day the inferiority of our sailors to those I have been accustomed to for the last 2 years in the coal trade – there are some good smart seamen, but the most of them are quite middling.

5 month 27. At 9 a.m. got under way and, with the wind easterly, sailed into the Downs, where we again anchored and sent ashore for our passengers and Captain, who were, we learnt, . . . gone to Margate for the day, which must prevent them coming off, tho' it is greatly to be desired, on account of the fine easterly wind which might be the means of sending us into warm weather, should it continue. 2 p.m., cleaned the upper and lower decks, and appointed 4th and 7th days for washing the gun deck throughout.

I quite expect to be very comfortable with my fellow officers, and have every reason to hope we are well met.

4 p.m. A boatload of water came alongside; hoisted it in and filled up our empty casks, after giving the [live]stock as much as they could drink for the last time.

Wind SSE, fine breeze and clear weather.

5th. Month 28. At midnight, after freshening from early on the last evening, it blew a gale of wind from the SE. . . . 7 a.m., a boat came off to inform us that, if a flag were hoisted on the signal staff ashore, we were to get under way and the passengers would come off, which was soon after done, and we commenced heaving but, the ship riding ebb and the wind ahead also, we got but very little of our cable after two hours' heavy heaving, but soon after, whilst blasting the messenger[31], the cable parted and we were under way, tho' rather unpleasantly. 11 a.m., the boat containing the Captain and passengers came alongside and [they] were hoisted in. Made sail and sent up top gallant yard and main fore royal; more moderate than before. Noon, filled the main yard and set all sail, fine stiff breeze, easterly with much rain.

1 p.m. Passed by Dover; every time the remembrance of the happy hours I

---

[31] Blasting the messenger probably means fastening the small rope bent onto the larger one, in order to bring it to the capstan.

have seen there is fresh as ever in my memory, and at the same time there is, connected with the passing [of] it, the different times and circumstances that I have been in the like situation. I looked back upon it with feelings I cannot describe, and the warm wish of my heart was that I may yet see some more happy days in it. I have so very many pleasant associations with Dover, that I feel a very great pleasure in merely a sight of it. We all feel an attachment to the place of our birth and childhood – not that I think we enjoyed it so exceedingly, for even then we have all had our little troubles, which in their way were great – but because we look back to it as a state so much to be desired, of innocence, quietness and peace, with no cares, comparatively, to harass and perplex in the way we find them to do now.

5th. month 29. Last night we got as far as the Isle of Wight; when off Sandown [?] the wind westered upon us and soon became quite a 'noser'; hauled in all fine weather sails and set down tacks [of] aft sheets. 8 a.m., tacked ship to the southward. The passengers seem to be good sailors, as I have heard of few of them being sick, tho' many I have seen but once, since they became our inmates. We hope, from the appearances, it will not last long. The island looks romantic and beautiful, but how differently am I situated to this time last year, when I was in the *Lady Frances* and [we] were obliged to go into Portsmouth, with many of our passengers sick of the smallpox! I am afraid I am in another leaky ship, for we now pump her every 4 hours. It may be on account of her being so long above water that it is in her upper works; if so, it will most likely swell and she will be staunch [i.e. watertight] again – which I humbly hope will be the case, for I hate pumping.

5th. month 29.[32] First day. Still off the Wight, with the wind from the westward and consequently foul. At 10 a.m. the word was passed to get ready for church at 11 o'clock; at half past the bell began to toll, seats were erected by putting planks upon pails and covered with colours, on the capstan a cushion with the books for a reading desk, and in the cuddy all the chairs in a row.

11. The men and the passengers were all seated and the Captain began by reading the morning service of the Church of England, the steward acting as clerk. After many passages and chapters of the Old and New Testament were read, the Captain blessed all hands and the service concluded. I was, on account of it being my duty, upon the poop, and I can truly say I looked down on the quarter deck with great satisfaction; it was an interesting sight. At 6 the bell

---

[32] Beck has mistaken the date here, and in his next entry – the voyage started on a Sunday, the 23rd, so the next Sunday must have been the 30th.

again tolled, and all the hands met in the cuddy for evening service.

5th. month 30. Busily employed in the hold, squaring the cargo and making all seaworthy; the passengers many of them very sick, and one or two of the young cadets wishing they had never left home. Poor fellows, they have had the pleasure of anticipation and hope; now they come to the reality, I think the gilding begins to be worn off. The missionaries are apparently studying Hindustani, as I see them frequently with those books in their hands. How much more beneficial will be their endeavours than those of the cadets, the one going forth in true love to their benighted brethren to preach the glad tidings of the gospel, to reclaim them from the errors of their superstitious worship, and in short to benefit mankind, whilst the others are bent upon the destruction of their fellow creatures, from whom they have received not the slightest injury. May the former meet their reward.

To the 6th. month 16. From the last date until this day I have been so very closely engaged, endeavouring to find the leak and consequently in the hold, that I have been unable to write anything, but I hope now, as all our attempts prove fruitless, we shall find more leisure time; if not, I shall be greatly disappointed in my India voyage. It is strange, but I never was in a tight ship, and I have to regret now being in a very leaky one. I do not entertain any fear, unless we fall in with very bad weather, in which case I am afraid she would strain.

We left the channel of old England on 31st 5th month, and on the 5th I saw the land about Cape Finisterre, tho' we were too far off to see anything distinctly. It appeared mountainous bold land; further we could say nothing.

I have seen several things novel to me, but as we shall most likely see more, I shall leave them for the present. Ther. 72 at noon.

17th. We are in the North East trade wind and I never found anything more agreeable in my life, the breeze is constantly in our direction – varying however, but about 2 or 3 points, and blows so steadily that it is quite a delightful companion; the heat, altho' great, I have not yet found very oppressive. In the daytime, especially towards the evening, it gets close and rather more troublesome, but still nothing worth mentioning; thin clothing is much in request, tho' many of our passengers have not yet diminished their woollen apparel, but I think there is a little bravado in it, on account of some old travellers making sport of them . . . complexions I think begin to darken a little, and for my part I expect to be completely tanned. Glass 75. N.B. All remarks [upon the temperature] will be at noon.

18th. Fine, pleasant trade [wind], going regularly about 5 or 6 knots, without touching a sail above 2 or 3 times in the 24 hours.

Saw for the first time a shoal, called by the sailors a school, of flying fish, their appearance is very pretty, tho' their flight is not so long as one could wish it to be. Their manner is to spring out of the water and flit like a bird over the tops of the waves for a short time, then drop and disappear. I should think the distance of their flight would be generally about 100 yards – but that must be, I conceive, according to their strength and size, unless (as it is said) they can fly only when their fins are quite wet. If so, I conceive their size would have no influence. They do not appear to be chased by an enemy of their finny tribe but I imagine, as they always fly from the ship, that it is her passing thro' the water that causes them to leave that element. . . .

19th. This morning, from one of the men being insolent to the 2nd officer, he was confined on the poop until half past ten, when, previously to the church service beginning, the hands were all mustered aft and then told by the Captain, surrounded by us, that as this was the first instance of insubordination that had occurred, he wished to let them all know that, if anything of the kind occurred again, the individual so offending should be most certainly flogged, for he was determined that, before he would suffer anything of the kind, he would lay down his life on the quarter deck. It had the desired effect; the man was turned to his duty, and all the men united in blaming him, as having behaved in an unseamanlike manner. 11, church service until half past 12, piped to dinner and served out extra grog. 8, evening prayers till 9. Fine cloudy weather and stiff trade . . .

20th. This day we were under, for the first time with me, a vertical sun, and I can say that I am agreeably disappointed as to its heat for, from having heard of being able to roast beefsteaks on the anchors, I had entertained no favourable opinion of the tropics – but I find at present but little inconvenience from the heat, except in the evenings, which are very close.

A martin has been with us now three days and seems inclined to stop; having abundance of flies on board, I expect he finds ours good quarters. I like its company much, as it seems to give an agreeable air to our ship, it is very tame, and orders are issued by no means to molest it. Leisure now begins to be a little more mine, and I have commenced working at navigation and am regularly on the poop to observe at 7 bells; I find great pleasure in it. . . .

21st. Shifted our course from SW, which has been steering a considerable time, to SWS [?]. Southerly fine breeze and beautiful clear weather, tho' very warm. I think [live]stock seems to suffer most, on account of their short allowance of water, and for myself I find 5 pints to be but a small quantity for washing and quenching thirst. I take care not to provoke it by eating but very little salt meat, indeed since we have been at sea I have not yet eaten any; a sheep killed daily, and sometimes a pig, affords my mess abundance of fresh provision.

We have been very busy all day observing by [?] lunar chronometers, and for Latitudes, and I find as I improve as an observer it grows more and more interesting, and I hope to be, ere I see Old England again, well versed in the theory of navigation.

Shifted all our second suit of sails for the old fine weather ones; it is rather late, but they not being repaired have been the occasion of the delay. . . .

22nd. Whilst time passes with us as it does now, with but little variety that can make it worth while noticing it, I have thought it might not be amiss to give an imperfect sketch of the life led on board ship trading to the East Indies, and altho' ours is not a Company's[33] ship, yet I believe few would surpass her in many respects, especially as regards the comforts of the passengers.

At 5 o'clock a.m. the decks are scrubbed with brushes and rubbed with a large stone and white sand called 'the great bear' for the purpose of making them white and clean. They are generally done by 6 o'clock, when two hands and the junior officers of the watch go into the fore hold and pump off 6 pints of fresh water to every man and boy in the ship; at the hatchway stand the various receivers, who dispose of it according to their several necessities. The cuddy servants place at each cabin door a pint of clear dripstone water[34] for each inmate to wash with etc., which is all they are allowed for the 24 hours; if they want more they must want, for no more are they allowed. At 7 bells or half past 7 the boatswain pipes[35] up all hammocks, which are the sailors' beds. They are immediately brought up on deck and received by boatswain's mate in each netting and then stowed away; the men who belong to the starboard watch have theirs stowed in the starboard side, those in the larboard watch in the larboard netting. By the time that is finished, it is 8 o'clock, the hands are piped to breakfast, and

---

[33] The East India Company was probably supposed to have the best ships.

[34] Dripstone water is rainwater.

[35] Edward Beck's footnote: Boatswain's pipe is an instrument with which he whistles, and by its different notes conveys orders, to go to dinner, to breakfast, to muster etc. etc., and is useful as it prevents the noise of shouting about the decks.

Time on board ship is notified to all by striking a bell for that purpose, and as each watch stops on deck four hours, a bell is struck as it is timed for every half hour. Consequently, at eight bells the watch is renewed and the bells begin at one for the relieving watch, and so on each half hour till eight comes round again.

all wears an air of cleanliness and comfort; at this time the breakfast is already in the cuddy, the cloth on, and the table well loaded with cold fowls, ham, hot rolls etc. etc., and in as tasty a manner as can well be. At half past 8 the urn is brought upon [the] table, the passengers summoned, and table duty commences; they generally sit at it about one hour (not being particular about the distribution of their time), when they leave it and separate, some to the deck and others to their cabins, where they pay mutual visits and sit lounging about on their sofas, couches etc. till tiffin, which comes on table at 12. It is generally biscuit and cheese with wines, spirits, bottled ale; after [the] cloth is removed they sit playing at chess or reading till the heat begins to be very great, then retire to a nap or study reading etc. on the quarter deck, where the cuddy chairs, tables and sofas are placed for those purposes.

Some of the young cadets amuse themselves by climbing up into the tops and about the rigging, spoiling their clothes, and it often affords a laugh to see one, who mounted dressed in a white jane[36] suit throughout, come down spotted with tar off the rigging, and chagrined to an extreme at their comical appearance. So much for the proceedings of the gentry; for a little of the ship's company employment, [see] hereafter.

6 month, 23rd. We have at last, in 10.8 N Lat., lost our NE trade we got for a beginning; this morning, a very heavy squall of wind accompanied with much rain – the commonplace weather, I understand of the latitudes near the equator.

I do not mind at times a stiff breeze (but I like fine weather best, like a greenhorn apprentice), but I am afraid of squalls, they come on so suddenly that they are much to be dreaded, and in the event of not being prepared, you stand a fair chance of losing your masts.

The thermometer now stands at 80 and 82 degrees and the closeness and heat below is almost unbearable, and when you come up on deck the breezes are, instead of being cool, quite hot. The perspiration is so great that it is unceasingly running down one's face and wetting thro' your handkerchief, pad and all. I bear it very well, but it is very relaxing, and the least exertion producing the most copious stream of perspiration.

Wind very variable. Glass this evening 86.

24th. Squally, unpleasant, close weather has now the ascendancy, the rains are very heavy and the squalls uncommonly strong. The glass stands at 82 and 3 and sometimes higher, but I have not seen it higher than [8]4 today.

To proceed with my sketch of the ship. At half past 8 the Boatswains pipe all

---

[36] Jane is the same as jean, a twilled cotton cloth or denim, as in our word 'jeans' today.

hands ahoy, which signifies that all the men are to attend upon deck, where they are employed, as well as the tradesmen, until half past 11 (or 7 bells, as we term it), when all the watch commence pumping, and continue to do it until none [i.e. no water] remains in the ship. At this time all the officers of the ship (who, bye the bye, are all acquainted when it is 7 bells) are upon the poop or where best, with their instruments, observing the meridian altitude of the sun. As soon as it is 12 by him, the Captain calls out, 'Strike the bell 8! Boatswain pipe to dinner, Boatswain's mates pipe to Grog!' Immediately the three commence whistling with might and main, and the fore part of the decks are in full flight[?], the cook of each mess getting the dinner ready, the caterers with their pots to receive the grog, the boys going backwards and forwards from the coppers, altogether make a bustling and, to a stranger, a ludicrous scene.

The caterers[37] receive, for each man in his mess, one gill and a quarter of raw, unadulterated spirits; the Carpenter, Boatswain, Sailmaker and Cook one pint each, and the 'awkward squad', consisting of the Butcher, Poulterer and Baker, half a pint. Their dinners consist of beef or pork, potatoes, flour, or peas and brown biscuit, their liquor they mix with water and, thus provided, sit down and eat as heartily and are as well content, as those who fare more sumptuously. As soon as they have eaten their meal, they leave the forecastle and come up on deck, to spend the remainder of their hour in smoking a pipe of tobacco or in going to sleep. At 1 o'clock the watch (which is half the crew) alone stop on deck; the rest spend their time as they please.

It may not be amiss, for the information of thou who may take the trouble to peruse this (should it and its author ever again reach Old England), just to explain a little how the watches are regulated on board ship. The officers and men are divided into two, the one denominated the starboard, or in land language right hand, watch and the other the larboard, or left hand. These attend to the duty in the following manner; let us say the starboard watch come up on deck at 8 in the morning, they will then go thus:

From 8 till 12 all hands on deck

12 – 4	Stard. watch go below
4 – 6	Lard. " " "
6 – 8	Stard. " " "
8 – midt.	Lard. " " "
Midt. – 4	Stard. " " "
4 – 8	Lard. " " "

---

[37] Edward Beck's footnote: The Caterer is the man who draws the allowance for the mess and delivers it to the Cook. He is generally chosen for his good foraging abilities; a dull, sleepy fellow would starve his messmates.

Thus it will be seen that the watches have alternately, by means of the dog[38] watches, 8 hours below all night and have, [the] rest of the 24, one day 6 hours to themselves and the next 10, being constantly varied by the short watches.

From 1 till 4 the watch is employed up on deck as most useful, the sailors about the rigging, the Carpenter and Sailmaker at their respective employment. At 4 the cuddy dinner is upon table and, tho' it may seem surprising, there is nothing more salt upon it than you might expect to find ashore; killing [live]stock every day provides the table with abundance of fresh provision. It generally consists of fresh mutton, pork, poultry, fish soup, pies, pastry of different descriptions, pudding, blancmange etc. etc. After cheese, a dessert of cakes, gingerbread, dried fruit, with wine of several descriptions; 2 hours generally sees dinner over and the company dispersed according to their different inclinations. At 8, tea goes on the table. At 6 the sailors take their beds below and, if it be moonlight, the evening generally concludes with music and dancing. At 10, the passengers take their wine and water with bread and cheese and retire to rest, and at ½ past all lights are extinguished and all on board hushed into a profound quietness (that is, in fine weather).

Still variable weather with heavy squalls and much rain; the squalls, of which I had often heard such terrific accounts, are not to be compared with those I have met with in my other voyages to the northward, they are perhaps heavier, but I dread them no more than I should the former.

We were surprised yesterday with a voice saying, whoever has meat towing[39] overboard [should] bear a hand and haul it in; on going up on deck, found that a monstrous shark was hovering about the ship, waiting for some prey. Having no hooks on board fit for him, we did not tempt him with a supper of pork and steel, as we otherwise should have done.

Neptune's works[40] are going forward, tho' so gently that we scarce see any of the implements. Knowing myself to have given umbrage to the Barber in the performance of my duty, I am preparing my mind for a rough scrape. Glass 84.

27th. We have had this day . . . many squalls and hard showers in which the

---

[38] Edward Beck's footnote: The dog watches are the ones from 4 to 6 in the afternoon and from 6 to 8, for the purpose of varying the hours of the men being up on deck.

[39] Edward Beck's footnote: The sailors' meat, being very salty, is, previous to its being cooked, put into a net or made fast with a rope and so towed, to correct the fault; it being served out to them for the day, it they lose it by a shark or another means, they must want.

[40] The ceremonies for crossing the Equator are overseen by King Neptune.

men have managed to catch some water for washing, my servant[41] having been pretty successful; I hope to profit by his industry in a reduction of my dirty clothes.

The flying fish have been this day very abundant, but what has pleased me much has been the sight of their adversaries the Albacore[42] and Dolphin. From our jib boom I could see them chase them in the water, where I think they are not very quick, and when they flew out the Albacore would spring out after them and, catching them in his mouth, plunge headlong again into his native element.

It is a most interesting sight to watch them. I think some of the Albacore could not spring less than 6 feet into the air after their prize, and their dive (after having secured it) is beautiful. They are, I should judge, about 4 or 5 feet long, with large side fins and tapered tail, colour reddish. Glass 83.

28th. This warm weather has at last compelled the most vaunting to lay aside their woollen clothing and to adopt a more suitable dress for the climate, tho' I have my doubts whether or not their laughing at proposals for doing it before have not been owing to their having a poor stock; for my part it has been a very weighty reason, tho' I have managed to increase my stock lately. At 8 p.m. my third hat took its departure over the ship's side in a clock calm, and altho' I immediately descended the ship's side, I could not get it, owing to the swell pitching the ship ahead at the rate of about one knot[43] per hour.

Of all the phrenologists who ever examined my head, not one had the sense to discern its property of losing its cover, for which it is most notoriously conspicuous, seldom going a voyage long or short without decreasing its stock of that most valuable article.

Glass 84. Very close evening.

From the constant variation of the wind from the north round to south we very reasonably conclude ourselves to be in the 'variables', a belief which is well supported by having to tack ship so often. Every time it is from the SE we conclude we have got the trade [wind], but it is squally, showery weather, I think, for it to be near us. . . .

---

[41] Edward Beck's footnote: Fearing you may be misled with the words 'my servant' I must tell you, he is one of the worst sailors in the ship, but notwithstanding a very useful fellow . . . [in] that he waits upon me, and gets my meals ready, cleans my shoes etc. etc., at the expense of the ship.

[42] Albacore is a kind of tuna.

[43] Edward Beck's footnote: A 'knot' in sea lingo is equivalent to one mile.

Abundance of fish have been about the ship today, but the adepts at the graip[44] lost all their dexterity on the blue waters, not being able to strike a single bonito or dolphin. Glass 83.

30th. Yesterday at breakfast the following letter was presented, directed to the Ladies and Gentlemen Passengers of the *Woodford*:

Ladies and Gentlemen,
It has been a custom for a long time for Father Neptune to pay a visit to all strangers that cross his line, and therefore we wish to inform you that he shall pay one to you as soon as you arrive there. We beg to ask a few clothes for himself and wife and company, for he is very badly off. He also has to say there is many of his children on board, whom he will think to shave. Wishing you a safe and pleasant voyage we remain,
    Ladies and Gents, your obedient Servants,
                Wm Rus.......................Neptune
                Thos Jenkins.................Mrs Neptune
                Wm Dewing..................Child
                Archibald Mcpherson.....Secretary
                Stephen Youdle [?].........Barber
                Wm Carter...................Doctor

As might be expected, it was immediately complied with and suitable dresses found for the company. Glass 83.

Preparations for Neptune's appearance become now more public. I have seen myself the iron hoop razor and the tin crown of the aquatic barber; at the sight of the former, I instinctively put my hand to my chin and inwardly confessed it had need be an iron one, to stand the operation of such an unmerciful instrument. I have also seen the list, upon which I stand foremost, for which I am not sorry, as I shall have the fun of seeing the others without their beholding me.

I would fain give the barber a bribe if I could, but it would be too great a concession to the old sour-looking friseur; however, I must manage to come off as well as I can. If they give it me, I must pay them off in my turn. The dread of it I hope will keep them within decent bounds, for of jagged razor one stroke would ruin the chin for ever and aye.

---

[44] Edward Beck's footnote: The graip is an instrument having 3 barbed prongs, like the representation of Neptune's trident, which is darted at the fish . . . which is thereby impaled and brought up into the ship. It requires long practice to make one adept.

2nd. Very heavy equinoctial rain the whole of the day, unaccompanied with wind, the sky very dark and heavy, but nothing very extraordinary. Got well wet thro' 3 different times.

I am exceedingly gratified with the opportunities our ship affords me of increasing my stock of naval theoretical experience, and after being used to 5, I do not know how I should like to be again in a ship without one chronometer. Between them and lunars, when they are to be obtained, one ascertains our position daily and correctly, and dare run with certain confidence anywhere.

7 p.m. As is our weekly custom, served out to the ship's company their extra gill of grog.

9. Beautifully clear, the constellations of the Southern Hemisphere opening on my sight, but more of them hereafter.

Glass steady at 82.

5th. Permission [has] . . . been granted by the Captain that the usual ceremonies might be commenced in due form, this evening being nearly upon the line. About 8 o'clock a voice was heard, of stentorian powers, hailing the ship with:

'Ho, the Ship, Ahoy!' the chief officer answering, 'Hello!'

'From whence came you?' 'From London.'

'What is the ship's name?' 'The *Woodford*.'

'How do you do, Mr Chapman?'

Mr Chapman says, 'Very well I thank you! How are you, Mr Neptune?'

'Quite well, thank you, sir. Have you any of my children on board?'

'Yes, several, who will be glad to see you.'

'Very well, sir! Then I will call tomorrow at 9 o'clock, so good night sir.'

'Good night, Mr Neptune.' 'Good night, sir.'

A pitch cask on fire being then set afloat, the God was supposed to retire, but whilst the passengers all crowded to see his departure and consequently lined the side, buckets of water from the main and mizzen tops and from the decks upon the group gave them a cooler, from his saline abode; drenched to the skin, they sought their cabins to shift their clothes, whilst a can of arak grog regaled the sailors, who are, as it were, almost in their entire liberty, except on duty. After tea, Nep and his Clerk called on the passengers etc. and managed to collect a subscription of £15, to be shared amongst those only who have gone thro' the ceremony before. For my part, thinking my chin too valuable to have it abused, I compromised with old Neptune, to be spared his 'barberism' for a golden George [i.e. a guinea] and a bottle of grog. The evening was cheerfully spent and not unbecomingly, tho' I regret to say an accident happened to one of our men who, falling from the pumps, cut his hand shockingly and, as he termed it, 'unshipped' [i.e. dislocated] his finger.

I can't but admire the manner in which he bore the pain, and tho' I sincerely felt for him, I could but laugh to hear him talking to the doctor, to whom he applied all the technical terms of his profession, such as: 'Doctor! Bear a hand and ship it, for it is terrible pain, but I suppose I must smile and bear it,' and when we were pulling it to get it to its place, he would say, 'Pull hearty and get it shipped, or get a luff tackle upon it!' However, after a deal of work and pain on his part, we got it replaced and in a sling, tho' I am afraid he will be for a long time on the doctor's list and, being a good man, I can ill spare him from our watch and my part of the ship.

Well, at last I have a pleasurable feeling, in being about to witness a ceremony of which I have heard various contradictory and some erroneous accounts, and looking out for a good sousing I retire to my cab[in], intending to prepare by 9 o'clock tomorrow to receive my august Father Neptune.

6th. At 8 this morning the work for receiving Neptune commences by stretching sails across the deck forward, to prevent strangers seeing behind the scenes. In the middle of the ship a sail was so hung up as to make, when filled, a large cold bath, across which was stretched a small spar or round piece of wood for a seat. At 9, two fellows dressed in a most ludicrous manner, with large patches of paint on their faces etc. and staves in their hands, ordered down the main hatchway into the foremost steerage all those who had never before witnessed the ceremony, myself amongst the rest – but wishing to see all, I escaped into the cuddy, that I might witness it there. In a short time, the sails being removed, the baker, who acted as piper, played up Rule Britannia and the men dragged our worthy Father from the waist [of the ship] round the decks to the scene of action. His carriage was a tub, with a seat in it upon a grating for Neptune and Amphitrite, with one before for the child and one behind for the servant; to it was attached a rope, by which it was drawn about. Their dresses were about as follows: the God had a tin crown, with a most curious dress of painted canvas; he had a beard of hemp and his hair of the same material, all dripping with water, hung over his shoulders nearly to the ground. Mrs Neptune had a fine figured gown on, lace cap, straw bonnet and white gloves, her hair also (of a darker colour, being some tarry rope) opened out into oakum, hung gracefully about her waist; the child was merely dressed in canvas, with some ornamental painting about his legs and face. The servant behind had on white breeches, white stockings, laced coat and a cocked hat. The doctor [had] a good hat, a black coat, white frilled and high-collared shirt; thus ornamented, and preceded by the clerk and constables, they made their appearance at the cuddy window, when Neptune complimented the ladies and, in a speech wherein was much of his technical language, begged them to witness the delight with which he would receive his children. At the conclusion, the barber, with a malicious grin, displayed an iron hoop like a piece of timber saw, a pot containing his lather (tar and grease), and a wire brush, at the sight of which I involuntarily put my head on my chin and descended to my companions, who were waiting to be shaved.

In a short time I heard: 'Constables, fetch up Mr Beck, the 3rd officer,' and in a twinkling I was blindfolded and led up the main hatchway – I must say, under a little perturbation of spirits. As soon as I appeared above, a general discharge of buckets of water upon me from all sides took place and I was then led to the bath, where, being seated upon the spar, I was requested by the doctor to take some of his medicines, which were pitch pills and tar water, but I neither spoke [n]or intended to, for fear of this being forced upon me. On finding his advice ineffectual, I was put under the hands of the barber who, unexpectedly to me, neither lathered [n]or shaved me, but merely pretended to; when he was done, Madam gave me a hard bite for a kiss and then, my legs being lifted up, I was soused into the cold bath and left to find my way out as well as I could.

In returning after, I was saluted with water from all observers, but I soon got a bucket and acted on the defensive. In this manner all were brought up and piped thro' the ceremony – some well used, but others well scraped, and whose chins bear witness of it at this time. What I enjoyed most was this: a party consisting of some passengers, the chief mate, the 2nd and the doctor, were enjoying the whole without sharing in the water, orders having been issued that none should be thrown upon the poop, but the captain, seeing the fun, said, 'Charge the poop!' Immediately, all buckets were filled and, when it was least expected, a general discharge took place, wetting everyone there but the doctor, who flew up the mizzen rigging – but, not wishing him to escape, I pursued and, from the mizzen top, sent down a rope to which a bucket was fixed, but, he possessing the advantage of strength, I was obliged to relinquish my hold and to see it thrown upon deck; still not liking to be beaten, I went out upon the crossjack yardarm when he, seeing I should succeed, decamped down upon deck – but I giving the alarm, he got a most comfortable ducking.

By 12 all were shaved, and Neptune having called to order, he remounted his car with his wife and attendants and, the piper playing Rule Britannia he was drawn to the poop windows, where some prepared brandy punch was served out and the ceremony concluded with a reel upon the quarter deck and 3 hearty cheers, as he was supposed to descend again to his briny abode. Glass 79.

11th. To this date nothing has happened worth recording, the Trade wind blows freshly and steady from the SE and we sail on with smooth seas and cloudless skies at about 6 knots an hour without touching a breeze[?]. Saw last night a ship to leeward homeward bound and, wishing to send home letters, bore away with our ensign flying, but to no purpose. She would not heave to for us – to our great disappointment, all having letters ready for the first ship we may meet.

As a proof of the clearness of the atmosphere, it is worth remarking that Venus was to be seen this day at 11 o'clock most beautifully clear, and the distance between the sun and moon's lines[?], taken for the purpose of ascertaining the Longitude, was to be observed with beautiful exactness; it afforded me the finest opportunity of taking a lunar distance I have yet had, and was not neglected. The weather is much more agreeable than it was; the Glass has stood steady at about 75 with fine, cool air.

12th. I am sorry to say our leak increased this day upon us and we have an increase of 3 inches an hour to pump out, which is far from agreeable, and another thing, which is certainly very singular, our mainmast has sunk 4 inches, a thing quite unaccountable. . . . At noon gained fast upon a ship ahead of us, set more sail and at 2 p.m. were within hail; she proved to be the *Britannia*, free trader bound to Bombay, all on board well, we exchanged passenger names but found no acquaintances. Kept our course and went from her like a shot. I think she was afraid of us, as she had all her guns set[?] out upon our side. SE trade but very squally, indifferent weather, 75 . . .

13th. Got our new apparatus fixed for the pumps, by which we managed to discharge, with two pumps, an inch per minute and shall be enabled to work 4 with the same labour, which is certainly a very great advantage. Total of water expended to this day 1,476 galls. Total remaining 8,476 galls. which, at a reduced expenditure on account of decreasing livestock, is sufficient for three months more and after, enabling us to increase the men's allowance one pint per diem, which they stand in great need of, on account of the leak they never having a draught at night. Water is indeed precious to us, as we are not intending to go into the Cape if we could possibly avoid it. I hope we may not, for my part, but go round at once, for the state of our ship makes it very desirable to get into safety with her, for if she makes 7 inches per hour in smooth water, what may we expect off the Cape at this time of the year? Glass 75.

14th. This morning some bad pickled salmon which had been thrown overboard was restored again in rather an unexpected manner by a shark, which we tempted to take a hook without a barb by a piece of fat meat being attached to it; we did not succeed in holding him the first time, but the second we managed to lift him out of the water and then to ship a running knot over him, by which means we secured him, but the rogue with his tail made a complete smash of our stern windows. We let him hang thus for about half an hour, whilst we communicated with a Brazilian brig, which we boarded and sent letters to England.

She[?] was from Pernambuco bound to Rio Janeiro in ballast, tho' our second mate, who boarded her, states she had on board 12 slaves which he did not see, but understood them to be aboard from the mate of the vessel. They sent us aboard some coconuts and unripe green oranges, and a bag of sand for the holystones.[45] Her name was *Silinus* of Pernambuco.

Our boat returned in a squall of rain, hoisted her up and made sail, having been lying to[46] for her to speak [to] us; after the squall we saw her lower her boat, and therefore hove to again. There came in the boat the mate and two black men, whose object was to obtain a few English potatoes, of which we gave them a bag, to his (the mate's) great satisfaction.

He was a fine, handsome dark-coloured man and was dressed in a jacket ornamented with our navy buttons and gold lace; he seemed delighted with the accommodations of our ship which were shown him, and departed highly gratified with his visit. Our second mate acted as interpreter tho', he speaking Spanish and the other Portuguese, it was with some little difficulty they understood one another. Glass 74.

15th. Strong breezes from the Nd and Ed, with heavy squalls accompanied by much rain.

For several days past our second and fourth mates have both been incapable of duty, so that the chief's time and my own is pretty fully employed, but I should think nothing of it, if it were not for the pumps, the continued clank of which every two hours is becoming truly painful and renders it necessary for the officers to assist the men; she has increased to ten inches per hour this day, but I hope it is only owing to the weather. We are now visited by birds (aquatic) quite strange to me, among which the Cape pigeon figures conspicuously, being spotted very prettily with black and white upon the back. I have tried to catch one, but hitherto to no purpose. One of the passengers has the jaws of the shark cleaned; the fish measured 6 foot 2. Glass 71.

16th. Another shark visited us this morning, about the same size as the last, accompanied by 5 pilot fish; the sight of them was exceedingly curious. The pilot fish were from 8 to 12 inches long, a plump round-shaped fish, dark body with white stripes; they attend the shark in all his motions, swimming above his large

---

[45] Edward Beck's footnote: Holystones are square stones used to polish the decks by rubbing them over it with white sand. The larger one, dragged by ropes, is called the Great Bear.

[46] Edward Beck's footnote: To hove a ship to is to arrange the sails in such a manner that part shall retard, as much as the other impel her, so that she remains nearly stationary.

fins and back, and attending him with unwearied assiduity; I should very much like to know for what purpose – it cannot be, I think, for the sake of sharing with him, as I observe they did not attack some pork which he after took that liberty with – much to the annoyance of our sailors, to whom it belonged. I noticed one leave him once, apparently to take something on the surface of the water, but what, I could not determine. Our sailors tried to get their revenge, but he would not take a hook. Glass 71.

17th. As the old adage, 'after a calm a storm,' so it has partly been with us, having been obliged to reef and shorten sail today with heavy, squally weather and foul wind; indeed of squalls we seem now to share pretty freely, but none of them particularly heavy.

Neglected attending Divine Worship today, being rather too much fatigued with my night watch, and with me most of the men absented themselves, most likely on the same account. I find myself but very poorly today, indeed I have not felt very well for a considerable time, having had a painful sick headache for that time. In the evening the southern pointers and the cross appeared very beautiful, but I cannot yet see any constellations to equal some of our northern ones. Magellan's clouds were also for the first time to be seen, they are exactly the same as the Milky Way, but very small. Glass 70.

18th. Stiff breezes and cloudy weather thro'out, nothing doing on board worth remarking. . . .

19th. The weather now alters very fast, it is so cool at night that in the course of a few days we shall be glad to put on our greatcoats when on duty. All the thin clothing has vanished and no more to be seen, I expect, until to the eastward of the Cape of Good Hope. . . . My situation has been rendered much more comfortable today thro' the kindness of Capn. Chapman, who has for several days given me charge of the ship every other watch, since the 2nd [officer] has been ill, but I am now confirmed in it and shall take it alternately with the chief and 2nd when he is well again. Altho' an arduous task, it gives me the situation I want to fill. Glass 70.

22nd. Last night a flying fish was found by the boatswain's mate in the fore chains; it was put up to auction amongst the passengers and fetched 5/- [five shillings]. It was immediately operated upon and completely spoilt in the skinning; I wanted him to let me do it for him, but he would not. He consequently spoilt the most material part of the wings.

It was 9 inches in length, 4½ inches [in] girth and its wings 5 inches; it was a plump fish, dark back, white belly and a small mouth.

We caught 2 Cape pigeons also, which I managed to skin admirably for 2 of the passengers; I do not intend doing any for myself until the passage home, when I shall take every opportunity of obtaining specimens. The Cape pigeon is 18 inches from tip of beak to the end of the tail, it has a black well-formed head, mottled black and white back and tail, white breast and black legs. Altogether a very beautiful bird. Glass 67.

23rd. Stiff and steady breezes from westward urge us on at a rapid pace towards the Cape, tho' I believe we shall not go into any of its watering places; we anticipate strong gales and cold weather, which we may very reasonably get, as it is the winter season there. I long to weather it and to be going to the eastwards; there is a talk of taking the Mozambique Channel, it is I think probable, . . . but barely so. Glass 70.

24th. Delightful sailing, all sails set and tearing thro' the water at a fine rate, the Captain and all the passengers in excellent spirits, looking for a conclusion of their voyage proportionately speedy or otherwise, as the rate of the ship at the time elevates or depresses their hopes. [At] 11 [was] performed Divine Service, myself absent, having to attend to the ship's duty; the wind heading us rather at the time caused a general shake of all the sails, I am informed much to the distress of the female part of the congregation.

6 o'clock, evening service, did not attend. J.J Gurney's book engaged me too fully to be able to, tho' I make it a rule generally to attend when in my power, as it encourages the men to do the same. Midnight, fine steady breeze and a beautifully moonlight night watch I have enjoyed. I have been leaning over the side, thinking on absent friends who are at this time most likely fast asleep in Old England, and whilst I have watched our ship ploughing up the waters and leaving far behind her foamy wake, I have been indulging myself in the pleasure of, and conceiving how delightful will be the speed of, her return; 'tis true we have been separated but 8 weeks, but time seems swallowed up in distance, and I feel as if I had been absent for as many months. Pleasant be their slumbers and mine, who will now return to my cabin. Glass 68.

25th. I hardly know what to write, there is so little variety passing on board . . . I do not wonder at passengers complaining of being tired, for with them having nothing to attend to, they must feel it a very tiresome kind of life; but with us who are fully engaged all day it is very different, employment makes it quite easy. Glass 67.

27th. It is a curious sight to have around the ship so many birds, as tame as pigeons, constantly attending upon us and picking up all that suits them from what is thrown overboard; should it be weighty and sink, they will dive right under the water and catch it as it descends. In addition to the Cape pigeon, we have now black hens[47] and albatrosses . . . the latter measure 11 feet from tip of one wing to the other, one of them flying directly over the ship gave me a good view of him, but I must catch one to describe him more fully; the Cape pigeon are so tame as to be caught by hanging a piece of twine over the stern, in which they entangle their wings as they fly under it. The skin of the ones I preserved were this morning thrown overboard, because there was an unpleasant effluvia came from them (at least so they say). They wanted me to do another pair, but I refused and let them fly. Glass 65.

Last night in my watch upon deck the wind, suddenly shifting with a heavy rain, carried away our driver boom, to my great vexation, and all this the fault of the man at the wheel, [who] got a lecture about it when I went to report[48] the time to the Captain at 8 o'clock, but as it happened in my going off the deck to acquaint the Commander according to my instruction, I quite acquit myself of all blame in the affair. The other mates are both better, the one does his full duty, the other duty in the daytime only. It is observable here that, contrary to the western ocean south of the equator, the wind veers with hard rain from the north west into the SW with fine clear starlight skies . . . it is easily accounted for, as it must reasonably be expected all the winds coming from the sun must be warmer than those coming from the higher latitudes[?] . . .

8th. month, 13th. Up to this date nothing has transpired worth remarking . . . Our second mate has again fallen sick and has been so for some time and is also likely to continue, so I am therefore fully invested with his duty until he recovers; my time is rendered less at my disposal on this account, having both his and my own duty to do, but I mind it not, if I can do his duty when he is unwell; I am sure I can do it as well if he was not here. I therefore think myself, should a vacancy occur in England, as entitled to the berth, if not in this ship, in some other; I must rise, and the sooner the better. The weather has been delightful and the winds quite moderate, the very variable rain has been scarce, but lightning most abundant every night for the last 8 days. Some of our men who are in my watch having got intoxicated and neglected their duty, after having previously

---

[47] Black hens could be frigate birds.

[48] Edward Beck's footnote: 8 o'clock in the morning and the same hour at night is always reported to the captain, who then gives any instructions he may have to the officer of the watch, to pass to the others for the day or night.

warned them and told them I would report it without any distinction of persons, I placed their names on the black list, in consequence of which they were punished, by their grog being stopped. They have on this account been rather rusty with me, but on following them well up I believe they have found out my character, and perceive that to fall out with me is grievously to their disadvantage for, as I told them at the time, I was charged with the 2nd's duty, so I have proved it good to them that, as long as I did my duty, I would see that they did theirs, and the neglect of it should be constantly punished until I neglected mine, after which I should take no further notice of it. When they grumble without occasion, I immediately find something for an occasion to do so, for my idea is, if a man does not know when he is well fed and treated and does not appreciate it, he should be taught, by using [him] in a contrary manner. There are one or two who, if I had my will, should be made to suffer, as they are constantly inciting the others to complain, but our Capn. is so good, that they escape what they richly deserve.

12th. 2 a.m. The lead going with bottom at 15 fathoms, with a hand on the fore topsail yard looking out for Madras light; we have passed 2 small native boats fishing, at the cry to the officer of the watch to keep clear of which, almost all the passengers came on deck, so anxious are they to reach terra firma. Half past 3, saw the light upon the lee bow, dist. 8 miles; shortened sail, waiting for daylight. Who can but admire the beautiful regularity of Nature by which, after being 3 months and 14 days from land, we are enabled mainly by our observations to run into a port exactly the same as if we had land in sight all the time! The long[itude] by chronometers on board ship, at anchor in Madras roads, two miles to the eastward of Fort St George, was 80, 23.32 E, which is but 5" from the true longitude. Can anything, I say again, be more beautiful?

At half past 7 we . . . [let] go our anchor in 10 fathoms; it was hardly gone before two fellows, apparently in the water, tho' afloat on what is called a catamaran, were seen paddling off, singing to the stroke of their work, and in a short time they were on board, but from a couple in a state approaching to nudity, what could be expected? But to my astonishment they lifted up a kind of straw cap that covered their close-cropped heads, and from thence presented the Captain with a number of papers, letters etc. etc., which they had brought off perfectly dry through the surf that rages on the shore, although their caps testified that they themselves had been thoroughly immersed. As they gave them to the Captain they, putting the palms of both hands to their foreheads, made a most submissive salaam to all that surrounded him.

The catamaran is simply three logs about 12 feet long, well secured together, in width about 2 feet 9 [inches] or three feet, with two sort pieces which form the

146

head of this float. They sit upon the soles of their feet with their legs bent under them and, astonishing as it may seem, will in this manner come to ships and fish, when the surf will not allow large ships to do so. There are always two upon them, both men or one man and a boy, and they always sit at the extremities; from the lowness of their catamaran they are constantly wet, and after standing in the sun a short time, you see formed upon their black skins a perfect coat of salt, more especially on the legs and thighs, the parts mostly in the water. This would soon no doubt destroy the skin and cause it to crack, but as a preventative they usually rub themselves daily with coconut oil, which not only effectually prevents it, but makes it completely supple and smooth.

The ship has been at anchor but a short time, before the decks are covered with natives who come from the shore, in another kind of boat which particularly deserves notice; they are sharp at both ends, about twenty feet long, and instead of being fastened with nails, the planks are merely put one to the other; to the seam is applied outwardly and inwardly a quantity of coconut husks. They are then with rope made of the same materials stitched together; thus, from their elasticity, they are enabled to bear the surf which rages on the shore and to bring off and land perfectly dry cargo and passengers. In the boat, as may be expected, is constantly a quantity of water, but bailing, and a quantity of bushes in the bottom, upon which the goods are placed, keep all dry. They are numbered and under the superintendence of the master attendant ashore; without such, there could be no communication with the land.

Now you begin to feel yourself in another part of the world; all around you black faces dressed, some in flowing dresses of muslin with turbans etc., others nearly naked, some painted with stripes on their faces according to their castes, some with great quantity of gold ornaments etc., some merchants offering fruits, clothing etc., some washermen, some offering themselves as servants, and all salaaming and jabbering away together, tell you instantly you are in quite another part of the world, in a strange land and among strange people. You treat all like Englishmen at first, but in a short time you are obliged to have recourse to a rope's end to drive the lower class off the decks, with their fish, fruit, parrots, monkeys etc. etc., and even then you will find them come up the other side offering their wares. Ask them what they are, their reply is immediately 'Marchant Sar.'

The natives are a small, delicately-limbed people, servile to a degree – at least those that visit the ship, a rope's end makes them run like sheep, tho' I would never allow the men to do it, or to cheat them, when I have charge of the deck, for I see no reason why we should abuse such a poor, defenceless race of brother men; I think it quite necessary to frighten them, otherwise, with words only, they would never quit the ship. They ask exorbitant prices for everything they sell, but they seldom get above an eighth part of it. Sometimes I have seen them ask a sailor for a fish he held in his hand a shilling; I have seen him immediately struck with it on the face and thrown at him. Shortly after, I have seen the poor wretch ask and get but the value of threepence for it – an infamy[?]. There is this to be said, they would get no more, or perhaps not so much, if taken to Madras market.

The appearance of Madras from the roads is very handsome, the houses being large, with high and numerous windows . . . the shore is covered constantly with a heavy surf, the roar of which at night, when the land wind comes off, is very loud. I could not get ashore, the chief officer having to go; I had at the time the charge of the ship, and some cargo being misplaced in the hold, I had no time to hove for the shore, tho' I must own I often, as I directed my eyes towards it, wished that I could have been spared for a day or two. I may perhaps on our return, but I think it very unlikely, as it will be so late in the season that our time will necessarily be very short there. I think it very tantalising, after being nearly 4 months at sea, to be so long in sight of land and not able to visit it, especially a strange foreign land.

The fruit brought off consisted of ripe and green coconuts, limes, oranges, shaddocks[49], pomelos, a curious type of gooseberries, and bananas, none of which I thought by any means excellent; having previously understood how much some had suffered by eating much fruit, I abstained from it, in a manner quite wonderful to myself. Fish is exceedingly plentiful and excellent quality; indeed, finer cannot be caught. Sharks are in great abundance, lying under the bottoms of the ships; anything tossed overboard soon brought them into sight. Swimming was immediately proscribed on our arrival, but I constantly am bathed by having water poured over me each day, about one doz. buckets every evening after sunset, the which I find both refreshing and beneficial.

Birds brought off were partridges 1 rupee (2 shillings) a doz., parrots, Java sparrows, marabou[?],[50] and several foreigners I do not know the name of. Animals were monkeys, mongooses, squirrels and jackals; three of the former are on board the ship. The Brahma Kite I must not forget to mention; it is a large bird like a hawk, with large talons with which it picks up things on the water and devours . . . [them while] on the wing. It is so very impudent, that it will take grease or offal almost before your feet. . . . I must also mention that the water every evening was full of that kind of jelly substance so common on the coast of England, only in the exact shape of mushrooms; they gave the water a most

---

[49] Shaddocks are large citrus fruit, a bigger type of grapefruit. Pomelos are also a type of grapefruit.

[50] Marabou is the Arabic name for the adjutant bird, the giant Indian stork.

disgusting appearance.

At daybreak and sunset a gun fires at the fort, before and after which no boats leave the shore. Every morning comes off to the ship beef, mutton, potatoes, and indeed most kinds of vegetables, supplied by a man called the ship's Cornucopiae, a name by which his receipts are always signed. There is nothing you want but the fellow will procure, if it be possible, and in quick time. The heat is very great, the thermometer standing as high as 87.8 and 9; we get the land breeze at night about 10 o'clock, but it is unsupportably hot, so that I can never sleep below, but on deck, when I think it is running a great risk of the heavy dews affecting you but, I am sure ... [if you] stop below, you are fairly parboiled in your own perspiration; you are always on the fidget to find cooler quarters, and it is not until you are perfectly overcome with lassitude you can get to sleep. Many of our men have been taken ill, but I am happy to say there has been no mortality on board, tho' many ships have suffered much from the cholera morbis, a scourge we are told [is] now raging in Calcutta. I must say, on the whole, I have not found the heat so unsupportable as I had believed it would be; it is very great but, although very oppressive, I had so fortified my mind about it, that I find I can bear it as well as most others. I think the worst of it is, that it so debilitates you that you never feel any inclination for reading, writing etc, and I am sure it is quite an exertion to write a page in my journal. It may be that working hard helps to increase it, but I do not know, the heat itself seems to give you a right of an evening to be lazy.

The morning, when we first get the sea breeze, I quite think the pleasantest part of the day, tho' the sun soon after rising gives a warmth to all around that makes one glad to get into a shady spot.

18th. Employed still in searching for some few missing Madras cases but with little hope, being afraid they are stowed where we cannot get at them. Bought some shells, nothing particular, on the contrary I am afraid they are of but little value – although I have given 5 rupees for them, which I am told is 4 too many. Had two parrots also given me, but before night I lost them, most likely stolen by the black chaps and, with their cage, sold to another customer. I do not mind the loss, because I intend what I procure shall be on our return to this part from Calcutta . . . feeling no desire to be burdened with them until our return homewards. It is surprising how their value decreases, when they become so common as to be bought a pair with their cage 1 shilling; very soon, nobody will look at them.

9th. month, 20th. We hove short, with the intention of going to sea with the sea breeze, but the Capn. and passengers not coming off, we were obliged to lower our topsails and veer away the cable. At 5 they came off, with many visitors, who partook of a well-provided supper on board and spent the evening with us. At 9 the latter went ashore, when we found ourselves, after parting with 5, again reinforced with 3 strangers from Bengal, a Mr Connolly, brother to our cadet, Mr Brown and a Mr Dalrymple. I should also notice 13 Native people, who obtained permission (thro' interest) to sail with us, as deck passengers.

At 12, the long-wished-for breeze came off the land, and after nearly getting on board a large French ship, we stood out of Madras Roads to sample our passage. We left the . . . [East India Company] ships *Coldstream, Wm. Money, Guildford* and several free traders, also some from Rangoon, with soldiers from the hospital there, where we understand from one of the sergeants they are dying by hundreds. One ship buried 79 on her passage from thence. From him also we understand that every preparation was making to prosecute the war with the Burmese with all possible vigour, at which news our young cadets all seem highly delighted; for my part, I am afraid of the ships being taken up to Rangoon with military stores.

After experiencing a succession of east winds for 7 days we at length caught the SW monsoon, much to our joy, having even shifted our light [sails] for our best sails, in expectation of those terrible gales so frequently met with at the breaking up of those periodic winds. . . . On the first of the month we began to find the water much discoloured; at noon, from the masthead made out the land, stretching for a considerable distance, very low, but from the clearness of the horizon very distinct.

One hand was kept constantly at the fore top masthead to look out for the pilot vessel and the land, and at night the deep sea lead was hove every ten minutes; long and weary indeed were the hours all through that and the succeeding nights; being upon the sand, leads in from 12 to 17 fathoms, no pilot to be found, and blowing fresh from the SW, we were obliged to keep beating to windward at nights and running in the day. At the word from the masthead, 'a strange sail in sight', we stood [i.e. made] for her immediately, but all to no purpose, until with great joy on the second night, after I had been in the chains heaving the lead for 4 hours and at the masthead I daresay 20 times, we saw, just as we were shoaling our water to come to an anchor, the blue lights which the pilots burn as their night signal. We immediately answered them with the same signal and hove to. Presently another ship, who had seen our blues, fired a gun and bore down upon us, and greatly deceived he was to find us in the same predicament as himself. She was the *Thalia*, Captn. Roden[?] from London, and sailed on the 10th of the 5th month with the Comdr. in Chief of the British E. India forces. All well. At daybreak we sail in the direction of the signal, 3 vessels, one of which proved to be the pilot brig, but without a single one on board. The other ships had them all before us; however, we took a leadsman who offered as a volunteer, a smart young fellow, and one that brought the ship up in a masterly manner. Immediately on his coming on board we bore away with light hearts and every stitch of sail set, for I have my person to judge if it was not enough to wear any person out, to be heaving the lead and pumping ship all day and night, for she was struck off the sand heads with a sea which made her leak about as much again as she did before; for my part, I think our men behaved exceedingly well throughout this trying time. For myself, I felt nearly fagged out, and I am sure I could not have stood it much longer.

The river is very wide for a considerable distance, but on getting to Sanger Island the land becomes plainly visible on both sides. Then we got row boats with 18 men who, much to the joy of the sailors, took the charge of the pumps. The poor natives received 5 shillings per day per boat and found out of it their own rice; miserable as they appear, whatever we have touched they will not eat, and even walking near them when at meal occasions them immediately to throw it [i.e. the food] overboard – to prevent which, they all go into their boats to get their meals, after which they wash their mouths and return on board.

At Diamond Harbour, where we anchored one night, we found the . . . [East India Company] ships *Marquis*[?], *Wellington*[?], *Minerva*, *Bombay* and *Sir Chas. Grant*; it is thirty miles from Calcutta and all their cargo is carried down to them in large boats called Burks, as they are of too great a draught of water to go up to the City. It is a most unhealthy part of the river, and there the cholera morbis, nursed by the surrounding marshes, the exhalations from which are of a most pestilential nature, annually carries off hundreds of our unguarded seamen who, foolishly giving way to the passion and stay[ing] off board drinking, exposing themselves to the sun in the day and the heavy dews at night,[51] thus find in a foreign land an untimely and premature grave. I wish not to say all the victims of that dreadful disease are thus predisposed for it, but I fear the proportion is very great.

Above Diamond Harbour the river Hooghly begins fast to lose its breadth, and the stranger begins to admire the verdant clothing of its banks, the lofty coconut tree with its naked trunk and large-leaved top, the sugar cane, the broad-leaved plantain, the dwellings of the natives, they themselves with their cummerbunds round their waists walking on the bank by dozens, the river crowded with strangely-shaped boats fishing or carrying cargo, all strike the eye of the European with admiration, and forcibly remind him that he is far, far away from his native shores, at the same time conveying that feeling of pleasure most entertain

---

[51] The so-called cholera was probably malaria; people expose themselves to mosquitos more readily at night.

when thus opening their eyes upon the rich variety . . . anticipated upon the voyage. Garden Reach[?], on the banks of which are the seats of the principal people of Calcutta, is a most beautiful part of the river, exceeding anything I have seen before, and serves to realise our ideas of Asiatic splendour and luxury. We were obliged to stay here until the tide made flood, as we had not [the] wind to stem the ebb; accordingly, our passengers left us in a passenger boat sent from town: many were, I thought, at leaving rather sad. The ship is the connecting link between the two countries; that link severed, the adventurer finds himself at once in a foreign land and amidst perfect strangers; feelings of this kind generally waken feelings hard to contain. It was thus with some of our passengers as they went over the *Woodford*'s side.

As soon as the tide of flood made, we weighed [anchor] and proceeded up. At the head of Garden Reach the town opens upon the view in an imposing manner, appearing truly a city of palaces, amongst which that noble structure, the Government House, appears with noble effect.

At half past 4 p.m. . . . we completed our passage out by mooring abreast Champoul Ghat, in which time we had, with one exception, enjoyed excellent health and much pleasure. 5 o'clock, the Boatswain piped all hands to muster, when our generous Commander thus addressed the men:

'Well, men, I thank God we have arrived in safety. I have called you thus together to say I am so well pleased with your conduct generally during the past passage, that I have made up my mind to give every man who conducts himself to the end of the voyage with the like propriety a bounty of £5, and now let me advise you to pay a little attention to what I say; do not go much ashore, keep sober, and out of punch houses, and let nobody entice you away from the ship [or], take my word for it, you will repent.'

One of my watch answered for the rest that they were much obliged to him, said they were never happier and better used and that, for himself, he was sure he would go home in her. Poor fellow! A short time after, he neglected his captain's advice, drew money, kept intoxicated, whilst it lasted exposed himself in a debilitated state to the heavy dews, was seized with the *Mort de Chien* (the most deadly stage of the Cholera) and in 10 hours was buried in the Baptist burying ground; . . . followed to his grave by all our men and officers excepting myself (having charge of the ship). An awful lesson indeed, read to those addicted to the like propensities; he was taken ill in the sail loft at 8 o'clock, was borne aloft by the mess mates, uttered, 'Mister Beck, I am dying may God have mercy upon my poor soul!', was taken insensible and a corpse, dismally altered in feature, by half past 4 p.m.

The next day we commenced discharging our cargo and, our second officer getting his discharge, I was promoted to his situation and very much to my satisfaction – may it be so also to my commander's. Our ship still leaking, we had from the shore . . . 20 Batta Lascars with their Serang and Tindal;[52] they are the native seamen and are such men as are, in my opinion, worth two of ours in this hot country for work. We have had them turned out every night 5 times to pump the ship, a half hour's job each time, beside keeping them hard at work all day, and yet not a murmur is heard from them, satisfied with plenty of good rice, with now and then a little in[?] boxes as[?] presents, they will work with unremitting perseverance and with a promptness quite astonishing to a European who is affected by the climate.

The city of Calcutta presents to the river a very magnificent and noble sight, the houses are such as in England we see in large parks, and to me they always appear, on account of there being no wood around them, as quite out of place. This feeling is very much increased on landing, as flights of crows are constantly on the wing about them, or picking up any offal in the street before you; protected by the Government, these and the Adjutants [i.e. storks] are so bold as to let you pass close to them without feeling at all disturbed. In a country like this, where putrefaction ensues in a short time after decease, where the natives are abominably filthy in their habits, and when an accumulation of putrid matter would inevitably in a short time produce infectious disease, we cannot but admire the bountiful provision made by our Creator, in so disposing the works of his hand that nothing, on examination, can be proclaimed wasted.

The Adjutant is an enormous bird with very long legs and bill, [on] . . . its neck hangs a huge pouch like a purse, it is of a bluish grey colour on the back, white belly and bare neck. It stands, I should think, about 4 feet high average, tho' some are much larger and such is their capacity, that I have heard repeatedly of their swallowing a leg of this country's mutton, and of a dead carcass come ashore with the reflux of the tide, in a very short time you will merely see the bones; they attach themselves to different houses, and long and bloody battles sometimes ensue, when the old frequenter finds one willing to dispute it with him; nothing comes amiss to them, they swallow all bones and, as the native servants will touch nothing from their masters' tables, it may easily [be] conceived, in so luxurious a country as this, how they fare.

So valuable are they considered by the Government, that 100 rupees is the penalty for destroying them, 50 for a kite, and 5 for a carrion crow; guess then their tameness. For a black person they never move, and but little for a white; when flying low they have an unwieldy appearance, but at the hot part of day in this cloudless, brilliant atmosphere, you may see them majestically soaring in the cool breezes of the loftier regions of the air.

---

[52] A serang is an Indian boatswain of a small craft, and a tindal is a petty officer of Lascars.

I should also remark that odious system of the natives committing the bodies of the deceased to the river. Whether too poor to bury or from religious custom I cannot say, but to a feeling mind it is certainly a most disgusting and deplorable sight, to see the birds devouring the bodies as they flow down the stream or are cast on the shore; indeed it is frequently necessary, after blowing weather or strong tides, to clear the cables of them several times a day.

But I was about to tell a little of Calcutta. I landed on the 3rd evening after our arrival, and as a description of my excursion may not be uninteresting, I will endeavour to describe it.

On landing, you are immediately addressed with, 'Palque Sahib? Palque Sahib?' by the palanquin bearers, numbers of which stand ready at each landing place, called Ghats; it not being very hot, I thought I should prefer walking, and therefore engaged with an umbrella chap for the afternoon at 2 annas or four-pence; he carries over my head as I walk a large, native-made umbrella which entirely protects from the sun the whole of my body; he also carries all purchases, to a certain weight or extent. Thus equipped, off I set, accompanied by my *sirkar*, a kind of ship's clerk but quite at the officer's service, and taken at this time to act as interpreter to the China bazaar, where I wished to purchase a few necessary articles I stood in need of in this climate. After walking through large streets with remarkably good carriage roads (for pavement is not needed when nobody but the lower classes walk), we arrived at the spot and entered a merchant's house, where I was soon seated on a couch and two persons immediately commenced fanning me. On my wishing to proceed to business and desiring them to show me the articles I needed, the master said in broken English, 'When Master cool, then I show.' I have reason to think since that the rogue, whilst I was being fanned, surveyed my features and thought he had a prize; after looking out what I required, I asked the price and was told 40 rupees. I offered 22 and, after much hard work, got . . . quite convinced I had a great bargain, and on leaving felt quite proud of it. After walking the Bazaar I felt surprised my *sirkar* was not with me, but as I returned the fellow met me, and begged me to compel the merchant to pay him his custom. Now this custom or 'dusting' is 2 pies or a halfpenny out of every rupee paid by his master, imposed upon the receiver of all money as a kind of acknowledgement for bringing him to his shops, but actually coming out of the master's pocket, and for the sake of this a servant will serve you if you do but little business, without any other recompense excepting what they manage by keen dealing. After seeing him righted, I took a palanquin, sending my *sirkar* on board with my purchases; I had a letter to a Lady Chowringhee [?] 3 miles from Calcutta, whither I proceeded. I found her carriage at the door, just going upon the Course, a fine road commanding a view of the river where the gentry of Calcutta resort in their different vehicles every evening to enjoy the air, and after presenting her letter, accompanied her, returning about 7 o'clock to tea. The Course was full of all the wealthy inhabitants of the city; amongst the rest I noticed the superior vehicle of the Governor, attended by three dragoons: the company was a motley group, consisting of Europeans, half-casts, and rich natives, altogether an amusing scene. Beside every carriage, whether gigs or whatever, there may be seen native servants, who seldom or never stand behind as English footmen do, then again, black drivers of curious vehicles, open palanquins with ladies etc. etc., the different costumes of the riders, to a stranger present an amusing scene. After tea and a most hearty welcome and invitation, I got into my palanquin and was taken to the riverside, paying half a rupee for the 4 hours I had detained my palanquin bearers.

The palanquin is something similar in its uses to a sedan chair, but it is borne and used differently; in the former, the rider reclines upon a cushion with a pillow for his head . . . it has also a drawer to put anything you please in, and the top of it for your hat. It is borne by 4 men, with a single pole at each end resting on their shoulders. They carry at the rate of about 3 miles or 4 an hour, the pay two shillings and ninepence employed per day of 14 hours and, being opened by doors at both sides, [it] is a very pleasant mode of travelling, as well as cheap. When the bearers find they have got a stranger, they go along towards the close of their work groaning and grunting most piteously, as if grievously oppressed, for the sake of obtaining a little extra pay; if you ask, on getting out of it, 'How much I pay?', the answer invariably is 'What Master pleases,' and let him pay as much as he will, they still ask more. It is surprising how well they can bear the heat and fatigue of bearing the palanquin in such a climate. Performing a long journey in the day, they not infrequent[ly] meet with accidents from the carriages, but a black man's life in this country is thought of little value. . . .

I forgot to mention two circumstances before, which happened in our passage from Madras, and as I consider them rather interesting, I shall thus put them down out of place. The first happened just about the Sand heads; our 'jolly boat' was lowered to try the current in a clock calm, but before the 4th officer was ready to go from the side, a fresh breeze sprung up; thinking it but a 'dapple', the Capn. gave orders to pipe to dinner, letting one hand remain in the boat as she towed astern. About 2 o'clock the breeze freshened and the 4th officer, after calling to the man to look out, slack[en]ed her tow rope – the fellow being asleep, and not sheering off the ship, she went under the counter and immediately stove [in] and filled, and before the ship's way could be stopped, she had capsized, and [with] the man, upon her bottom. The tackles were immediately overhauled for taking her up, and 3 of our young fellows jumped overboard to turn her for hooking on, but just at the moment their aim was nearly accomplished, the man at the wheel carelessly let the ship go right round upon her heel, and she immediately got fresh way, leaving, in a short time before we could get the main yard slack, the 3 out of 4 as far astern as we could see. The 4th and myself, with 3 men, immediately jumped into the cutter and cut away her lashings; we were lowered away and succeeded in picking them up, but just in time – for one, not catching any of the gratings, oars etc. thrown overboard, was just sinking as we approached – he caught fresh life and with joy entered the boat. We were directed to him by the others who, having oars etc., were not willing to be picked up first, knowing their shipmate had nothing to support him. When we got back to the ship we found the 'jolly boat' on the poop in two pieces, being old, and not able to bear hoisting full of water. Broke her up and burnt her; received the cutter and made sail.

The other was the death of our female passenger Mrs Ray, a missionary's wife who had been ill all the voyage; she was a native of this country, but converted to Christianity by her husband. She had accompanied him to England for the benefit of her health, and died 2 days before we reached Calcutta; she was interred in the river at a place called Haltah, the ship being hove to and divine service performed by the Capn. The coffin, not being weighty enough, floated, much to the grief of the afflicted husband.

6th. of 1st. month 1826. I have, as will be seen, written nothing lately; I have felt no inclination. I may now just state as reasons that the ship, whilst in dock at Hourah, required all my time to look after [her] as, our 4th officer being discharged and the chief ashore, [a] good part of the time the duty devolved principally upon me. I felt in the performance of it a great pleasure and, with a wish to deserve my promotion, endeavoured to discharge my several duties with all the ability I was master of. After hauling out of dock, where we had received very large repairs (having been in nearly 4 weeks), we took in nearly 300 tons of bag sugar and 3,000 of rice, which was stowed and all cleared for light freight under my charge as 2nd when, to my astonishment, I was told by E.C. that another young man was going home as 2nd. Conceiving myself unjustly treated in thus being superseded, I requested my dismissal, which, not being granted and finding I should have to go home as 3rd, I was reluctantly obliged to descend a step and take up my original post, tho' I cannot describe what I felt, after having performed the duties of 2nd officer so long, being introduced as such to gentlemen on board, and [having] been looked upon as such by all the ship's company. I was told I should not repent it, if I went home – that remains to be fulfilled. Mr Mullins, who holds the situation, has my warmest wishes; the tender feeling he evinces towards me under the circumstances makes appear light that which, with a supercilious person, would be intolerable; we are in one cabin and are very happy. I keep a watch and do all as heretofore, but still the honest pride I felt at the thoughts of going 2nd is never vanished, and in being superseded I feel as if, to others, I was disgraced. I now feel I have but the duty home to do as 3rd – when home, I am such no longer. We left the pilot at the foot of the river on the 15/12 mo. and, after a tedious passage of 13 days, arrived at Madras, [where] . . . we stopped until the day before yesterday, discharging and taking in cargo for the Cape and London. We had 21 passengers from Bengal. . . .

I cannot tell the joy I felt when we turned our face homewards. When I saw us again once more surrounded by the dark blue waters, thoughts of home and of absent friends crowded upon me, and I felt my heart light as the shores of India receded from our view. Farewell, thought I, to thy bright skies, welcome the blue waves! Home, thou art home, be thou ever so homely! Sickness soon prevailed among our passengers young and old.

[The dairy concludes at this point.]

Part V

Second Voyage to India

Journal of a Voyage in the ship Woodford

On our return from India on the 23rd of the 5th month 1826, the ship *Woodford* was tendered to Government, for the purpose of taking out convicts to Botany Bay or elsewhere, and was accepted, with orders to prepare accordingly for the reception of stores for the colony and water, provisions, etc. for the prisoners, their guard etc. as also for the reception of passengers. She is a ship of 548 tons register, with a very fair height in her [be]tween decks and was, when taken up for the service, fitted up with 27 cabins for passengers to and from India, in which trade she had always been before, and bore the bill as an excellent ship, being always full of the first-class people who were going to, or returning from, that part of the world.

The part appropriate for the convicts was from the fore part of the main hatchway to the fore part of the fore one; from there to the bows was appropriated as an hospital for their sick, and fitted up accordingly. Abreast the main hatchway, to fore part of the after hatchway of the starboard side, was fitted up for the soldiers or guard, and on the larboard side was the part appropriated to the seamen etc. belonging to the ship; from the bulkhead, including the latter spaces right aft, were the cabins for the officers and the passengers – in the whole, 8 cabins; the poop accommodations for the Captain, Surgeon, Commander of the troops and part of the colonial secretary's family, remained the same as when we were in the India trade.

From the 21st until this day we have been employed fitting out the ship, the convicts' prison etc., which government does at its charge. The lower deck or prison is divided into bed places, each for four men and supplied with 4 mattresses, 4 blankets and 4 pillows. Before each row of bed cabins is a seat fore and aft for them to sit on, they not being allowed to get into their sleeping places during the day. At 11 Mr Ferguson joined the ship and took charge as pilot, cast off and with a fair wind ran down to Gravesend; brought up at half past 4 and veered away upon the hempenbower[53] [sic] to 30 fathoms, all made clear for sea. At 7

---

[53] The bower is a small anchor.

Capt. Alfred Chapman and Lady, Miss Ellen C. with servants and baby, and Mr [John] Beck[54] joined the ship as passengers round to Portsmouth. Wind WNW, strong breeze and cloudy weather, came alongside King's Craft with powder.

Employed making ready for sea, received 30 barrels of powder for the use of the guard. . . .

At 4.0 p.m. Capt. Edward Chapman joined ship, up anchor and made sail; half past 9 brought up to the wharf, fine breeze with south easterly appearance. Daylight, weighed [anchor] . . . brought up in 7 fathoms from Sandwich, WSW 1 mile. 3 p.m., weighed again and ran through the downs, landing Mr Culman, our pilot, in a Deal boat. Set stud sails on both sides, light breezes and clear moonlight night. Ladies squeamish. 9 p.m. South Foreland N and E and E. 3 miles. 11 p.m. abreast Dover, strong flood tide to stern, making little way. 7.30 a.m. turned the hands out to reef topsails, strong breeze from the northward, Dungeness NE and E. distance 9 miles. Ladies quite sick, my brother John in excellent tune and spirits and really a most admirable sailor, eating as heartily as any in the mess. 1 p.m., sighted sails off Beachy Head, strong breeze and short off land. . . . Ship in good trim and sailing well. It was to my brother a fine morning seeing Beachy Head, and I think it will be some time before he forgets the grandeur of the scene. The breeze strong, the sea covered with foam thro' which the ship going about nine knots an hour, and the lofty headland partially covered with mist, combined together to produce a scene which, to one unaccustomed to such scenery, could not fail to be both novel and grand. I felt a pleasure in seeing such evident enjoyment depicted in his countenance, tho' I feared once or twice, as I looked at him from the forecastle standing in the sleeting rain and wind on the weather side of the poop, he had lost [his appetite] . . . however we met at table, and both did our parts. As we passed Hastings we were employed together fancying our brother and sister R. and K. there, and wishing them as much pleasure as we were enjoying together. 5 p.m. got a Portsmouth pilot, Mr Love by name, who took charge, but owing to the wind being cut he could get no further this evening than St Helen's roads, where Capt. Alfred Chapman and suite left us in the pilot boat for Ryde.

11 a.m., up anchor and turned to Spithead with a strong northerly breeze brought up in 7½ fathoms, Portsmouth church N and E, Pembridge point SSE 1/2 E. Squared the yards and made all harbour fashion. Found at an anchor HM ship *Ganges*, 70 guns, *Blanche* Frigate and *Heron* brig, *Phoenix* convict ship, bound to Van Dieman's Land, getting in a new foremast, having sprung her old one after leaving Spithead.

---

[54] John Beck was Edward Beck's brother, who joined the ship to keep Edward company over the first day or two of the voyage.

In the afternoon Capt. C., my brother John and myself went in pilot boat to Ryde, took tea with Capt. Alfred and went in the Newport coach to that place. We enjoyed our ride as much as could be expected, though being late in the evening we could see but partially around us. We took up our quarters at the Angel Inn and, after ordering beds and supper, sallied forth to see the capital of the Isle of Wight – which I think, as to the size and appearance, was greater and fairer than we expected to find. I doubt we gained but little local knowledge – tho', much to our landlord's loss, very sharp appetites, which caused great destruction amongst his lamb chops etc.

After fixing our route for the following day we retired and slept most soundly, rising at half 7 to breakfast and fresh exertions.

After breakfast, harbour dues, etc. paid, we, in a very excellent chaise drawn by an excellent nag, servant behind us, got under way for Shanklin Chine. I think we both agreed that it was the most beautiful ride we had ever taken, the country was truly beautiful and at that time of all the most charms, when the land bore upon its fruitful bosom the gladdening crops of ripened grain, which were in many places yielding to the sickle. The lad behind, one found of the greatest use possible, for it is a feature of the Isle of Wight roads, their being constantly crossed with gates, which it would be a great bore to have to open ourselves continually.

We put up our horse at the village of Shanklin and walked to the Chine, where I think we were most amply gratified in the beautiful prospect that opened to our view. I cannot describe my own particular feelings; they may easily be imagined by those who have ever been seated upon the top of a cliff by the side of a brother or relation, the last of all he was to meet with until the termination of a long and uncertain voyage over that wide ocean that rolled beneath them. I felt a kind of melancholy pleasure, which must have been mutual, from my brother's proposing that on that spot we should meet in fancy, which with me has often been the aim, and long will it be ere the recollection of those few hours we spent together will be eradicated from my remembrance. After satisfying ourselves with the Chine this while, we walked up to the village; we got lunch at the Inn and walked by the cliff to Bonchurch over a small part of the undercliff, which was exceedingly pretty, read a few of the inscriptions on tombstones, lines by travellers in the church porch, etc., etc., and returned much gratified to Ryde by another road, in time for the evening steamboat for Portsmouth, where my brother was just in time to obtain a place in the heavy night coach, in which he left me for London. I soon after fell in with Capt. Chapman and with him went over to Ryde, and here let me record the kindness I received from them all whilst I was at Spithead, being a constant visitor at their Inn and one of all their parties of pleasure which were made up ship visiting, etc. etc. We went aboard the different men-of-war, and particularly examined the *Ganges*, of 70 guns, which was fitted for the flag of Rear Admiral Hotham for the South American station and expecting orders daily to sail. We received our 100 prisoners on the 25th and drew for them daily their allowance of provision at the victualling office, consisting of beef and vegetables; their friends had leave to visit them, and many were the affecting sights one almost daily witnessed of distracted wives, mothers and sisters, who were taking their last farewell in this world: the unfeeling remarks made by some of them on their relations leaving the ship was a full proof of the depravity amongst them, and of the terrible effects of vice upon the human heart, which entirely destroys every fine feeling of the man and degrades him below the brute creation. They were, as they came on board the ship, put into their berths and messes of 6 men each and cautioned as to their behaviour, to show the necessity of minding which, the Dr. punished an offender the 3rd day with a doz. lashes. Our boatswain that day, on being ordered to flog him and refusing, and his mate also, were ordered into confinement to be taken ashore and punished for refusing to do their duty, which so frightened the former that he consented, but immediately after was discharged, much to my satisfaction, for he was a poor fellow, and he made an excellent exchange for a capital, clever one.

6th 3.0 p.m. Sent all the prisoners' friends out of the ship, bumboat men etc., and so all clear for weighing. 3.30, got sailing orders, hove short and set all sail; soon after, Capt. Edward Chapman and passengers joined the ship, accompanied by Capt. Alfred and Miss C. who came to see us off, up anchor and proceeded to sea. At 4.30 Capt. Alfred and sister left us, after bidding us all adieu, and returned our three cheers which we gave as they shoved off from the ship.

Turned to as soon as we got thro' St Helen's roads to [secure] the passengers' cabins, who felt immediately the [need] of their beds from the motion of the ship. As we passed through the roads, one of our passengers from India last voyage came alongside with some ladies and dined with us; we were delighted to see each other again, for he was an excellent fellow and a great favourite. 8 p.m. Durlston [bearing] NE, fine breeze off the land.

7th. We have made a good run today, getting as far as Portland with but a scant wind. Dr Dickson assembled all the prisoners today upon the quarter deck, and told them the manner in which he would treat them if they behaved well, and what would be the consequences of disobedience, admonishing them to endeavour to merit a good character from him, which would be of great service to them in the colony. 11.0 a.m., performed Divine Service, concluding with a sermon. Men very attentive and orderly.

After service mustered the crew, gave them orders not to know a prisoner by name or hold any communication with them, if they were guilty of impropriety to them, report them, when they would immediately be righted, but on no account to strike or abuse them. The which orders all promised to obey. Served out grog for the men to drink success to the voyage with.

Passengers this voyage Mr John (?) Burnett, Colonial Secretary, Mrs Burnett, Misses Mary, Henrietta, Charlotte, Gafry (?) and Mary Ann Burnett, Capt. Meyrick, Commanding Officer of Guard, Lieut. Berkley, 2 daughters, Mrs Meyrick, wife of Capt. M. and child, Mr Dickson, Surgeon Superintendent and 4 servants.

Took our departure this day from the Start Point, bearing NE distance 13 miles; never did any point get more feeling looks of last farewell than were thrown by our passengers who, as the land receded from our view, left the deck, overcome by the intensity of their feelings, plain indeed as it [is] that they are no willing wanderers from their beloved country, but evident that [for Mrs Burnett], with the exception of her children and husband around her, it contains all that can make life desirable for her.

8th and 9th. Passed this morning through a great many ships homeward bound but, not speaking [to] any of them, could not send a line home. Everything is going on very comfortably, the prisoners behaving in a very orderly manner and much to the Superintendent's satisfaction, with the exception of one prisoner who, growing rather too warm on the subject of rations . . . his antagonism . . . being observed by the constable of the deck and by him reported, the offender was pinioned ankles and wrists, and his allowance stopped till he becomes sufficiently contrite; the next offence will be punished with a flogging, a repetition of which I should feel sorry to see. Their irons will soon be taken off if their conduct is good, they look forward to it with pleasure and, I have no doubt, will make themselves very useful to us in the duties of the ship. Got sights of the sun and moon, by which we find not one of the chronometers has kept the rates given by the maker of them.

10th. Beautiful clear weather, glass standing steadily very high, from the lightness of our breeze and the rolling swell generally to be met within this famous Bay of Biscay. Oh, the ladies have found themselves, though reluctant, obliged to keep their beds and to absent themselves from our table; our number consequently at that post this day has appeared very thin. Mr Burnett, the Colonial Secretary, has made up his mind, from the fear of cutting himself, not to shave for the passage; from the strength of his beard now, I conceive he will in 4 months have a very patriarchal appearance, if he keep in the same mind. Today the superintendent knocked off about a doz. prisoners' irons, much to their satisfaction; the alertness of their movements after showed their pleasure in the release of their legs from such bondages. Cape Finisterre.

11th. of 8th. Same weather as yesterday till 5 o'clock, when it shifted to rather a misty atmosphere but soon cleared up with a fine breeze at NE, and when the bell struck 6.0 I left the deck, with her walking away, about 6 knots, all stud sails low and aloft. At half past 11 a.m. a letter bag was closed, a vessel bound to the eastward being right ahead, distance about 4 miles, hoisted our colours and approached as near as the wind would allow, but he was not civil to bear down to us or even to show his flag, so we are obliged to proceed with disappointed expectations. The bag remains closed in case of another opportunity presenting, which we all anxiously hope for, as when we get into the trade [winds] we are soon out of the track of all homeward bound ships.

12th./8. Throughout the whole of this day we have had a strong 8 knot breeze from the NE which is helping us forward at a fine rate; such a breeze, with so many on board consuming water and provisions, is invaluable indeed, altogether it is a most prosperous beginning to our voyage: our ship is as tight as a bottle, which, to us who for a whole India voyage were used to pump for ¾ hour out of 2 or 3, is a complete luxury. As we have had quite a fresh blow [?] of wind today and one that has certainly tried her, I think we have every reason to believe she will continue in so desirable a state. The remark of the old saying of sailors: 'Carpenters are the loss of more seamen than gales of wind!' will apply to the *Woodford* and to the *Constantia*, as in both instances our leaks were entirely through the neglect of the shipwrights. Ther. 68. Madeira S.25.25W. Sympis. 30.33 Dist. 734 miles. Strong breeze and cloudy.

13th. The strength of the breeze last night, combined with the motion of the ship, which upset some furniture that was not secured in the ladies' cabins, quite alarmed them, even to that degree that a messenger was dispatched to the Capt. to inquire if there was any danger, and it was not until they met us at the breakfast table and heard our rejoicing in the breeze, their fears entirely subsided.

At 2.0 p.m. spoke the *Prince Regent* of Dartmouth, bound to that place, a small fruit schooner and rather deeply loaded. We gave our name and requested to be reported all well on her arrival; we should have sent our mail on board, but there was too much wind and we were unwilling to lose one moment's running wind. We exchanged longitudes, with a difference of 30 miles. Ther. 69. Madeira S.26.4W. Sympis. 30.24 Dist. 539 miles. Strong breeze and clear.

1 4th. The breeze seems inclined to carry us into the trade [wind], as it still is as fresh as ever. Saw about 2.0 p.m. a brig ahead, up colours and got our longitude chalked upon a plank for him but, as he did not heave to, but crossed our bows about 4 miles distance and did not, as we neared him, which was very fast, show his flag, we kept the *Woodford* her own course and soon ran him out of sight. Yesterday one of our lads, being found in the double offence of stealing wine and getting drunk with it, the Capt. ordered all the apprentices to be called and made the Boatswain punish with a doz. which made the dust fly in clouds out of his jacket, thereby yielding a double benefit, the cleansing [of] his jerkin and the amendment of his manners. Orders then were issued to keep him in confinement on the poop and to feed him on bread and water for 3 days without any of his messmates communicating with him. Ther. 70. Madeira S.24.16W. Sympis. 30.43. Dist. 373 miles.

15th. The Surgeon today detected some of his charges breaking the chain that communicates with the irons on their legs; by way of teaching them to be content, he double-ironed the defaulters. He also found they had made the ankle rings oblong so they could slip them over their heels, the whole of which he rounded again; as long as they continue to misbehave, he will liberate no man of them. At 6.0 p.m. departed this life one of the worst offenders on board, his disease a malignant fever, in consequence of which he was interred shortly after with the usual ceremony, the Surgeon reading the service. It was the most beautiful night that can possibly be imagined, and a most impressive scene. The moon was shedding a path of splendour upon the scene through which our ship was ploughing her rapid course, whilst the divided wave rolling from her prow seemed like liquid fire. As the body was dropped into its watery grave I thought the solemnity of the scene impressed all around. Ther. 70 Sym. 30.39.

16th. At 5.30 p.m. the island of Madeira bore from the deck S.30W. Dist. 32 miles, the thick mist over the highland prevented our seeing it before, altho', had it been clear, we should have seen it at once, it being very bold and lofty. We had no distinct view of it until the moon arose, when I think as fine a view surrounded us as ever I remember to have seen. The breeze was strong and we were carrying a very heavy press of sail, under which our ship staggered in fine style past the land, whose rugged promontories were finely delineated, from the circumstances of a dark cloud hanging over them, whilst the whole splendour of the moon's beams were directed toward the quarter where they jutted into the sea. The ladies stopped upon deck until a later hour than usual and, as I heard nothing of the pianoforte, I concluded the sight had raised those feelings which the sight of terra firma so generally does in the heart of the unwilling wanderer from their beloved country. . . .

17th. Our fine fair wind still continues, all goes on very comfortably with all parties, not a single unpleasant occurrence has as yet disturbed the harmony on board the *Woodford*. Seasickness not quite gone, but much on the decline, except among the poultry which, much to the sorrow of the table, still continues to show heavy bills of mortality. My chronometer seems to be going very well, giving us the longitude to within 2 miles, but not at the rate given by the watchmaker – nor, indeed, do any of them, however, the being able to determine our exact situation has enabled us to at least know the error, but the rate must still be unknown, until some other land shall give us the power of saying positively how they are going. Mean of lunar observations east and west would satisfy us, but we cannot say positively we shall be able to get them. Ther. 76. Symp. 30.22.

18th. Considered ourselves this day as having the NE trade wind, but we are therefore now pretty well sure of a speedy passage as far as the equator; should we when there get speedily into the SE trade, we shall in all probability make a quick passage out, as we are almost sure of westerly winds after we get to the southward of 28 or 30 south. Our convicts are all behaving very quietly and giving us no trouble but they do not yet satisfy the Doctor, who still keeps them in irons and says he intends to until he can pick out the worst amongst them, which effected, he will liberate the better and give them their allowance of wine, which they have not yet received, it being left to the Surgeon's discretion to serve out. I think them abominably lazy, I had thought they would have been glad of a job, but I find they would rather be excused. San Antonia S.27W. 780 miles, Ther. 70. Sym. 30.26.

19th. Found this morning in the chains, a number of very curious kind of cuttle fish emitting a very dark inky matter, a most curious animal and very disgusting in appearance; should have preserved one, but I had no bottle, nor could I procure one. Immense shoals of flying fish are now constantly seen around the ship, our constant companion in tropical seas. Got hooks and lines fitted for catching their enemies the dolphin and bonito, as well as shack hooks and grapnels, for spearing the former. This afternoon, a convict was tied up for the offence of collaring a constable and refusing to obey orders, and punished with 2 dozen lashes, which on account of the Boatswain's strength left visible impressions upon his unfortunate back. I had hoped the first would have been a sufficient warning to the refractory fellows but, as it proved otherwise, I was glad the rogue catched it severely – for it is a most painful thing to be obliged to witness, and the less often, the better. Ther. 77. Sym. 30.24.

20th. At 11 a.m. the Surgeon performed divine service before prisoners, guard and ship's company, and concluded with one of Cooper's sermons. At 6 in the evening after tea, the Captain had service in the cuddy with the passengers and ship's Company and those of the guard that chose to attend.

A flying fish earlier this morning flew into the chief mate's cabin, a very acceptable present to the ladies, who had long wished to see one.

Mrs Burnett, who has been some time ill, seems to be worse today, the rheumatic pains in her face increasing to an alarming degree. I know not how to account for it, but she is the fourth case of rheumatism in one shape or another since our leaving Portsmouth; we miss her company much, as she is [a] very intelligent and agreeable lady. San Antonio S.25W. 483 miles, Ther. 77, Sym. 30.28.

21st. All well. Ther. 77 Sym. 30.

Heavy squall rose this morning between the poor second mate [i.e. the author] and the Captain. Seeing what was coming, he [the author] prudently made all snug for it and bore away under bare poles, when it cleared up, rounded to upon a better tack than ever, settled the difference and made all sail. It was the first breeze, and I mean it to be the last, as far as I am concerned; I must confess in this instance it was all ny fault. Fine light breezes, expect to see the island of St Antonio tomorrow evening or next morning.

Flying fish in great abundance about the ship, . . . few dolphins or bonito, saw a few ship jacks, but they would not take a hook baited with white rag for a flying fish. Ther. 78 Symp. 30.11. San Antonio S.15W. Dist. 102 miles.

23rd. I find today that the 'starting' (as it is called on board ship) or, if you please, 'rope's ending' our drunken apprentice got the other day had not the effect intended, for today he was quite intoxicated and wanted to jump overboard. It being the second offence, the lads were turned out to punishment and the delinquent, by then lashed up to the mizzen rigging . . . was stripped to the buff and punished with the cat, with ½ doz. from all the other 6 apprentices, and 3 doz. done and pretty severely administered; he sung out 'Peccavi', pleaded the fault of his head and begged to be excused, but it would not do so, the which seeing, he bore the last dozen without a murmur and travelled up to the main top gallant yard to spend the remainder of the afternoon. At 7, anointed his back and turned him to his duty. San Antonio S.16W. 30 miles. Ther. 78 Sym. 30.10

24th. Very light winds and a loss of the trade, consequently making but little progress; saw a great number of dolphin, but could neither hook nor strike any of them. It will be a very serious thing to our prospects, the loss of the trade thus early, as we shall, in case of long calms and variables, so expend our water, as to be obliged to go into the Cape to replenish our stocks. . . .

25th. Caught this morning a shark, very small and young; he took bait immediately and was soon cut up into slices for the sailors' and prisoners' dinners; being young he was, I have no doubt, good eating. I am sure he would make excellent curry. Still, light airs, inclinable to calm and little prospect of a breeze, all looking so still, and a scene as more to resemble a lake than an ocean. . . .

26th. Calms, calms, sails flapping against the masts, becoming hot and bad water to drink, O Father Thames, purified be thy waters! Thermal 82. Symp. 29.96.

27th. Found down in the hold, to our great joy, a machine which no one knew the use of or to whom it belonged, but . . . [which] proved to be a water purifier; set to work immediately, and drank weak wine and water all the afternoon, by way of fetching up leeway. It is a most simple tin pump, at the top like a Dutch oven, with shelves or partitions full of holes; this, which as the water is raised it runs through from division to division back again, by which means it is purified by the air and all its unpleasant smell taken from it. So great was its value considered, that it was proposed at dinner to drink the inventor's health in a bumper of his purified waters. What pity he knows not the honour done [him]. Thermal 82, Symp. 29.98.

28th. 11 a.m., Dr Dickson performed divine service upon the quarter deck to the passengers, prisoners, ship's company and guard, concluding with one of Cooper's sermons. 7.0 p.m., Capt. Chapman had evening service in the cuddy with all who chose to attend, concluding with a sermon from the same work. The prisoners' behaviour was orderly and very attentive, and I think on the whole their conduct is very good, although the Doctor will not allow it, or serve them out their wine, or knock off any more irons. 2 of them have had them taken off, on their volunteering for the hold, and proved themselves very serviceable in that department in the serving out water, provisions, etc. One fellow, for his misdeeds and assault and battery, is in confinement to take his trial at Van Dieman's Land. Thermal 83. Symp. 30.

29th. This morning got reported to the Captain, for the first time since I have been an officer, for neglect of duty. Mr Rybot's complaint was that I left the deck with the stud sail half lowered down, not a tack out, and the braces all gone with the yards all swinging about. It was a malicious design upon my character but my Captain knows me, I have been on board the *Woodford* 17 months and, I hope, am an improving officer. I've been relieved by Captain C. many hundred times, who never had to say of me that I left a thing to be done; it was well for me, I was no stranger, or I might have gone to leeward; but I hope this has, instead of injuring, done me a service.

4 p.m. spoke the *Lady MacNaughton* of Calcutta and the *Charles Grant*, a China Ship by whom we sent letters to England. The *Chas. Grant* had been ashore at the Straights of Sunda, and got much injured. The son of Mr Bush, né Garratt, was on board as midshipman, to whom I sent word his friends were well, and begged him to report [from] me as Garratt. Thermal 81 Symp. 29.94.

30th. Caught 2 sharks, one 9'6", the other 5'4", clock calm and desperate hot. Therm. 83 1/2 Sym. 30.0.

31st. Got a strong westerly wind with a heavy head swell, saw a ship ahead and gained on her fast, but did not get up with her by dark. Split the main top sail and unbent it, got the 2nd one to the yard; this strong breeze ill agrees with the old sails. Thermal 82 Sym. 29.94.

9th. month, 1st., Split the fore top sail in a strong squall with continued heavy rain, after it was over and the canvas dry, hauled it up and repaired it in the top, hardly hoisted when it gave way again, let it remain with another . . . against it . . . [if] it goes all together, which I hope will be soon. Owing to the strong breeze and heavy swell, many of our passengers seasick and nearly all prisoners and guard. Full platters, poor appetites, and plenty of hearty messmates, the order of the day. Cuddy table half deserted, hot soup in ladies' laps very uncomfortable. Thermal 80. Symp. 29.97.

2nd. Still a strong breeze, and much seasickness observable on account of it. I know not when they will get rid of it entirely, but it must be fine weather first. Thermal 80. Symp. 30.1.

3rd. Saw a strange sail to windward hull down; less wind and sea, consequently less sea sickness. Mr Burnett's cook, I fear, is near her death, the Dr. saying that she has got the liver complaint, at which rate she might as well be exposed to a tropical climate, I think, as her own fire. My chronometer for the last several days has ceased to go well and is on the contrary going most infamously; I should, with no other, feel no kind of confidence in it. The rest of the watches are going very well and keep time together admirably; I know not where the fault is, but it certainly is a grievous one. Ther. 79. Symp. 30.3.

4th. Strange sail in sight again this morning, maintaining her position. Got a very fine breeze about 10 o'clock that enabled us to steer S by E, set out stud sails and gained on the stranger. At 9.0 a.m. it commenced raining, with every appearance of the wind shifting into SE, it would be a blessing indeed to get it, for we are now in as little as 17 degrees west, and therefore in a fair way for going well to windward in the trade. Midnight very heavy, continued rain and very threatening appearance to the eastward, got the . . . stud sails in and saw all clear for a top sail haul. In these tropical climates the symprisometer is so little affected by changes that it is of no use to us; I should like to know a satisfactory reason for it, for I am sure the most sudden changes are found between the losing and gaining a trade wind. Ther. 79. Symp. 30.2.

5th. Served out this day at noon for the first time a gill of wine to each prisoner, which had the effect of cheering up their spirits to a small degree. Nothing worth recording. Thermal 78. Symp. 30.

6th. Tacked several times, but to little purpose; found ourselves at noon in sight of yesterday's place. Got the boats thoroughly fitted for going round the Cape. At midnight in my watch, I was caught aback with a heavy squall from the SE, got the ship round upon her keel and turned the hands up about ship. Stood to the westward ½ hour, then tacked again and did no better, eastward on one tack, westward the other, will make us a long while getting to the southward of the Equator. Chronometer going very bad. Attribute it to the heavy head sea and pitching; none of the others in the least affected by it. Thermal 80. Symp. 30.8.

7th. Still a foul wind and heavy head swell prevents our making much headway, and I should think it very likely to be another [month] before we get across the equator. Our passengers are still seasick at times, especially Mrs Meyrick and Henrietta Burnett, who are frequently absent from the cuddy table. I attribute it to the ship being so light and lively that her motion so affects them. Obtained a victory, observed three sets of lunar observations, each within 5 degrees of the Captain's; I hope therefore soon to be able to call myself a lunar observer. It is certainly the most gratifying thing imaginable, to be able to determine without any other aid than a sextant our position upon the globe within a few miles. The confidence felt by a good lunar observer must be invaluable, and I shall never feel satisfied until it is mine.
Chronometer going infamously.

8th. A prisoner detected stealing 6 half-crowns from a fellow rogue, so that the old adage 'honour among thieves' must fall, it being extinct. The Doctor told them, on giving them their money, that he won't hear no complaint about it if lost or stolen, consequently he will get off. It must be for the pleasure of thieving, for where can he spend it? Southerly winds quite foul. Thermal 76½. Symp. 30.9.

9th. Strong squally weather, but no better prospect of the SE trade, the ladies still sick. My chronometer again came near to its rate yesterday, but as it is so fickle we do not use it to determine the longitude: the mean of the other 3 (which are going admirably) are alone used, and certainly they do credit to their makers.

Served out to the convicts to mix in their wine and water, ½ ounce of lime juice and sugar, to be continued. Therm. 86. Symp. 30.8.

10th. Dr D. performed service on the quarter deck before the prisoners, guard, ship's company etc. as usual. Saw a strange sail to leeward, proved to be a brig, something like a man-of-war. Wind still foul, with very squally weather at nights. Consider our ship very weakly manned, which is rather a misfortune, seeing we are likely to go to so sickly a place as Batavia. My chronometer again came to its rate this day, about minus 6 degrees daily, and I hope will keep so. Prisoners now receive their regular allowance of wine, lime juice and sugar, mixed together at the rate of a pint each man, which must be a most excellent and wholesome beverage. Several of them have had attacks of fevers and one nearly carried off with apoplexy, but Doctor bled him profusely, which restored him – but he stands, I believe, but a poor chance of seeing the place of his destination. South west winds, no prospect of trade. Therm. 77. Symp. 30.8.

11th. Strong squalls between the chief and third mates, the former having, in the most unjustifiable manner, reported Mr Govey as being so intoxicated last 9th day evening, that he did not think it prudent to have him in charge of the deck. I came up in my watch to see if it was the case, but believed him, in my conscience, to be as sober as myself, so took the liberty of speaking to the Captain, thinking it such a cruel thing for a young man to be so grossly vilified; was pleased to find Capt. quite satisfied himself, and that he had ordered Mr Rybot to be more cautious in future how he acted. Under such a rogue no man's character can be safe; utterly despised by everyone on board, not spoken to by many of the passengers, detested by the apprentices, I know not where he finds pleasure in his life; I am sure he cannot say he has but done his duty for his consolation; his conscience, like him, [is] another story. Ther. 77. Symp. 30.10.

12th. Have not yet got the trade wind nor any more prospect of it, except a strong SE swell. Saw, for the first time in my life, a most beautiful solar halo, more beautifully prismatic than I ever saw before. A knave amongst the convicts this day, for a wager of 2 shillings, did eat 6 men's allowances of plum pudding, about 7 lbs within an hour and, to the amazement of the rest, drank afterwards a pint of salt water, certainly the best thing he could do. The Doctor allows of nothing of this kind, but as it is done in the watch below and they keep a good sentinel to observe when he is coming, he never can detect them. If he did, he would make their backs rue it, for he thinks no more of giving a man a dozen or 2, than of eating his breakfast. Ther. 77. Symp. 30.3.

13th. All going on well, several convicts ill of a low fever, the rest in good health, our own ship's company and soldiers quite well, excepting an ordinary seaman, who has been ill all the passage. The cleanliness preserved among the prisoners must have a very salutary effect, their clothes are scrubbed twice a week regularly and, as they all pass before him [the surgeon] as they receive their pint of lime juice, wine and water (may it not be called punch?) and he is in the habit of not giving it them if dirty in their person, he is quite certain of their being washed once a day – for they would think nothing of being handcuffed a week, but stop their punch, and they are immediately punished to a desirable extent. It is a melancholy sight and I cannot accustom myself to see it with indifference, the degradation of so many fellow creatures who, hobbling about the decks with their irons rattling at their heels, seem to be quite indifferent to it. Therm. 75. Symp. 30.9.

14th. At 1 o'clock turned the guard out under arms to punish a prisoner for disobedience of the Surgeon's orders. The guard, as usual, was ranged on the poop deck above the convicts, who were all drawn up on the weather side of the quarter deck to witness their fellow flogged. As soon as he was stripped and seized up to the grating, the Doctor gave them some general advice respecting his orders being obeyed, then told the boatswain to do his duty. A few strokes fetched blood from the poor wretch's back, and before he had received the second dozen allotted him, he must have felt it most severely if his back told tales. He was sent in handcuffs after he was cast loose onto the forecastle, where I saw him an hour after, singing and whistling away as unconcerned as ever. He sung out most loudly but to no effect, no mitigation got he. I am obliged to be a witness, and I therefore wish it would have the effect desired. Therm. 76. Symp. 30.8.

15th. All well, with a complete foul wind making very little southing indeed. Therm. and Symp. as yesterday.

16th. Foul wind, low spirits amongst passengers, livestock decreasing fast, what pity people should eat and drink more, when it is such fine weather and the ship not proceeding on her course; spliced the main brace at 8 bells, by way of seeing the sailors enjoy the evening. Ther. 75. Symp. 30.11.

17th. Got the SE trade; better ship's appearances by 50 per cent all round. Performed divine service in the fore and afternoon on the quarter deck and cuddy; to me it is always a most interesting scene and has, in my humble opinion, a very admirable effect upon the men's conduct, to whose credit I may say I have hardly heard an oath amongst them since the first week or two; the effect of example is very great, and shows how desirable a good one should be set. Ther. 65. Symp. 30.13.

18th. The people requested to keep Neptune's holiday as usual with the accustomed ceremonies, but as we had prisoners on board as well as the soldiers, the Capt. very prudently told them he could not decide to it, but they should be made quite comfortable and have the day to themselves. At 8.0 gave them a proper allowance of grog to commemorate the eve of their crossing the equator: the young midshipmen got up a whimsical kind of a play in the steerage; whilst they spent the evening in dancing and singing, not a man got intoxicated, but kept their watches with the usual order, except that the first watch, instead of sleeping, was kept awake by the watch below who, joining them in the fine moonlight, kept up their amusements till 12 o'clock.

Strong trade this day, with a run of 184 miles – quite a novelty of late. Ther. 75. Symp. 30.3.

19th. The following letter was addressed to the ladies and gentlemen passengers in the *Woodford* outward bound:-

Ladies and Gents,

This is to inform you that Commodore Neptune will excuse the Customaries if the Ladies and Gentlemen will abide by the usual customs of the ship's company.

Signed . . . Commodore Neptune.

A broad hint for the little presents usually given the men to prevent being shaved;

however, I believe they got nothing, which I think savours a little of meanness for a trifle, as being customary, whilst it conveyed pleasure to the people, would conciliate their good offices, often required at extra hours; they have a great deal of trouble with passengers in general, and I think a trifle spared them is not badly applied and is never forgotten by them whilst they are on board, but generally repaid by the good will manifested towards them; a sailor hates any appearance of meanness, and seldom scruples to express [this] in his blunt manner, if an opportunity offers.

Our young middies, who went last voyage with us, were not, however, to have their fun spoiled. 'No! No!' said they, 'We were well shaved, and will shave our newcomers!' So they got all the apparatus into the steerage and, after well tarring their faces, shaving them etc. etc., took them up on deck, to the great amusement of the passengers etc., and there soused them in a tub of water. The people had the day to themselves and employed the greater part in what they term 'getting a blow out of the ship'. They had as much grog as they could reasonably be supplied with, and a double allowance of the best provisions. I never saw a ship's company so happy together before; we have not yet witnessed a quarrel amongst them but, on the contrary, great harmony. Ther. 73. Symp. 31.11.

20th. All well, strong trade . . .

21st. Fine steady trade and clear weather with but very little to vary the monotony of sea life, which to many of our passengers seems very irksome. Ther. 75. Symp. 30.4.

22nd. This morning a couple of prisoners (for want of better amusement) had a quarrel and fought; one of them, a complete savage, bit about a large mouthful out of the other's cheek, and left it hanging by a bit of skin for the Doctor to repair. I suppose they will both get flogged, unless the Surgeon is more mercifully inclined than usual; at least, I should not like to run an equal chance. A booby [bird] has been about the ship for the last day or two, but we cannot find where it roosts at night. There is a reward for his apprehension, dead or alive. Ther. 75. Symps. 30.13.

23rd. My birthday – one year older, ¼ of a year wiser and . . . not a tenth part of one better, I am sorry to say. Indeed I am afraid I am making little else than leeway. I wish the retrospect of the past may have the effect of stimulating me to a more earnest attempt at amendment of manners. The rogue who committed the assault yesterday on his fellow's cheek is condemned to be fed upon a pound of bread per day and water only, by way of experiment; I am heartily glad of it, for I am tired of bleeding backs.

Got some excellent lunar observations, which give us most satisfactory errors to our watches and consequently the greater confidence in our longitude:

C.C. sights	{Capt. C's O.S. No. 547	Slow 11"
	{Mr Govey Lex	Slow 8"
	{E. Beck's	Slow 10"
E.B.'s sights	{Capt. C's O.S. No. 547	Slow 14"
	{Mr Govey's	Slow 17"
	{E. Beck's	Slow 15"

rate allowed to this day 17" slow.

24th. Fine, strong breeze, and much seasickness amongst the passengers, on account of the ship's motion; they are much to be pitied on account of its lasting so long. The Doctor today detected a constable stealing, in company with one of the hospital men, a number of comforts such as tea, sago [?] etc. out of the sick bay; he immediately put them into double irons, and stopped their wine for the voyage. Another fellow, for abusive language, is put upon bread and water for a month. We have been exceedingly unfortunate in our livestock, having lost 6 pigs, which to our little family is 98 days pork provision. There is every reason to fear we shall come short now in that essential pork provision. I hope, however, we shall have plenty for the ladies; gentlemen may get their salt beef . . . aboard. Ther. 78. Symps. 30.13.

25th. Miss Mary Burnett, a very interesting sweet girl about 18, seems to have made a deep impression upon our Captain, and it is rumoured, even publicly, that we shall have Mrs Chapman passenger to England with us. She is a great favourite of mine, and I think one a young man, so inclined and only wanting an object, would soon fall in love with. However, a short time will soon completely satisfy me about the matter, and tell the wondering world of the *Woodford* the truth. Such a subject on board a ship where there are plenty of females is worth anything, and it is to be hoped it will long remain clothed with a little obscurity, that they may not want [for] amusement in that most delightful (to them) of all their subjects, LOVE. I wish with all my heart it may be true. Ther. 72. Symps. 30.20.

26th. Very fine weather throughout the day and squalls at night and always, in my watch, just as the moon is rising. The news is now confirmed, Capt. Chapman marries Miss Burnett on their arrival in the colony and brings her with us to England; the servant, who is now with the family as nurse, is to be her servant home. I hope it may have weight towards preventing our going [to] Batavia. Ther. 70. Symps. 30.33.

27th. Nothing but the intended marriage seems to occupy the attention of all parties on board the *Woodford*. The Captain has received the good wishes of all the passengers, and seems no little delighted with his prospects. We are seldom obliged with his company in an evening now, he spending all his time with his Mary. Run these 2 last days 190 miles per observation. Ther. 69. Symp. 30.32.

28th. The rascally prisoner, who was punished with 2 dozen lashes the other day, was detected stealing sugar and money from another prisoner. The Doctor, after long deliberation whether to flog or otherwise punish him, fixed to give him daily bread and water till his arrival in Van Dieman's Land, and to handcuff him to prevent his doing the like in future. Fine breeze and clear weather. Ther. 65. Symps. 30.33.

29th. Made a fine run today with a good deal of easting; looking very wild but, the glass standing very high, there is no fear of a change.
    There is proof of the value of symprisometer [i.e. barometer]; were it not for it standing so high we should, from appearances, these last two nights have had reefs in our topsails and consequently [have lost] both their services, when there would have been no reason for it. Ther. 66. Symps. 30.41.

30th. Fine fair breezes are wafting us along at a rapid rate towards our destination, and I should think it very likely we shall be off the Cape in about a fortnight; I hope we shall not have to go in for water, but I think it is at present very uncertain. I got such a thrashing, with the fiery southeasters last homeward bound passage, that I do not wish to have the pleasure of beating into the Bay against them. We attempted twice to get into the anchorage but both times, about three o'clock in the afternoon, just as we were accomplishing our object, the white cloud which gathers on the top of Table Mountain and is a sure warning (distinguished by the name of the Devil's tablecloth), came rolling down the sides . . . bringing with it the most violent south-east wind, which tore our sails and made us bear up. On the second trial we lost an anchor and were obliged to go to sea, but happily got a leading wind in, and anchored the next morning. Ther. 65. Symps. 36.36.

1st. of 10th month. Performed divine service as usual, morning on the quarter deck, evening in the cuddy. Doctor Dickson reads prayers and a sermon also, every sabbath afternoon in the prison and twice in the week. Fine strong breezes still continue, amazing 170 miles a day. Ther. 65. Symps. 30.40.

2nd. Set all hands today to work upon two new topsails, a fore [?] and main one, which we are now in want of in case of an accident. All on board quite healthy, which is a great pleasure when there are so many.

The climate is quite changed from that fine, bracing, refreshing air one breathes in England, tho' the ladies complain a good deal about cold, but still taking no exercise; if they do not, they will be half starved [for warmth], for we have no fires for them to sit round – nor shall we have, all the voyage. With north-west, strong breezes.

3rd. We are now favoured with the company of abundances of Cape pigeons, Cape hens and the king of seafowl, the Albatross. We have caught two pigeons, which were released again, after the ladies were gratified with a look [at] . . . them. I certainly think them the prettiest aquatic bird I ever saw. The thermometer fall makes my night watch very, very cold, but thanks to S. Marsh, the stout clothing he has provided me with, I intend shall defy it.

4th. This evening was enjoyed a theatre in the steerage and Shakespeare's tragedy of whatever it was [Hamlet], or at least the ghost scene in it, was acted before an overflowing house and amidst thundering applause. All went on very well until, Hamlet forgetting his part, the curtain dropped, and then such a roar of laughter commenced that they could not be persuaded to try it again. However, to make some kind of finish, they persuaded the sailmaker, who was half seas over, to appear before the audience and sing, which he did, in so droll and ludicrous a manner that the ship rung with laughter, nobody thinking he had been drinking, though he acted the returned sailor to a[n] azimuth. I remembered the Query,[55] and fear I plead guilty to the attending a place of amusement.

5th. The making of the new sails getting on famously, the Captain ordered the men extra grog, which by some roguery or other made half of them drunk. One man, who had slept it off by the time he had to steer in my watch, being nettled that I should enforce his going to the wheel, not thinking it his turn, chose to yaw the ship about like a collier and was insolent into the bargain, upon which I turned him from the wheel and reported his misconduct; in consequence, he is

---

[55] Probably a reference to a Quaker document forbidding attendance at places of amusement.

now in confinement or durance vile upon the poop, fast to the mizzen mast as a warning to all offenders.

6th. Sailmaker drunk, disgraced him by turning [him] out of the petty officers' berth and allowing him about a 6th part of his grog. Strong squalls at times, otherwise fine breezes and fair. The symprisometer still keeps very high and the thermometer falling fast. . . .

7th. Immense shoals of porpoises around the ship, proceeding from the NW, give us reason to expect the wind from . . . [that] quarter. The shoals of these black fish[56] were the largest I ever saw, and it formed no small feature of the novelty to see them, as if with one impulse, leap together out of the water a considerable height into the air, appearing more like a flock of black sheep than anything else I can imagine.

A number of grampuses favoured us with their blowing and spouting abilities for a considerable time. . . .

8th. Performed divine service as usual. Symprisometer, after falling to 30.28 at 2.0 a.m. with very unsettled winds and weather, rose by 10 a.m. to 30.30, where it has stood all day, though I should have thought we were going to have a change with a breeze of wind.

9th. The symprisometer fell last night to 29.90 with squally weather and rain at 2.0 a.m. The wind suddenly shifted from NNW to SW, with heavy rain and a very strong breeze; turned the hands out, and took in a single reef of the topsails. Daylight more moderate and finer, with the symprisometer rising fast; made all possible sail again.

The ladies were quite alarmed last night; hearing the Captain's voice on deck and feeling the ship heel over a great deal, they conceived there must be danger. [I imagine] that they were soon convinced to the contrary and slept well after it . . . they not being at breakfast. Ther. 65. Symps. 30.32.

10th. Fine strong breezes with cloudy weather and heavy swells from the southward and, I think, every appearance of a shift.

In overhauling our cables today, we found one of them nearly half cut through in a most unaccountable way; we were obliged to cut and splice it. Ther. 64½. Symps. 30.19.

---

[56] 'Black fish' probably refers to dolphins, though strictly speaking dolphins are mammals, not fish.

11th. Last night our drunken sailmaker, who had been making rather too free with the grog, pitched head foremost down the after hatchway, broke his nose and nearly knocked one eye out; he laid himself up against the bulkhead of my cabin and, whilst he was bleeding like a pig, trolled out most lustily the burthen of some old naval song, in which are the lines:

Oh grog is our larboard and starboard
Our mainmast, our mizzen, our log,
Ashore or at sea or in harbour,
The mariner's compass is grog.

He would have concluded, had not the Doctor arrived, who plastered him up and sent him to his hammock. Ther. 66. Symps. 30.26.

12th. James Johnson, a prisoner, having behaved in a disorderly manner and used threatening language to a sentry, was this morning condemned to receive 2 dozen lashes at 10.0 a.m. The prisoners were, as usual, mustered around him and the guard under arms. As he came along the deck he met Mr Owen the boatswain, whom he begged to be merciful, and whilst he was receiving his due he merely winked his eye to him and, said Mr Owen, bore it manfully. The boatswain flogged hard, but he was well provided for it with a thick skin and it made little impression. Ther. 65. Symps. 30.30

13th. At last the wind has headed us, and it has become what we term a complete 'noser', north one, tack south; the other fresh provision vanished like a ghost from the table, excepting one good joint for the ladies, and other passengers got my salt beef tacks aboard for the first time [in] the last 18 months or 2 years; remaining stock 3 pigs, 5 sheep, 2 dozen fowls, 6 geese and 15 ducks. Ther. 65, Symps. 30.26.

Turn[ed] to and cleaned ship fore and aft and scrubbed the paint work. Got reported again to the Captain by my friend Rybot, because I would not send him up a swab from my lower deck, the cleaning of which is under my superintendence and was then going forward. Got a good wigging from the Captain, and a most triumphant look from the chief, which so elated him that he forgot how to observe the latitude at noon, being only 29 miles south of her true places. I was desired by the Captain to tell him, convince himself of his [Rybot's] error by getting another latitude immediately, which he did, and was satisfied of his mistake. Tables now turned, and he received orders not to observe again, if he could not do it correctly; my correction caused me no pain, his (had it been mine) would have made me half mad. Foul wind, low spirits and cold weather, monkey jackets in good request for night watches. Ther. 63½. Symps. 30.28.

15th. Last night, whilst we were at church in the cuddy, the sky suddenly assumed a stormy aspect . . . accompanied with a great deal of lightning. As soon as service was over, we were turned out to reef topsails and I think I may say that, when on the topsail yard reef, I never saw such terrific lightning or heard such tremendously loud thunder, in my life and experience. The whole heavens seemed to be in one blaze, which continued very long, whilst streams of liquid fire seemed raining down upon the horizon in this form. It rained at the same time very heavy, with a good deal of wind, and glad was I to see it clear up and turn out only a thunder squall. Plenty of wet jackets etc. but, the ladies having been mindful of us in the cuddy and prepared plenty of good hot mulled port, we were soon lifted into dry clothes and enjoyed their company but, more especially, their good things. Woman, lovely woman, is indeed a treasure aboard ship! Ther. 63. Symps. 30.28. (Symps. 2 a.m. 30.30. 4. a.m. 30.28. 4 p.m. 30.26. 6 p.m. 30.20. 8 p.m. 30.10., after the squall 10 p.m. 30.18, midnight 30.26.)

16th. Fine breezes from the north-west with delightful weather, all possible sail set; we have this day passed the meridian of the Cape, and have remaining 5,760 miles to perform before we reach Hobart Town. I expect it will take us 5 weeks to the island; happy shall I be when we are delivered of our unfortunate freight and once more a clear ship; however [if one] has had the pleasure of taking out prisoners [he] will not desire the job again, I imagine. My chronometer, from a losing rate of 7" per diem, goes now to mean time, being quite affected by the change of temperature; it is to me rather mortifying.

I believe it is pretty well fixed for us to return from Sydney to Van Dieman's Land, and so through the Bass Straits up to the Strait of Sunda to call at Batavia and, if we cannot get a cargo, to go to Singapore; if we get a freight soon, we shall be home, I imagine, within the year. Ther. 64. Symps. 30.20.

17th. Fine breezes from the westward, but a strong current against us prevents our sailing very great runs. The Doctor this morning released a great number of prisoners out of the iron of one leg; his opinion of them is that they are a hundred of the worst characters to be found amongst the condemned on board the hulks, and undeserving the kindness of being unshackled altogether.

18th. The wind this afternoon at 4 o'clock from dead aft drew right forward with strong breezes, small rain and dirty appearances; took in the first reefs of topsails and reefed the mainsails. Some very large brown birds making very bold with the ship, we got up our guns to have a shot at them; I fired once and, in putting in the next charge, some fire left in the bottom ignited the powder and it went off; it knocked in the powder flask and black[en]ed my hand but did me no injury, though I must reckon it a narrow escape of severely injuring, if not of losing, my hand. Ther. 67. Symps. 30.6.

19th. Fine strong south-west breezes going about 8 knots per hour. The birds which have accompanied us so long are not to be seen now, and a solitary Albatross or two form our only acquaintance with the feathered tribe.

We intend sighting St Paul or Amsterdam,[57] or perhaps both, as they lie on the route towards our port; it will afford a little variety and give us new departures. Midnight, just going up on deck to keep the solitary middle watch. Fancy a ship with all sails set low and aloft, the ½ of her crew (the watch) all sleeping on the deck, a man steering and myself walking alone on the poop with a fine sea around me, and above a beautiful clear starry vault with the moon in all her splendour, and you have an idea of the *Woodford* and the situation of your humble servant, and I can truthfully say that, lonely and solitary as it may appear, I can reckon many happy hours spent in this manner; at such times I seem to have memory of the happiest hours of my life again, and how irresistibly do these recollections of absent friends pursue their way to the best fullness of the heart.

20th. Every appearance of a breeze at noon, 3.0 p.m. strong breezes and clear weather, 5.0, the wind took us all aback in a heavy squall, the wheel ropes gave way and we split our fore top gallant sail, 6.0, in first reefs of fore and main sail and reefed the mizzen top sail; very squally, with much lightning in the SW Symprisometer falling. Symps. 30.6.

21st. At daylight more moderate, out all reefs and made sail, strong breezes and clear weather, going about 8 knots and ½ per hour.

4 p.m. Very unsettled appearance at stern, turned the hands out and took in 1st reefs of topsails, reefed and furled the mainsails, ½ past 10 took in 2nd reef of main topsail, ship rolling very heavily over the long sea. Dinner table making bad weather, pea soup capsized and a clean sweep of plates, knives, forks, etc. However it must blow uncommon hard before I'd lose my dinner, so jammed myself up in one corner and made a good one, on roast pork and apple pie.

22nd. Performed divine service in the prison and cuddy, it blowing too hard to have it on the quarter deck. A poet of early date says:

---

[57] Amsterdam and St Paul are two isolated islands in the Indian Ocean.

> Our paper, pens and ink and we
> Are greatly tossed about at sea.

and I think I can agree with him, for I am obliged at this moment to write jammed up between a chest and my writing desk; squally weather and a falling glass. Ther. 65. Symps. 30.14.

23rd. Strong breezes and squally weather; last night about midnight, whilst reefing the main topsail, [the] clew gave way and the men were all obliged to get out to the yard arm to prevent the sail knocking them off the yard. They . . . at length got an opportunity and six got into the top. The squalls were terribly heavy, and we who were on the fore topsail yard were obliged to go off and stop in the top until it lulled again. Captain Chapman unfortunately very unwell and ought to be in bed, but obliged to attend on deck. Symps. fell to 29.92., with very heavy appearance and much lightning.

24th. Very strong breezes from the westward, the symprisometer as low as 29.90, very continued heavy squalls, some of them heavy enough to tear the masts out of her, at 5 o'clock the main topsail gave way, hauled it up and repaired it, double reefed and set it again. Split the fore topsail at [?] fore topmast; stay sail, unbent it and got a new one out. 4.0 p.m. the symp. rose again and before 10 o'clock was up to 30.21, but no better appearance. We have had a good deal of hail with some of the squalls, and bitterly cold air. Got the dead lights on the lower after windows, the ladies all abed and frightened out of their wits. Midnight, double-reefed the fore topsail, reefed and furled the mainsail, squalls coming one after the other, strong and heavy, with lightning to the westward, indeed I thought several times the topmast would have gone over the sides. Glass rising fast, but no improvement in appearances.
Symps. 6 a.m. 29.90, 9 a.m. 29.91, 12 noon 29.95, 4 p.m. 30.0, 8 p.m. 30.12, 10 p.m. 30.21, 12 midnight 30.24; depression [?] of not knowing when this weather will become fair after the recovery of the glass.

25th. I never was better pleased in my life than when I was relieved last night; the anxiety I felt under the press of sail we were carrying I cannot describe. I am sure no one can be easier than myself when, in my judgement, the canvas is equal to the breeze, and no one can be more miserable than I when I think the ship is carrying too much sail . . . in my humble opinion it is in the end a folly, as this ship loses in bad steering what she gains in her speed, besides the additional wear and tear. I should just notice that, when at dinner yesterday we felt the same motion as if the ship was touching the bottom slightly, the Captain immediately jumped on deck, as we have laid down in the charts as very doubtful lots of shoals etc., but there was no appearance whatever of shoal water, and we concluded it must be the rudder. Evening, out all reefs and set the stud sails fore and aft, with an appearance of light winds. Symps. 4 a.m. 30.30, 8 a.m. 30.31, noon 30.34, 4.0 p.m. 30.36, 12 midnight 30.38.

26th. This morning it fell, light winds and nearly calm, and about noon it became perfectly so. Some fine albatrosses settling near the ship gave the officers of the guard an opportunity of trying their skill at long balls with the common musket, at which the sergeant completely beat them and, I must say, amazed me with the correctness with which he fired to an immense distance; he nearly struck twice, but the motion of the ship was against him. Ther. 64. Symps. 30.39.

27th. This morning I thought there was as fine an appearance of a steady breeze and beautiful weather as could possibly be, but . . . the track of the weather predicted otherwise, and that most truly. It is now 8 o'clock p.m.; from all possible sail we have now got double-reefed topsails, reefed mainsails, royal masts and yards down and everything made snug for a breeze of wind; dark stormy clouds are rising in the north-west with vivid lightning, and a hollow-sounding wind mourns in the blocks of the rigging. Our last breeze, to those who desired before to see a gale, has had the effect of satisfying them . . . they would be willing to forego that pleasure and fancy what it would be, and I believe (if the truth was known) they are inwardly frightened at the thought of another blowing match. Mr Burnett says he will take to his bed and not quit it until it is over, should we have a gale of wind. Got good sights of the sun and moon and very satisfactory.

Glass remained at 29.96 for all this day until 4.0 p.m., when it rose, by midnight to 30.2.

28th. Glass at 8.0 a.m. 30.8 blowing a gale of wind at north-west with a very heavy sea, the wind being right aft makes her roll very heartily and has caused several contusions. In the morning watch, the liquor cask was broken open and a quantity of rum stolen, the thieves or takers all apparent from their drunkenness. At noon searched all their chests and, having found a quantity in one of the fellows' possession, who is a noted rascal, got the bilboes [i.e. prisoners in fetters] up on the poop and put into durance vile hand and foot, with the comfort of having bread and water only; the rest of the watch have their grog stopped until further orders. Whilst at dinner today the table, with all upon it, fetched away, though with but little loss and immense laughing on the parts of the party. I cannot imagine a more exquisite scene for a caricaturist, dishes and tables flying to port, ladies' shrieks, longshore people holding on by the stanchions with terror in their countenances, whilst the sea birds were intent on saving their dinners only; . . . then assisting to secure all afresh which, when accomplished, general fun succeeded to (what many would fain make us believe had not been the case) desperate fright.

29th. More moderate, out all reefs and set stud sails, fine breeze and much swell; at 11.0 a.m,, whilst performing divine service in the cuddy, the ship, taking a tremendous roll to starboard, capsized nearly all the congregation, which had such an effect upon the visible muscles of all present that, at the words 'Here endeth the 1st lesson', the Captain thought it better to end altogether. 8.0 p.m., whilst carrying the lower stud sail in the first watch, the man at the wheel let the ship come right into the wind and she filled again; she carried away the boom and we lost about 2/3rds of the lower stud sail, which with a bang went into 3 pieces.

30th, 2.0 a.m. In my watch, thinking [that] although at the time . . . a moderate breeze . . . it [was] looking suspicious, I furled the top gallant sails and reported it to the Captain. By the time he came up on deck, it came on like a clap of thunder, and we had to double-reef the topsails and furl the mainsail. I found the smps. had fallen to 29.80 in the Captain's cabin; my own I had not observed, on account of not being able to leave the deck. Strong breezes throughout the day, with much sea. As we approach the islands of St Paul and Amsterdam, we renew our acquaintance with large and numerous descriptions of aquatic birds, Cape pigeons amongst the number very numerous. Got the lumbago, a shocking partner at reefing. Ther. 66.6, Symps. 30.1.

1st of 11th. At daylight the island of Amsterdam was right ahead and at half past 7 we were abreast it, a small barren island with that volcanic appearance most of these islands in the middle of the ocean have, though but partially. I consider these opportunities of renewing our acquaintance (tho' but by night) with the land, as some of the most pleasing incidents in the voyage and worth remembering, for the train of pleasing reflections brought in by them. It is an amazing relief to the eye, after it has been for months with nothing to gaze on around save the heavens above and waters beneath, to rest upon even such a barren, desolate-looking spot as Amsterdam. We got no meridian altitude yesterday and, the ship having gone farther to the northard than by our calculations, we took it for St Pauls (which is to . . . the southard of it), but our latitude corrected the error. Our longitude was out 2 miles, the ship being east of account. I imagine 3 more weeks, running as we have lately done, will see us at our port. Ther. 66, Symps. 29.90.

2nd. Today the symprisometer fell lower than it has done all the voyage, to 29.56, with a dark, threatening appearance to the northard and much lightning. 3.0 p.m. turned out the hands, double-reefed the topsails, reefed and furled the mainsail and, to cut short this lingo, made all ready for a gale of wind. 10.0 p.m., after a heavy squall, the wind flew into the south-west and we were in fact disappointed, for it was merely an 8 knot breeze all night and we might have carried all sail; this remains to be accounted for, and until then I should think it must be accounted a failure in the instrument.

3rd. The symps. up to 30.8 with cloudy weather and cold southerly wind; a hail shower we had this morning was heavier than usual, and bitterly cutting. Two of the prisoners today (who have hitherto conducted themselves well and been at work in the hold), having some rum improperly given them by the ship's steward, one of them got drunk, but I cannot think the other was; however the Doctor accused him of being so, and he persisting in it that he was not, the Surgeon collared him (I think very improperly), upon which the prisoner desired him to desist or he would hold him off, which he did. The Doctor immediately had him up, and the rest of the prisoners, the guard turned out and [the Doctor] stated the offence, telling the rest he would punish them worse than giving them 4 dozen, which the prisoner in question was to receive if ever the offence was committed again. He then ordered the constable to seize him up . . . when . . . he declared solemnly the Doctor had struck him, and that he would see if he could not obtain justice in the country. He received the 4 dozen lashes without a movement of the body being perceived or a single alteration of countenance, and then dressed himself. I am inclined to say I would not have had him punished had I been the Captain, but have confined him to take trial in Hobart Town, when my impression is the Surgeon would have been in the wrong; for, from having him [the prisoner] in the hold a good deal to assist me, I know him the most civil and quiet man I could wish for, and I cannot think him drunk, because he had had but one glass of rum, whilst the other had been getting some before, of another person. The punishment for a prisoner thus lifting hand to the Surgeon would, I imagine, put his life in danger, unless it could be proved that he did it in self-defence. I am sure, almost . . . that the latter was the case, for I know the Surgeon's hot temper and have seen him just about to strike once before. Ther. 65. Symps. 29.79.

4th. This morning the Doctor released nearly all the prisoners out of irons, excepting . . . those offenders of yesterday, who are doubly loaded and handcuffed and confined on the forecastle; now this I consider an act of injustice, because one of them said he was drunk when the Doctor charged him with it. . . . 2 or 3 instances have occurred before of the same offence, and were punished by stopping their wine, while this poor fellow is double-ironed and his wine, beef, pork and everything else stopped from him. However, I cannot set myself up for a judge of these matters; those ought to know best that have had to do with them before. Ther. 64½. Symps. 30.29.

5th. Performed divine service as usual, morning and evening. I find this day as precious as it is ashore as a day of rest and abstraction . . ., altho' not so much . . . [nor] can it be on board ship as on land, yet it bears a proportion [i.e. of rest and abstraction] which to me is very grateful. A line, which was towing overboard today, I saw had a large bird[58] attached to it, having entangled itself in flying past it; we hauled it in for inspection and then, after notching his feathers to know him [again], released him again; he measured 6 feet from tip to tip, had a large head, bill and eye, the latter very brilliant and prominent, its colour was a dusky black, with lighter feathers round the neck. When upon the deck at liberty, like all sea birds, he had not the power to rise. Threatening appearance to the NW, with a falling glass. Ther. 62. Symps. 30.0.

6th. Last night it came on strong and heavy from the NW, with tremendously heavy squalls of wind and rain. Mr Govey sick, gave the chief and myself 8 hours more duty between us; myself very unwell, back nearly broken with rheumatism, which makes my duty as a leader in a gale of wind doubly painful, but I am determined I will not give in until I am not able to sit in a chair and look out for the steerage of the ship. Afternoon finer weather, made more sail, but the glass uncommonly low and I am sure we shall yet have a heavy gale of wind, though we are carrying much sail – I think foolishly.

[Marginal note] Symps. fell today from 30 before midnight to 29.22, which I should like to know if not very remarkable. I never remember to have seen so wild an appearance in my life, the sky was certainly awful to look up to, and I could not help contemplating it with a kind of fear I never did before.

7th. A very heavy gale of wind came on this morning at 11 o'clock a.m., split our sails and plagued odd joisting. I cannot write at such a season, so must leave descriptions till a better opportunity; in bad spirits from my poor unfortunate terrible complaint, which going aloft and getting wet thro' ill suits.

---

[58] Probably an immature albatross.

8th. Blowing fresh, yet going about 8 knots per hour but steadily compared to yesterday, the gale has been heavy and uncomfortable from continued rain, which is ten times worse than any breezes. Saw some seaweed this morning, tho' but a small quantity. We have had none of the Burnett family at table today, all of them being in bed. Miss M. Burnett, our intended Mrs Chapman, has been unwell 2 or 3 days, the faithful swain has had therefore an opportunity of showing his anxiety for her recovery. Water getting very bad, and worst of all brackish; it spoils the tea and everything else.

9th. Strong breezes and squally weather seems to be the sum of all I have to remark. In the evening took in single reef and made the ship snug for night, a very necessary precaution, in my opinion, in these latitudes and with a low glass. Midnight, strong breeze and thick weather, Miss H. Burnett fortified me this night with some hot mulled or spiced port, a most comfortable warmer for a cold night.

10th. Poor Mr Burnett, who during all the last blowing weather has obtained no sleep, has been taking opium pills and is in a dreadfully nervous state; they have not had the effect of making him sleep and have therefore had a terrific effect upon him. He says he believes, if this weather lasts, he shall be taken ashore in a strait-jacket. He declares he would sooner lose his life than come to sea again. Not much wind all day, but towards night very strong again. Ther. 62½. Symps. 30.

11th. I suppose tomorrow week, if this breeze continues, will see us off Van Dieman's Land; we were yesterday in the longitude of Cape Leewin, on the coast of New Holland. From the time of our leaving the line we have not had a foul wind 12 hours, but have [been] running as constantly as if we were in a trade wind. The westerly winds appear to me to prevail in the southern latitudes more than in the northern hemisphere; it would be useless trying to get home so far against them.

12th. Performed divine service as usual in the cuddy. The Doctor, thinking it too cold on deck, has had his 'dearly beloved brethren' in the prison. We now frequently see quantities of seaweed of the large-leaved kind and yellow-coloured, a sure indication of our being within no very great distance of land. The weather seems now to be more settled than lately. The symprisometer steady at 30.10 and moderate 3 degrees breeze, which is a great luxury to Mr Burnett. Last night, one of the larger apprentices having beaten a lesser, he was sent to the top masthead to look out for squalls all night; he is not yet allowed to come down. I suppose, from just having seen him there (11.0 a.m.) this is what I call a 'cooler' for immoderate courage and will have a good effect, I should hope. 4.0 p.m. Yesterday night, whilst the ship's steward was under the after hatchway, a chest fell from the lower deck upon his bare head and cut it dreadfully; we immediately got him up and the Doctor dressed the wound, which he says he would not have had for one thousand pounds, so I consider it to be bad.

13th. Light northerly breezes, which makes us willing to believe we shall not arrive so soon as we calculated, but as all our calculations are made with this proviso, 'If the breeze stands', we are never to be accused of giving passengers wrong information. Yesterday the prisoners were all called aft and asked if they could read or write, and if they said 'yes' it was proved, by making them write their name or reading a verse or two in the Testament, but of the 99, forty could read and write and 19 others read only; all the greatest rogues wanted [i.e. lacked] both acquirements generally. Ther. 68. Symps. 30.0.

14th, Still, almost calm, the last pig died yesterday, a sheep remains; when that dies, farewell fresh provisions. Blow, my sweet westerly breezes, blow, and send us into the latitude of lowing herds and squeaking swine! No cheerful sounds of the cock's shrill clarion now welcomes morn; the stalls, all deserted, now echo no more the bleating of sheep, whilst our old cow, after surviving all her woolly friendly with an emaciated countenance and ribs staring through her skin, looks mournfully at her calf, without a doubt thinking, 'Thou wilt soon be motherless', a thought which seems mutual, from its hanging its lower lip and its hair all standing on end, proclaiming that the famine is exceedingly sore in the land. N.B. they have had no hay the last week, but have been fed with mashes etc. to keep them alive. Ther. 68. Symps. 29.98.

15th. Foul wind, which is sickening [?] yet not without comfort; if it shifts it must be for the better, being now due east. I cannot imagine a much more trying thing for the temper, than being placed in a situation where much respect is expected to be paid to a superior officer, who is one you cannot help despising from his wanting every requisite claim to it. This reflection arises from the unwarrantable behaviour of Mr Rybot to me in endeavouring continually to make my conduct appear to the Captain in the worst possible light, and although I am sure my wish has always been to be upon easy (though not familiar) terms with him and forward his views as much as possible, yet I believe from pure envy he is constantly aiming to destroy the good understanding existing between the Captain and myself; did it arise from my being exempted from any part of my duty which fell upon him to perform, there would be a cause, but I am sure so far from it is the true state of the case, that a great deal of what properly should be performed by him, falls to my lot (I mean in the theoretical part) and I am sure, if I held the situation of second in command of a ship, I could never be easy if I were not the person to whom the Captain looked up to for judgement in the navigating of her. But it is our duty to make good come out of evil if possible, and I know not [but] that we may frequently gather as much instruction from the errors of some by avoiding them and their consequent effects, as we may from the abilities of others, and I hope (from what I now feel) that, whenever I may be called upon to fill that situation, I may always, if I observe little errors or omissions on the part of those under me, act in a more brother-officer-like manner than tale bearing to the Commander, by mentioning it to themselves. Ther. 66. Symps. 29.86.

16th. The symprisometer fell last night to 29.32, we shortened sail and this morning got the breeze from the northard stiff and strong, double reefs etc. Contrary as the winds were yesterday, and little as we had the last 24 hours . . . we managed to make 3½ degrees of longitude, which inclined us to think there must be a current here to the eastward, which I believe will frequently be found where winds blow continually from one quarter. Most likely we shall be there next week, about the 21st. of *Moore's Almanack* style, a day before or a day after. The cook took sick today, and consequently there was a bad dinner for the after guard; in small vessels he is dubbed Doctor and, I think, very appropriately, for to him we look for restorations when nature feels exhausted. Finished today Boswell's *Life of Dr Johnson*, a most entertaining work, not merely on account of Johnson alone, but also contemporary literary characters. I cannot say I felt what his biographer wished his readers to feel, profound admiration of his character; I admire his talents, but dislike the man.

17th. Fine breeze from the north-west, began painting ship outside to smarten her up for harbour, ran last 24 hours 240 miles, the greatest day's work this passage. We now look forward to a speedy arrival; after being 15 weeks at sea, one week seems comparatively nothing.

18th. Smartening up with paint, oil, tar, etc. in every direction, but unfortunately as usual it rained, and has run all the side black into white etc.; I expect after all our pains we shall look about as fine as a half-scraped carrot! Wind northerly, hearts light at the thought of soon parting with the thieves.

19th. Performed divine service in the cuddy and prison, all comfortable and clean in braid, sailors in their white duck trousers and frocks [i.e. tunics] and their clean Scotch caps, give that Sabbath-like air to the ship which the country people under similar circumstances do to a village. Tomorrow we bend cables and unstow anchors.

20th. At daylight saw no land, the sun at rising gave us no view of it, but as soon as the mists cleared away and the sun got above the horizon arch, the high bluff land of Van Dieman's was visible from the deck. Its first appearance is as exactly like the coast of Scotland as can be, and forcibly reminded me of Caithnesshire. Yesterday at noon we saw a strange sail ahead, by one o'clock we were near enough to communicate with signals. She proved [to be] the *Leander* and said she was going into port (Van Dieman's Land not being in her vocabulary), and he should steer E by S; we told him our longitude and corrected his course to eastward, which he steered. This morning it was as much as we could do to see him. At 9 o'clock we were close in with the land, whose bleak, sterile aspect to the southward pleased the unfortunates but little; this sight of the place of their destination was the means of calling forth the only curiosity I ever saw them evince. All dangers are here seen, and we run between small rocks, with tremendous squalls at times, in perfect safety. As we got further to the eastward the land in the valleys began to look more fruitful, and when we rounded Tasman's Head, the entrance into Storm Bay, I think the scenery was as interestingly grand as I ever remember to have seen. Midnight, blowing very hard, lying to for daylight, squalls at times very severe; we have reefed no less than 3 several times within the last 12 hours and then shook them out again. 'Blow a Southwester and let's get up!'

21st. Made sail again this morning with a foul wind but, by watching favourable times, we got by 6 to the foot of the river and commenced our acquaintance with this part of the world by welcoming the pilot on board the *Woodford*, who soon brought up to an anchorage; he came in a whale boat manned with 2 prisoners and 2 emancipated convicts. One of the prisoners, on coming on deck, was immediately recognised by a prisoner and surrounded with eager enquiries after the situation they were doomed to fill. At 7.0 p.m. we came to an anchor in 18 fathoms, close under the land. When the watch was set the pilot came into the cuddy, where he was pretty soon beset with enquiries from the ladies and they plied him without mercy, so that one could not get one word in edgeways for about 2 hours.

22nd. At daylight, up anchor and made sail; when the anchor came off the ground, she drifted into deep water and a famous job we had to get it up. Mount Table, at the foot of which Hobart Town is situated, had in the early part of the morning a grand appearance, and indeed altogether the scenery is strikingly beautiful, and a charming relief to the eye that has for 16 weeks, with but little variation, rested on sky and water.

23rd. We have kept underweigh all night, but to little purpose, though before dark last evening we were in sight of Hobart Town. The naval officer boarded us about 6.0 and Mr Burnett left us in the pilot boat; we got a fair wind for about an hour, which put us in a fair way for getting there in a few minutes, but it soon failed and, a strong breeze coming down, we had to turn into the cove, where we let go our anchor, after a passage of 16 weeks and 3 days from Portsmouth. We found here the *Hugh Crawford* for London, the *Leander* which we spoke [to] at sea and which had arrived 2 days before, and the brig *Venus*. Lots of gentlemen holding official situations have been coming aboard all day, and the acting secretary mustered the prisoners by tens and asked them if they had all received their rations and if they had any complaints to make. Three made complaints, whose names were taken and [the complaints] will be properly attended to; they [the officials] all expressed admiration at the clean and fine appearance of our ship and of the prisoners; the prison and hospital were inspected and highly approved of.

Hobart Town is situated at the foot of a mountain whose giant form makes the town look very diminutive, but as you approach and come close to the quay it has a pretty, tho' straggling, appearance and the houses, all built upon light and modern plans, give you the idea immediately of being in a youthful colony, an idea that perhaps first takes place from seeing spots partially cleared, and a house just rising amid the stumps of felled trees. The church has a large appearance from the cove, but I must say no more until I take a trip ashore.

24th. This morning the official persons came on board and took the height and particular marks of the prisoners, asked them their place of birth and about their crimes, how many times they had been convicted, whether they were married and what family, if they had any relations here and where, asked them whether they had received their rations and if they had been humanely treated by the Surgeon, Captain, officers, people of the ship, and took all their answers down. They at the same time asked the Surgeon about their behaviour, and he told them about their characters from gaol in England, hulks[59], and on the passage, but gave them no advice. At 2.0 p.m., whilst weighing the stern anchor, the boat nearly capsized and shot me overboard; I swam up to the attendant boat and got

---

[59] Hulks were ships with their masts removed (or shot away). In the 18th and 19th century they were frequently used as prisons.

in, in quarter less [than] no time, and as we could not get it [i.e. the anchor], I went on board to shift [it], first sending away the boatswain and three boats' crews, to try it in another manner. I had hardly got up on the poop to look at them, than she capsized again with us and sent the smaller boat over, too, sending about 13 or 14 men into the water, 5 of whom could not swim; 2 who could, threw off their jackets and swam to the cutter, [got] up into her [and] cast her adrift and picked up the rest, two of whom were only to be seen by their hands above the water.

It was truly happy to see them all dripping safe on board, gave them all a throat-warmer to prevent their catching cold, and went back and righted the boats, to do which the swimmers jumped into the water again and, by main strength, got up the long boat to the gig, [which] they soon righted. Got the news that we are freighted from Sydney to England direct; most agreeable to all, and has raised my spirits today 20 per cent. The mountain, like its namesake, covered with a cloud, which I think foretells rain and squalls of wind, for that is the weather we have had since we first sighted it, and terribly uncomfortable it is. Passengers yet remain on board.

25th. Wet drizzly weather. The *Hugh Crawford* sailed for Sydney, to return here again to complete her cargo and take in her passengers.

We are to have home with us Mr Hamilton, the acting Colonial Secretary, and his lady and a Miss, I forget her name, and if we get any at Sydney we shall again make a party home. The prisoners are to leave next two days.

26th. Performed divine service in the prison and cuddy. Several persons in office called and left their cards with Captain Chapman and the officers of the guard. Dined with us today Mr & Mrs Hamilton, provisions all excellent (which we get from the shore), but the beef is but lean. The cloud not upon Mt Table today and, as I thought it would be, fine weather; the fragrance from the shore as the sun got up was quite refreshing and makes me regret stopping on board, which we are compelled to, until the thieves land. Dr Scott, the colonial surgeon, brought on [board] a nosegay for the ladies, but nothing strange or rare, many of them wild flowers.

27th. This morning, at half past 8 a.m., all the prisoners were landed; whilst in the boat, that was to convey them from the last link that united their native land and this place of their exiles, they seemed very low-spirited and lost a good deal of the assurance they always possessed in so large a degree. Broke bulk and began discharging government stores. . . . Ther. 66.

28th. Discharging cargo, convicts from the shore in charge of a corporal knocking down the prison. Fine, clear weather, with slight showers now and then. Vegetables, which were sent on board from the government gardens, excellent except carrots, some of which, though fair to the eye, were as hard as a stick within. Ther. 68.

29th. This morning the corporal of the guard fell down the main hatchway and severely hurt himself; his wife, who witnessed it, immediately fainted away. We immediately sent ashore for the doctor, who pronounces him much injured. At 6.0 p.m. a boat ¾ mile astern of us was seen to capsize, the chief mate immediately went away with our cutter and 4 hands and . . . another boat which happened to be alongside, to the assistance of the sufferers. It proved to be the naval officer's boat; [he] had been floating on the water and . . . was just able to keep up when our boat pulled him up; she had upset in a squall whilst in stays, and it was fortunate for them . . . [we were] so near [that] they could be observed and assistance rendered. A signal has been up for a ship in sight – but what, we have not yet learned. Ther. 63.

30th. To 2nd of 12th month. Discharging cargo and passengers' baggage, carpenters fitting stalls upon the lower deck, for the reception of 1,500 sheep for Sydney; also getting wood ready for the same in the hold. Arrived the colonial brig *Amity* in command of a lieutenant; a man-of-war in distress proceeding to Cape Leewin with a detachment of the 39th regiment, I understand, to watch the motions of the French in that quarter. Thers. range from 65 to 82, consequently very variable weather, with strong breezes at times. Fish here in great plenty; bait and put the line over, and you immediately catch a small fish, very sweet, and nicely boned.

3rd. Little did I think when a schoolboy and [looking] upon the chart of the world that hung in ample size upon the wall pointing out the distant land, that my lot would be so cast as to know it, with others, more intimately; this thought arises, amongst others, as I am sitting upon a huge oak tree to which, as to all of its size around, the settler has applied his forest thinning. Far below is Hobart Town, the cove and the Derwent seem many miles [away]; on my right Mount Table, clothed at the foot with a forest, the trees of which decrease in size [with altitude] until they terminate in bush and leave the naked rock covered with snow; on my left a mountainous tract, the foot of which cultivation has beautifully clothed, and at my back fine, undulating country, greatly cleared and brought into cultivation. I have altogether as beautiful a view around me as can be conceived; the birds are singing about me and I am highly delighted and enjoying to the full the pleasures of a foreign land though, were it not for the recollection of the voyage and the absence of a friend, I could easily fancy myself in Britain, [were it not] that, whilst the top of the mountain has snow upon it, in this valley all [is] summer, and whilst in England it is 'come stir the fire and let's draw in', here am I in . . . light dress as warm as toast, waistcoat unbuttoned and hat in hand, leaning on [a] friend's palings and, with an impudent face, spying out his land. As I walked towards the little house of refreshment, (do not think I am [implying] public house, for it was not one) I met an open-countenanced fellow leading a fine horse and dressed quite in our country's sober fashion and, wanting somebody to enquire a little of, got into conversation with him, first about his charge, then where he came from, and soon found no great way from Hitchin, from Shillington, from whence he said he had been transported for 7 years for pheasant and game . . . shooting, that he was tired of it and intended coming home as soon as possible, for which purpose he was saving money. I told him that wages [at home] were very low etc. etc., but he said his friends were very well off and that his own folly, not want, had led him to his punishment; he begged me to take a letter, which I promised and, giving all good advice (seasoned with a shilling to add to his savings), travelled on. From his respectful, unsoliciting manner and from his charge, I have no doubt he is amongst the best of the class [of felons], some of whom, as they pass, insult and rot you with their looks, or pass some impudent remark, beside being dirty and noisy, and [are] in fact people no one would like to meet on a dark night, complete out persons [i.e. outsiders]. I soon after met a Sussex farmer, who had come out as a settler but had got a bad grant of land and is now a bailiff; from him I could learn nothing about the lie [?] of the country, except that the Derwent was there, such a mighty fine run of water, as broad as from here to that there. . . . The rest was all about filling out cattle . . . when the grass got better, and killing as fine beef as there is in England, so I left him, and got a steak at this aforementioned [refreshment] house, and a pint of rich London porter, for which I paid only 3 [shillings] and 8 pence, a kind of forbidding welcome [from the owner] and an encouragement to wear large and well-supplied pockets. However, I got from him 2 fossils in limestone from a quarry 2 miles further inland, one of them very good; he also put me in a line for the ship by [way of] the river, where he said I would find plenty of shells, and thanks to him, he was right, for the rocks were blue with mussels, and the sand white with cockles; so much for the shells of Van Dieman's Land! At the top of a hill behind Hobart Town which commands a very fine prospect the Governor is building a house, the garden for which must, from its appearance, have been long in cultivation; the stone of the building, which is very good, is quarried close by, which makes it very convenient. And now to conclude, as tea is on [the] table; . . . the scenery was grand, the ground in places good, though in others [there is] very little depth of soil, the stock bad, flowers numerous – but few, uncommon, shrubs, the reverse; people scarce and some very civil, others as impudent as they dare be, but on the whole I think it to be a place a man might be happy in, and one where he will enjoy in his own [life] time the fruits of his labours and not, like America, be only working for posterity. But he must not dislike prisons, to live among thieves.

Half past 4, I have got on board and dined and sat me down to write a little more of what I have seen. I walked down from the hill, when I passed partially [?] cleared land full of cattle, to New [?] Town, which is a little scattered village with a good deal of well cultivated land about it, with heavy crops upon it and adorned with an elegant and tasteful mansion, the residence of the Attorney-General, the grounds of which and the gardens are . . . hedges of geraniums. An arm of the river runs before it and gives it the advantage of water carriage to Hobart Town, from which it is distant 2 miles. There is also another very extensive house and premises, the property of a man who was transported and who is still a prisoner of the crown, the only title they allow themselves to be called by. The garden was full of flowers which yield no perfume – and luckily, so I think, otherwise it would be quite overpowering. The kitchen [garden] partition was teeming with gooseberries, currants, green peas, beans and indeed all kinds of vegetables and fruit.

7th. Today dined at his Honour the Colonial Secretary's, where I heard tomorrow Captain Chapman leads to the altar Miss M. Burnett; spent the evening with them after seeing them on board the ship, and ashore again when they had been to arrange about the cabins, and when I most sincerely regret to say I lost a watch, the gift of a dear relation (who, from his honourable years, I can scarcely hope to see again when I return), as well as a seal, a present from two of my very intimate friends. I lost them whilst leaning over the quarter [deck] ordering the cutter round to the side, my fob being shallow and it slipping out. I have made every attempt to recover it, but in vain; however, I shall not desist, if I can procure a dredger. One of our men today, on being struck by Mr Rybot on refusing to obey his orders to put a stranger over the side, is confined upon the poop, to remain there until the Captain chooses to release him. The people on coming on board complained they could not live with Mr Rybot. . . .

8th. This morning from the ship saw the party going to church at half past 8; when the ceremony was over, fired a salute with 21 cannonades and dressed the ship with flags from masthead to deck. As soon as we had fired, I ran ashore to breakfast by appointment with bride and bridegroom at Mr Hamilton's, who was the Colonial Secretary – and as gentlemanly a man and as kind as I could wish to meet. I wished them joy, and presented them with the mutual good wishes of all on board for their happiness etc. We sat down to a very excellent breakfast, at which I was the only stranger, and afterwards saw them off in the Governor's carriage to New Norfolk, 22 miles distant, where they stopped to the 13th. Everything was provided on board to make all parties happy and Jack lived like gentlemen, so much to their satisfaction that a dry fellow exclaimed, as he carried his cake to his messmates, 'I wish our Captain would marry every week, if this is the plan!' They were allowed no spirits but beer, and a fiddler, so that they were very merry and, I am glad to say, without anyone being drunk or quarrelsome except Mr Rybot (of which I expect to have to say much hereafter). At sunset we fired a gun, at dark burned blue lights at each yardarm. In the cuddy we had an excellent dinner and the company of two gentlemen from the shore, tho' 3 hour before it was ready; I took my gun into the bush, where I shot about 10 parrots and parakeets of the most beautiful plumage, which I regret to say I could not preserve, from its coming on heavy rain and wetting completely through [and] spoiling all my birds for the purpose.

And now for poor Rybot, but 'tis a long story, so I must e'en mind my pen.

The fiddler had been called down in to the steerage to play to the midshipmen who wished to dance. Mr R. came down and ordered him out, they (to avoid disappointment) sent [some] one to get his flute, but in the meantime vented their spleen upon the chief mate by pushing down his door and a desk fixture on it; hearing the laughing he jumped down into the steerage and in an instant, seeing Ensign Berkeley looking into his cabin, he struck him at the back of the neck and he fell towards his bed place; [Mr Rybot] repeated his blows, until he was prevented by the third mate and steward. I am happy to say I was engaged with Captain Welsh and his friend in conversation about the colony at the time, and heard nothing of it until Captain Meyrick, stepping out of his cabin, began to upbraid Mr R. with his conduct and threatened to prosecute him for it, at which Captain Welsh said 'It is time to be off,' and, it raining, I went to procure them coats etc. which, when they had put on and gone from the side, I returned, but all was quiet; Mr R. in his cabin and Mr B. (who was bleeding) and Captain M. in theirs. I immediately myself set the watch and went to bed, determining to know nothing about it, except what I have related from hearsay, and not from questions asked by me. If it be true, it will read R. a pretty sound lesson. Ther. 67.

8th. (cont.) All I related last night proves to be correct and, as Captain M. assured him, he this day got a warrant made out and constables apprehended him and took him ashore, where he had to find bail for his appearance on the 12th next, but to appear tomorrow with M. and B. to see if it cannot be brought to an arrangement – which, I fear, will not be the case, from he having so often offended the officers of the guard. Mr Govey the third, the steward and cuddy servant are subpoenaed for witnesses on the prosecution. Ther. 89.

9th. At 11.0 all parties attended, when it was decided to appear on the 12th before the Commandant. The officers have engaged a solicitor, as well as Mr R., so the expenses will prove heavy, and as he cannot procure a single witness and yesterday confessed all about it to the magistrate and has only to hope for a corner to slip out, I am afraid he will go to leeward – for which I should be sorry, though I should like a lecture read to him, as I think it would do him good. Sharp, one of the apprentices, on being questioned if he knocked the desk down by Mr R.'s solicitor, said 'No,' though he certainly did do it, as many can tell. Ther. 70.

10th. Went ashore after dinner and took my gun, saw a good deal of country with but little game until, as I returned, I shot a black swan. On getting on board about 10.0 I found the Captain had been on board, had spoken to Mr Rybot and discharged him, for which I was sorry, as I think he will be sufficiently punished without [that]. Ther. 69.

11th. This morning the Captain told me to consider myself chief officer of the ship, and that he should introduce me as such to the ship's company. I spoke about R., but the Captain would hear nothing for him, but I dare say he will take him again, on our return here in another 6 weeks. We are to take 15 desperate convicts to Port Jackson [Sydney]; the trial does not come on until the 15th. Ther. 81.

16th. This morning at daylight fired our signal gun for sailing, and came to sea. The pilot left us off the foot of the river about 9 o'clock – then a beautiful fine morning, now, at 8.0 p.m., we are lying to off Van Dieman's Land with a heavy gale of wind directly in our teeth. I regret exceedingly to say that, whilst reefing our fore topsail in Storm Bay in a very heavy breeze of wind, Douglas Graham, a seaman working his passage to Sydney, a quiet, well-disposed man, fell head foremost from the topsail yard overboard and never rose again. We lowered the cutter immediately and the boatswain, a sailor and myself went immediately astern, but could not find him. It blew so hard that we could not fetch [up alongside] the ship again. The Captain wore the ship and took us in tow, whilst they again wore upon the larboard tack; I thought we should have lost her whilst hooking on, the ship pitching a good deal and sending spray flying from her; however, we got [the cutter] hoisted up and secured again to the quarter, then furled the fore and mizzen topsails, mainsail [and] jib, and tied her to, under the main topsail and fore sail.

Still lying to, blowing very heavy, which makes our 800 sheep very uncomfortable, but on the whole I think they do very well, and I hope we shall land nearly all in good condition. We also received at Hobart Town 13 most notorious prisoners, hardened murderers, or rather accessories [to murder], who are going to pass the rest of their days at Norfolk Island, where they are treated with the greatest rigour and work very hard; they are all ironed, and we have therefore that horrid jailclanking in our ears. Our party now consists of the officers of the guard, Mrs Chapman, Col. Balfour of the 40th and three children and Mr Wright, a New South Wales merchant, so that we still muster pretty well at table – or rather shall do, for at this time they are all sick. 4.0 p.m., it fell less wind and became [a] fair trade [wind], all sail and stood to the northard, spirits up one hundred per cent.

18th. Made 90 miles, all going on very comfortably on board and I hope will continue to do so, sincerely desiring that I may be able to avoid the errors of my predecessor and to give satisfaction, and although I know very well the berth is one I am not, in my own opinion, capable of filling in a proper manner, . . . I hope the will for the deed will be taken for a time, and that my endeavours to fill a very responsible situation properly may be attended with satisfaction to myself and then, after doing my best and using every exertion to forward the interests of my owners, I shall calmly look forward to the event, not doubting of a reward. I am afraid it is my temper which, being none of the best, often rises, to the vexation of those about me, and greatly so of myself. So, Ned, remember 'A soft answer turneth away wrath,' and 'Be not hasty unto anger,' are two old and excellent proverbs.

19th. Anyone imagining a Captain saves [on provisions] by seasickness ought to have been at breakfast this morning, to be convinced they are at fault! To see the wreck of a table, but a short time before covered with bread, butter, eggs, mutton chops, sausages and nice things for the ladies, to tempt them, poor things, to take a little, would have been sufficient to undeceive them of this! I am sure we ought to have a quick passage, or else famine will pay us another visit, excepting in the way of mutton, of which we have a very good supply at hand. I really thought Pharaoh's lean kin had appeared again in the persons of our passengers, tho' not in the similitude of a dream but in the reality; for I believe, had it not been for fair shame, they would have been happy to have enjoyed a 2nd edition. This day we are off Bass Straits, with beautiful weather and fine breezes from the southward. Ther. 60.

20th. Progressing, tho' not very rapidly, owing to very light variable winds. Yesterday morning I caught a shark of the blue species, measuring 10 feet and weighing between 3 and 6 cwt.; we had to get a tackle to hoist him in. I quite thought myself sure of a very large pair of jaws with famous teeth, but some one or other (of the soldiers, I believe) tossed the head, backbone, tail, fins and all overboard, so that I am disappointed. Ther. 64.

21st. Ther. 67. We expect to be in Sydney the day after tomorrow and then commences our labour; I would sooner be at sea 10 times the length of time. It grows warmer and I have no doubt we shall find it hot enough at Port Jackson, but that I do not care, for all I desire is to be away again pretty quickly, being fearful our having to return to [Van Dieman's] Land will retard our journey home a good deal. It is not yet decided whether we return by the Horn or the Hope. I hope for some things the former, for others the latter.

22nd. This morning at day break saw the land of New South Wales from the deck; 39 miles from Sydney, we have been sailing for the port ever since, but have yet, at 6 o'clock, a long distance to go, which makes me imagine an error in our meridian latitude. Ther. 74.

23rd. A fine day with a strong breeze, but as foul as can blow from the northward; we have therefore no hopes of getting there until the wind changes, which I hope for most sincerely, as the sheep are beginning to die very fast, having lost 13. We have seen a good deal of the coast, which has nothing very remarkable about it, being in some places low and sandy but mostly cliff, and covered with bush, which makes it look but very unpromising. We yesterday found out one of our ordinary seamen in secreting a key that belonged to the grog cask, which had been lost some time, and which the possessor has made frequent use of [for] procuring liquor. Being fully convicted, the hands were turned out, the gratings rigged, and the prisoner seized up, when he received one doz, and [a] half of lashes. The people seemed very mutinous about it and two of them, being insolent, were confined upon the poop; it will, I think, show them they can be punished, and that [they] will not act improperly with impunity. Ther. 76.

24th. Light variable weather, found ourselves at daybreak 10 miles to leeward of last evening. Exchanged signals with the *Phoenix*, a ship from London on the same service, who has to take in her prisoners at the Cove of Cork or Dublin; she sailed the day after we arrived at Portsmouth, so we have beaten her [by] one month.

We are in sight of the head of Port Jackson, which is rather mortifying to be with a foul wind; lost last night 11 sheep, and how many we shall land no one can tell, if this warm weather and light winds continue. Performed Divine service on the quarterdeck. Last evening one of the prisoners was discovered making a saw out of a knife, but we cannot say for what purpose. Ther. 79.

25th. 10 p.m., all's well! We are in Sydney Cove, the finest harbour in the world, with delightful scenery and the best accommodation for shipping, being just the same, where we lie, as if [we] were in a dock. We found here the *Warspite* 74, *Success* and *Volage* frigates; Commander Brisham [?] who [had] hoisted his flag in the former, died three days before our arrival; his lady and daughter, who are in the ship, are expected to proceed to England. The merchantmen are about seven ships, some with prisoners and others loading for London; we all be within hail of each other without any inconvenience. After entering Port Jackson River, the sides of the river appear very delightful in many places, ornamented with handsome villas with verandas, as in all hot climates, and I think it on the whole a more pleasing, tho' not so picturesque, a scene as the Derwent presents, the latter being much more grand than the former. Furled sails, spliced the main brace and went to bed.

29th. I have been ashore and little do I like it, there is a feeling oppressive to the spirits in these colonies similar to that felt in a jail, everyone you meet you call 'convict' in thought as you eye them, else there are some good houses, good barracks for soldiers, good roads and good things – [though] at the same time [at] a good price. I called upon an attorney to deliver a packet of letters, he showed me into his office, chatted a little with his coat off, asked what news of England, satisfied himself, then made me understand 'I wish you to be off'. I took the point, and left him; and thus I was repaid for taking a packet which, as I was told, would give me an introduction into a gentleman's house, where I should meet with the greatest hospitality and in fact be quite at home! So much for bothering yourself with letters, to save a person 10 shillings expense at 20 shillings worth of bother to you! I like an acquaintance in every place, it gives a knowledge of localities one cannot otherwise obtain; here I thought to get one, I am mistaken! I had an idea shells and various curiosities were cheap here, now it is a fact that there are none to be procured in the place, I have tried in several directions and have obtained none, nor do I think I shall; the price of a New Zealand chief's head I asked, and was told 15 dollars.

10th of the first. After [a] good deal of bargaining we are taken up for the conveyance of the third regiment of infantry, or Buffs, to Bombay; tomorrow we leave this place to go down to a bay a short distance off to fetch our fresh water, there being but little to be got here, and that not certain, which is a great defect to the cove.

11th. We are now in a delightful bay called Rose [?], surrounded by hilly land close to a delightful and picturesque place called Viper Point, the residence of the naval officer but (on account of a destructive and extensive fire) sadly wasting the advantage of wooded surrounding land. We are obliged to roll all our casks a distance of three quarters of a mile, and that thro' the burnt trees, the dust of which blackens all our people of the watering party, so that they appear like scamps, more than like sailors.

28th. We are now out in the fair way for a start. That I have given no description of this place I can but allow, but when I look back on the past, and when I remember that I have been at work mentally and bodily from the day I arrived, I cannot charge myself with blame for writing less. I therefore beg the family of Beck, and all its branches that may peruse what here [?] is recorded, when they come to this part to put it by, [if] . . . they are . . . perfectly wearied, and then remember, 'they feeling no interest to read such stuff', to believe me that I had as little to write it, and thus we shall both be satisfied. *When* I publish, no such excuse to be admitted [?].

I am not able to say much of Sydney, having been on shore into the town but three or four times, my time being fully occupied on board; so that . . . will give an idea of what immense information [we] one thousand leagues blue water travellers derive from our voyages! We leave here for Calcutta tomorrow; after the troops' stores etc. were embarked, we received advice from the Government of our destination being changed from Bengal, which is a great advantage, but . . . whereas, as in all contract business, the former agreement being rendered null and void we have been able to make better terms, and now have twelve hundred [pounds] extra, [this] . . . is little enough. The soldiers are kept in excellent order by their officers and we are more quiet and less cumbered than I expected to be, but still I shall feel happy to see their backs in Calcutta.

29th. Lying to in Port Jackson, for the Captain to join the ship, we have fired 2 guns for him, but to little purpose, for he appeareth not; the ship is surrounded at this time by boats containing the friends of some on board – washer wives, rogues and rascals of all degrees, who have followed us down here (5 miles from Sydney) to see their friends off, to get their money and etc. Oh, the rascality of a washer wife! How can I describe it? They bring the things on board when they know the owner has not time to overhaul them (on account of getting under way or what not), and when the poor fellow gets to sea, he finds he is cheated in all directions! The Captain comes. Farewell, Port Jackson, to thy fine harbour and scenery. Farewell, Tom Piper's watering place, honester be thy people, cheapness to thy shops, better beef in thy stores, and thou shalt yet have [?] a fair name with the wanderers of old ocean!

We are again at sea, and in as great a mess as may be imagined, from the deck [being] full of sick men, women and children; all are sick, excepting two of the officers, who hold out well. For myself, the coming to sea has increased my spirits tenfold; after what I have gone through in harbour, I now look forward with a blessing to something like peace. I care not for the storms of nature, they are more familiar to me than the constant unhappiness attendant on a situation that give[s] you no satisfaction. Once again I go to visit the East: 'tis not often I go where I expected, and this adds once more to the . . . [time] ; however, in about ten months yet I hope to see the light blue western lands of England again, tho' it is still probable we may have to look elsewhere for a freight than Calcutta. Still, a fair wind to us is my warm wish.

6th. For the last week poor Beck and his companions in the enterprise have been tossed by the angry elements in a most tedious manner, having been lying to under a mizzen stay sail for these three days. Today we have a respite and the long-neglected pen is again in hand, tho' a heavy swell makes it very uncomfortable writing; but at sea you must consider such things trifles, and happy is he that has nothing more to complain of; for me, I am full of anxieties and unhappiness, I see my rigging, that ought to have been secured in harbour, unfit to bear the violence of the gale, and the masts all cracking for want of being properly secured, but I must console myself with the remembrance that my wish was overruled by an order peremptory to let it alone. If we have much severer weather we shall find out our mistakes.

11th. We are again in Hobart Town, the scenery of which I admire as much as ever, the long ranges of hills, the lofty mountains, dark forests and noble river all delight the eye that has for some time been resting on the agitated ocean. We are going to fill up our water and procure a few necessaries for the troops, [such] as potatoes, flour, etc. The band have hard work here – for the Colonel, who is proud of it, loves to display their prowess to the many listeners ashore. They just now, at ½ past nine, concluded with ½ an hour performance on key bugles. We have had a beautiful day, and look forward to the morrow with pleasure, as a day of rest [i.e. Sunday], I am inclined to think that the majestic Mount Table, tho' magnificent, is a very unpleasant neighbour to Hobart Town, from its collecting[?] so much vapour and discharging it in showers rather too frequent to be pleasant.

12th. Cleaned ship throughout at 11. Capt. Chapman came on board and performed Divine service, troops and seamen all present, very squally, rainy, unpleasant day; wrote to Sister Lucy, to go by the *Crawford*.

13th. Received our water and provisions; I myself have been ashore all day forwarding the former, which is procured with difficulty by ourselves, and I think it does reflect great discredit on both colonies, when the Governors can command so much labour, the great want of convenience for watering ships, altho' it might be done at little expense.

14th. 8 p.m. Once more cast loose, to find our passage to Calcutta and for a time to be exiled from the rest of the world. So at least it will feel to the numbers on board; to me it gives no trouble, for I look upon my ship as my home, and am never better pleased with her, than when she is in the element she is designed for.

22nd. From the last date to the present nothing particular has occurred, save the usual calamities of seasickness and loss of appetite, occasioned by the unpropitious winds which have driven us about no little, but in a short time I'll warrant them all to fetch up keel way, and make the stock decision, 2 reefs. Two reefs, furled mainsail and jib, heavy seas, tremendous squalls, split sails, severe contusions, leaky decks, wet beds, no appetites, dinners spoilt, milk capsized, bad water, sprays flying over and wetting thro' thick clothing, lee lurches, weather rolls, cotscreens drawing, hammock lashings stranding, shelves falling, Captain grumbling, mates echoing, boatswain swearing, sailmaker drinking – but I see the page will not hold the catalogue of landlubbers' complaints at the weather, so must omit the rest!

23rd. Also above.

24th. These foul westerly winds seem neverending. When we shall weather the western extremity of New Holland, I do not know; my venture of livestock seems in a bad way, from the severe weather accompanying the cold southerly. Westerly [?] breezes; 'Reef topsails!' is now the daily cry, and nightly one also. Ther. 65.

25th. Fresh day, blowing weather and no prospect of a change for the better, unless the new moon of tomorrow should favour us. My cabin is at this time a complete aviary; in one cage are 5 Lowry parrots, one king parrot, 2 rosellas[60] and 1 Maria Island parakeet, added to which I have a magpie, a cockatoo and a kangaroo; to complete the whole I had originally 2 more parrots and another cockatoo and [a] kangaroo, but they are now defunct, and if I get home 2 of what remain, I shall think myself well off. The range of Ther. from 68 to 65 for the last 8 days.

26th. Fine weather, with little wind. The band, I conceive, do not prefer such, as it causes them no little exercise, morning and evening. All well, which is pleasant with so many.

3rd. month, 4th. Tremendous gale of wind, with constant heavy rain and lightning, came on this morning and played old gooseberry with us. Ah, ye comfortably seated Friends in your snug [Quaker] meeting house at Hitchin, whose walls are impenetrable to the howling blast and watery deluge, how little think ye of your absent member, who is now surrounded by the roaring elements, jammed up in a corner of his cabin, writing (for want of better amusement), waiting to be summoned to dinner, which he earnestly hopes will not be shipwrecked – but I'll be with you by July and have the laugh on you yet!

10th. From last date we have been knocking about with foul winds and low spirits until today, when Boreas with his blast on sackbut [?] has threatened all our sails to fill and, like a good fellow, [is] keeping his promise by urging us forward at 7 knots per hour; sadness has given way to gladness and the voice of moaning [?] is found no more; . . . whereas from the change of weather it doth appear that, from a fear of having it [i.e. their soup] in their laps, the passengers, [as] in the late tempestuous weather, [are] taking a 2nd edition at each dinner time. Black Jack, the cook, has to give notice that he must either have more fresh water allowed him for the purpose of making the said soup, broth, or whatever you please to term it, or else he must make it of inferior quality and, the former being found the lesser of the two evils, he is hereafter to receive 10 galls. for the said purpose, by order of the Captain and E. Beck, chief mate. . .

13th. Weathered Cape Leewin after an absence from the SW extremity of Van Dieman's Land of 4 weeks, of which I may safely say, we have had 3 weeks of continued gales of wind with heavy seas, and in fact all those benefits contained in the catalogue of the rough side of seafaring life; now we look forward to a change for the better, soon we hope to get to the SE tradewind and turn our head

---

[60] Rosellas are a type of Australian parakeet.

towards the East. Welcome indeed will be the steady trade [wind], when we can proceed quietly upon our way. Throughout the heavy weather I must say the *Woodford* has behaved right well, we have had no pumping and I consider that a great blessing, for at times I have thought she would spring a leak, owing to her labouring so heavily in some of the gales. I wish her a continuation of health to the end.

15th. Quite unexpectedly, we seem to have got the SE trade [wind] strong and steady; from a continuance of lightning and from the appearance of the clouds, some days back we had reason to believe we were upon the verge of it, and we are not disappointed. Now we have got into finer weather, the Colonel promotes by all possible means the exercise of his detachment [of troops], and among the rest of his plans is one of having every evening one of his band with a fiddle, and one with a fife, playing to all who choose to try the 'light fantastic toe'; both sailors and soldiers are therefore to be seen stepping to the different airs, and that to a degree that gives me an idea more of labour than of pleasure; however, I have no doubt its effects towards promoting health amongst them are most beneficial.

24th. Great time between dates, but having only a little more paper left I must be sparing of it, and what can I write about, no more than I can sum up in a small space? viz strong trade winds averaging 180 miles per day, sulky weather, and an expectation of arriving about the 20th or 25th of next month.

4th. 6th. Since writing the above, we have had two births in the ship and, I am very sorry to say, 1 death: the former, two sons born to two soldiers and the latter, an ordinary seaman who has been ill nearly all voyage from rheumatism and fever, the former of which, in the head, carried him off when (poor fellow) he least expected it, he considering himself very much better (but a few hours before) than he had been for a considerable time. There are a number of melancholy feelings fastened in the heart when on board ship the bell tolls [for] the assembling of all round the deceased shipmate, to see the last duties performed over one who has been your companion thro' many a stiff breeze and weathered the same gales; one to whom, from our insulated situation, you cannot help feeling a regard, and it is a loss that can be felt when the number is so small. Our men all attended the committal of his body to its watery grave and showed by their attention to the service that they felt it a loss, altho' of one who had, comparatively speaking, . . . been [of] but little assistance [?] to them; at the conclusion, as they retired, the solemn [?] expressions dropped by some of them [spoke] to the fact, tho' in their rough manner, 'Poor Bill, it's 8 bells with him!',

'He's lost the number of his ship!' [?], 'He'll get no more grog this voyage!'

The range of the thermometer for the last 8 days has been from 85 and 6 to 90 and, from its being 3 days out of those [8] perfectly calm, the sea more like glass than water, we have found the heat very oppressive and, I think, none more so than the soldiers – who, from not being used to salt provisions, find 6 pints a day for everything but a short allowance. Such a scene as occurred yesterday at the scuttle hole I shall not soon forget; all of them, men, women and children, crowding around it, in spite of the sentry stationed there to prevent it, giving one more the idea of a set of shipwrecked wretches than otherwise, and [it] was such that the Colonel was quite offended and made the men fall in, kept them there a considerable time, and has made him order [that], instead of their allowance [of water] being put together, every man, woman and child [is] to receive its allowance served out to it, like all other rations. In the way of fishing we have been very successful, having caught 2 sharks and about 8 or 10 dolphins, the latter of which, after their colours at dying being admired, obtained a better fate by being served up at table, and I think them very excellent; from one of the sharks, 8 feet long, we took off a sucker, which is a most curious little fish, possessed of amazing adhesive powers; its under jaw, throat etc. are full of small furrows by which it sticks to the shark, its gills are on the top of its body and it is of a brown colour. I have preserved it in spirits, with the intention of carrying it to England.

Gymnastic exercises amongst the troops seem now to be the order of the evenings; some feats of agility I have witnessed amongst them that were quite astonishing, and leave me no amazement at those mountebanks who, in days of yore, at fairs and such places of vain amusement stirred up my boyish wonder and made me believe them almost miraculous. Our tars, not liking to be left in the background, last evening took the shine out of the redcoats on the slack rope, but at nothing else could they equal them. They caused us great diversion and, I almost venture to say, tho' we partake not of the benefits arising from the exercise of their muscles, we obtain almost [?] [an] equal degree from the laughter they occasion us, which makes all sides shake again, with peals both loud and long.

6th. Hitherto we have had a very harmonious voyage but, I regret to say, it has today been disturbed from some misunderstanding between the Colonel and a Captain of the troops. I hope however it will be settled amicably and we may finish the voyage in peace.

8th. We have crossed the line today and found ourselves at noon 31 miles N of it; should we get the monsoon pretty quickly, a short time will see us in Calcutta – and we had need to be there pretty quick, for nearly all the fresh stock is expended and I know not how the gents will manage upon 'salt horse' as we term beef. They complain greatly of thirst now, but then I think they will do so doubly; if we speak [to] a ship we may procure a sheep or two. All we bought in Sydney were rotten and, I am sure, not fit to eat.

9th. Tremendous thunder and lightning throughout the morning, one of the lads standing by the chain [?] [of the] main top sail received a slight electric shock in his foot, which did him no harm. The relief to the atmosphere was immense, and the sky, after a discharge of heavy and continued rain, assumed a more pleasant appearance. Made the 1st move towards preparing for harbour, by getting in our sheet anchor for stocking.

Began today to show signs of a tedious passage by proclaiming no more beer, no more claret, no more port wine, all being expended, and then to end [?] the matter they all complain the water is so bad they cannot drink it; but necessity, I warrant, will soon bring them to admire it and they may yet have to be glad, that they can get even 3 pints of that per day, instead of 5, as at present.

10th. This day died the infant girl of one of the passengers at 11; it was buried in a small coffin made by the carpenter. The funeral [was] attended by great part of the soldiers aboard, all the wives on [the] bridge [?], dressed as well as they could from their small stocks. Last night, or rather this morning, it rained, thundered and lightened in an awful manner and quite frightened all our animals on board, who expressed by their various notes their feelings on the occasion. I might remark, as to the former part of this page, that at the time the burial service was being read over the infant, a magpie I brought from the Derwent began to sing for the first time, which our people took to be quite ominous – but what of, I am at a loss to determine, unless of its being a future whistler.

11th. Banyan days have commenced – instead of the old breakfast, mutton chops, preserves, fish, etc., etc., there appeared this morning only salt beef, which makes the 'after' gents [i.e. passengers] look very sour; we old junkers mind it but little – not but that we like fresh best, but 8 hours' watch always qualifies the stomach for whatever is to be found, even tho' it be but a sea cake.

Last evening I heard a civilian joust [?] about [food] soon running short; [they had] paid forty pounds each and had expected to have plenty of everything etc. etc.; all indications of a breeze which, unless some ship is so good as to come our way and supply us with a few articles, I expect will take place daily. I hope, however, we shall manage to get thro' it. The row between themselves was amicably settled; I hope there may be none between the Captain and them.

16th. We seem to have arrived here at the very shift of the monsoons, for these

209

last 5 days we have had complete contrasts between the northerly and southerly a winds, accompanied with continued thunder and vivid lightning all round the horizon. Yesterday we got at noon a fine southerly breeze, and I hope we shall at noon today have made a degree, which will be a complete novelty to us and lightens the hearts of all on board, for the soldiers are tired of shipboard; the sailors are in turn tired of them, and nothing will keep up good understanding and unity amongst them but a fair wind – which, as we have it now, I hope [it] will stand and give us a good push behind (for being absent so long), and there is another good reason for wishing to be . . . [at Calcutta], viz, but two weeks' water on board ship, which makes it very anxious work for the Captain and Ned Beck.

Good Friday was duly observed, altho' an absence of Hot Cross Buns, [which] did not grace our breakfast table. Divine Service was performed, as usual on 1st days [i.e. Sundays], on the quarter deck and the band played some sacred music, very beautiful and pathetic, but I cannot say I quite admire to hear such beautiful hymns sung in public by men who we daily observe, thro'out the week, swearing and otherwise behaving very opposite to the doctrine of that God in whose praises they are employed singing . . . during Divine Service on the Sabbath. But I set not myself up in judgement upon the practice; it seems with [i.e. to] me . . . ridiculous, [but] as we [all] have very different views upon different subjects, the best plan, I conceive, is to let all follow their own opinions. . . .

17th. Lots of fish about the ship, tried my luck but caught nought; I never was an expert hand at the trade [of fishing] and I think I shall carry it [i.e. this lack of expertise] with me thro'out [my life]. 'Tis rather mortifying to look from the jib [boom] upon dolphin, bonito, albacores [i.e. tuna] etc. etc., chasing the flying fish and not be able to take a meal off them, but as I could not catch, like Reynard I was led to exclaim, 'Well, never mind, they are a coarse kind of fish,' and go without. Weather very hot and uncomfortable on a/c of no wind, having lost our breeze again this morning. Well, patience, as the old proverb says, patience works miracles, so sit me down and read 3 chapters in Job to acquire more than I at present possess of the great essential for every sailor; let me advise anyone who thinks of trying his fortune on the rough bosom of the ocean to carry aboard a good stock of it, so that he be not reduced to the common extremity of having 'a good growl to ease the mind', as at sea it is commonly termed. Indeed, I would venture to cut away the mainmast, on condition of a sailor being found who was not at times a grumbler; 'tis a spice [?] mixed up in his nature, and one I am so accustomed to, that my common saying to them is, 'Growl you may, but go you must, my boys!' as I order them to some unpleasant part of their duty. Yesterday there was a long argument between the Capt. and

210

some of the officers about the legality of corporal punishment being inflicted in a merchantman; I have often heard it discussed, but never heard it satisfactorily settled, tho' I should much like to.

20th. 2 p.m. I am now a prisoner to my cabin, confined to it for the following reasons. I about two weeks ago was ordered by the Captain to carefully survey the hold and report to him the quantity of water remaining, which I did; a few evenings ago (2, I believe) Mr Govey and myself were called in, [for the Captain] to hear our opinion about the quantity remaining, which seemed satisfactory – but as a further satisfaction, we were ordered to survey it again. I did it, he fell into high dudgeon and sent us both to report the quantity to him, which was done, and being more particular, even to ½ an inch in the dry depths of the cask, we made a few gallons more – I think about 28 or 30 only. On going into his cabin to report this quantity, he ordered me to give it him on paper . . . signed by myself and Mr Govey, which was done. At the time, he was making the plan of the ship, which, when finished, he came upon the poop and began upbraiding me with child's play in the matter and said he was sick of me, which worried [?] me, and I retorted rather sharply; he said, 'Do not insult me, Mr Beck!' I said, 'I do not insult you, but I will not be upbraided without reason.' He said, 'Do not answer me, sir, I want no reply from you!' I said I would answer when I thought myself wronged; he then ordered me to my cabin, which I immediately complied with. In looking back upon my conduct upon this ship, where I have been 2 years and 3 months, I feel nothing to condemn myself for, and I suffer, I cannot help it – will bear up against it all. I have my feelings, but I trust they are, as regards my duty, more omissions than commissions; let me bear testimony to his general kindness to me at the same time remarking that I never took advantage of it – and I will take care he never shall, on that account, take it of me. I think he has, in this instance. I did not survey the hold with the mercenary feeling of a person getting 6 or 8 a dip [?], but with a warm feeling of anxiety, for fear we might run short of such an indispensable article as water, and I can positively declare that my return was correct; that there has been a greater expenditure than there ought to have been, I am fully aware – but that it has not arisen in any way thro' my neglect, I can satisfactorily prove, and would have proved (and endeavoured to have traced it to its proper source) had he condescended to have asked an explanation, and in which way I accounted for the deficiency; that he did not chose to do, but publicly, on the poop, upbraided me with [accusations about] a line of conduct that I should scorn, as a chief officer of a ship, to act upon, and then – because I have more spirit than to bear being bid to [?] silence, like the common soldier or sailor, I am to be publicly disgraced, in a ship where I have heretofore, from my old and ever respected commander, received approbation. If I am confined long, I know I shall suffer in health, the weather being oppressively hot and my cabin so much confined; the passengers have kindly offered me the use of theirs, and of books or anything they can supply me with, for which I feel very thankful. They have also interested themselves with the Captain about me, but (as I suppose he expects me to write to him and beg pardon, which I never will do), I can look forward to nothing but confinement to Calcutta; tho' not close, for I know that the Dr will represent it to him that, if I am debarred the deck, I shall soon begin to suffer. About 5 o'clock our steward, who a short time ago was taken with a fit of apoplexy, was seized with a paroxysm of madness and ran after the ship's steward to the after hatchway, he calling out for the Dr all the way, when at my door, seeing by his eyes what was the matter, I pounced on him, calling out for assistance, which soon arrived tho' not before I had received some heavy blows from him. When overpowered his arms were secured, tho' he gnashed his teeth with all the frenzy of perfect madness and screamed dreadfully. When it subsided a little, the Dr bled him freely, and he has lain till this time quiet. 11 o'clock.

21st. The steward still very ill and I am afraid he will have to be put into a straitjacket, to prevent accidents.

23rd. Another child has died today and will, I suppose, be interred this evening; from what I see of soldiers' children, their education, their habits etc., I should be inclined to think it a most happy release. It being the anniversary of the King's birthday, the troops were all paraded under arms and a glass of extra spirits served out to them, after which the band struck up the National Anthem, and the while concluded with 3 cheers from all present; I am told there is a strange sail, ahead or astern, I know not which.

24th. Here am I, poor pilgarlic[?],[61] confined to my solitary cabin, whilst all around me is life and gaiety, on occasion of a firm breeze and our near approach to land. Much friendship has always been professed for me by E. Chapman – and here is a proof of profession, how far it is with him to be depended upon! This is the 4th day I have been confined in a manner I consider arbitrary – I cannot tell his intentions, but I suppose I shall be discharged, as soon as the ship arrives in Calcutta. I have not communicated with him in any way or begged pardon; that, as I said before, I will not do – he surely does not want both to punish me [and] that I [should] concur . . . and besides an apology from me – which I conceive as much due from him – if he does, he will be disappointed.

---

[61] A pilgarlic was a bald-headed man or other poor creature.

The officers of the detachment have kindly offered to give me, before they leave the ship, a letter in which will be stated the high terms in which, but a short time before, and during the passage . . . Captain Chapman has spoken of me – so that I hope to pass into any other ship with good repute. I must confess I would rather leave the ship now; I have been disgraced, which I never was before in any ship. I cannot return to my duty with that earnest feeling I had before, I consider that towards E.C. I can entertain but one opinion, which is, that he is a fickle man and one where professions are not in the least to be depended upon. I have in the present case asked advice, and everyone says that he ought, the same afternoon or next morning, to have returned me to my duty, in which case I should have attributed to warmth, a great deal of what I now consider to have originated in a worse feeling.

3 p.m. A brig is right ahead, Mr Govey is about to go on board to hear the news of the country if possible, she looking as if she was from Madras or some place on the coast. [He] spoke [to] her as she passed but, [she] being manned entirely with natives, did not board her.

25th. A strong 8½ knot breeze is driving us along famously towards Calcutta; all is therefore, on the part of most, lightness of heart at the thought of a speedy arrival at our long desired port.

8 p.m. After a very long uncomfortable day on my part, occasioned by constant headache and sickness, I was obliged to send the Doctor to represent my case to the Captain, which he did, in the most gentlemanly manner. Captain C., after a long rigmarole story, in an endeavour to place my conduct in as bad a light as possible, desired him to inform me from him that, if I had had any feeling for him at such an anxious time, I should have gone to his cabin and have settled it. I immediately replied by letter, stating to him the heartfelt satisfaction that was mine in having done my duty, acknowledging my error in the improper retort of my reply – at the same [time] telling him I had shared his fortunes for a long time and had always understood that I also did his friendship, tho' I was led to believe had I [truly shared his friendship] it would have led him earlier to have forgiven an error, arising from my temper getting the upper hand.

26th. The pilot brig is right ahead at an anchor. I have received no communication from the Captain and I suppose I shall not, since how arbitrary is that law that allots to so trifling an offence so rigorous a punishment! I should state that he would not at first hear anything about my coming on deck, but, on the Doctor insisting on it, gave permission for 2 hours of an evening, provided I did not keep in his sight – which I should have taken care to avoid, having not the slightest wish to annoy him. He also told Dr K. that he had a letter written to his brother Alfred that he should send immediately on his arrival, that would immediately cancel their attachment, which he said they had for me – truly, if what I have done has that effect, 'tis an attachment the loss of which will be very small; if with that he thinks to frighten me, he will find himself completely deceived. I would think less of it, if he would be content with the true statement of the case, but as he has made considerable additions I cannot feel towards him as I otherwise should, and what I think is the best of the story is, that he has endeavoured to persuade all I am very ungrateful that he has brought me forward from being 3rd to be his chief officer, and that I have nowhere else to look for the command of a ship but to the house of Chapman, when he very well knows that I never asked for a single favour except the 1st berth I got (which was 4th) [i.e. fourth officer], and [if] . . . I asked him for another, I am sure it [would] . . . be hard times with me. Should our differences have the effect of my losing the esteem of his brother, I shall have deep cause to regret it, for a more gentlemanly, honourable, kind and affectionate commander, I shall never have the pleasure of sailing under; I would sooner go 3rd with him, than chief with this fickle young man.

27th. The pilot is now on board; we saw 3 brigs at daylight and stood for the weathermost one, but she had no pilots on board her, therefore bore up for the 2nd, who sent us one and a leadsman, or volunteer, [who] is in training for a pilot. He brought with him newspapers of most dates and, what was far more acceptable, a sheep and 2 brace of ducks and fowls, which will tend to make the officers in good humour. Whilst making sail in the afternoon, . . . [Govey] complained of the slackness of the men, saying that there was but one efficient officer to look after them, and that he must have more exertion made, which vexed the Captain much, and he attended himself on the poop; he, the Captain, complained to Govey, tho' [it was Govey] in the 1st place who told him that he could not do all himself, at which he turned on his heel, and did as I have mentioned above. Got talk with the pilot in the evening, who tells me things are very dull and flat in Calcutta. 7.30 p.m. Came to an anchor in Iaccamo Channel. In getting, or rather endeavouring to get, the anchor when the ship was just over it (from the jump of the sea, in which she broke the iron hauls [?] of the windlass) . . . they were obliged to unshackle the chain cable and slip it, leaving the anchor behind. 7. All possible sail set, and a fine breeze.

3. Brought up off Diamond Harbour after a pleasant run up. At 10. Mr Ben [?] came to me and said he had news to tell me, which was that he had effected a reconciliation with the Captain and Cdt. Cameron, and that, after they had all told him they could not think of leaving the ship without seeing us reconciled, . . . he [the Captain] said he should be happy to shake hands in the Cd. cabin –

which was done at 11 o'clock, and I was restored again to liberty and life – for 6 such days, I never spent in all my life! Ther. 96.

29th. At 10 got under way, with a fine strong breeze up the river, everything very delightful and cheering. Off Fullah the Captain went ashore [?] and fetched off a quantity of good wines and beer, which soon set all in good humour together; towards me again he is as frank and free as ever. 12 p.m. Anchored off Casley [?] bazaar and, I regret to say, lost a man of the cholera at 3 in the morning following, 30th, and in the next day 1 woman, 1 man and such a distressing scene I never wish to witness again; our quarter deck was covered with people at 10 at night who were being bled and medicine administered and then immediately sent to the hospital, many of them with death in their countenances. This day the Inspector of Hospitals mustered the people and said they all looked remarkably well. Ther. 96.

5th. month 2nd. At 12 last night called up to see the cook's mate, told he was very ill, got a light and found he was, and had been for 6 hours, attacked with cholera, immediately bled him and got him into a warm bath, which eased him of the spasms, which were excruciating; gave him 60 drops of laudanum in brandy and oil of peppermint, but it was quite evident from the first [that] no human power could save him. He lingered in great pain and expired in my arms at ¼ to 8; so severe was the attack, and so short a time does the dreadful disease take to carry off to the grave the strongest constitution! The doctor that I had sent for arrived shortly before his decease – but, on reading the progress and symptoms that appeared and which I had put on paper, he immediately said, 'I could have done no more for him than you have done,' which was comforting to me.

3rd. Yesterday went ashore, 2 men to the hospital with cholera, the disease is marching thro' the ship and will, I am afraid, thin our numbers before it ceases. My situation can be better conceived than told, with no surgeon on board, 2 miles from Calcutta and from the shipping, and all around looking to me for medical assistance; unable, with some of the cases, to get even other assistance than the 2nd officer's to bathe them . . . (on account of the people's fears lest it be catching). I am quite worn down, and so dreadfully nervous that I cannot even sleep without dreaming of lancets, doctors, dying or [the] dead. My life is, however, in the hands of that Almighty being who created me, and it may please Him to take it, but I humbly pray Him to spare it to be of use to my shipmates, and whilst He grants me health, they shall always receive all the attention and care I can give them. But if it pleases Him that I no more revisit my native land

and that I leave my bones thus far from all so dear to me in it, I pray Him to bless them all and to give them to feel that, in my last moments, the remembrance of them soothed my last hours.

4th. Lost 2 more, those sent to hospital yesterday; they both died shortly after in great agony, one of them a man universally beloved by his shipmates. Our people, dressed in their blue jackets and white trousers with straw hats and black ribands, followed him (covered with the Union Jack) to his place of burial. Thinking to do them good, gave them a month's advance and 3 days' liberty ashore, but I am afraid it will, with drink etc., be the death of many of them. I have got just one more case, I think, on board, but the doctor will be here shortly, I hope.

5th. The man mentioned above has not the cholera, I am glad to say; if he is not better tho' tomorrow, he will go to the hospital.

We are taken up to go to the Isle of France, Madras, and in fact a trading voyage, so that when I shall be home, if I escape the cholera, I do not know. We take in rice [?] tomorrow and get to sea as soon as possible.

Got on board 40 Lascars to get forward with the work and caulkers, carpenters etc., so that with painting, tarring, rigging, caulking, cleaning and docking, poor Beck's hands are full of business, and it requires no small care to keep clear of the sun, which is here positively necessary.

8 p.m. A man has come on board with cholera, so that tonight will be a pretty busy one, I expect. Midnight: the doctor bled him and dosed him with laudanum, but I am sure he will die.

7th. Lost today, by the cholera, one of the best shipmates that ever trod ship's deck; he lingered from 8 on the 5th until 1 p.m. this day when, with his hands clasped in attitude of prayer and eyes lifted towards heaven, he peacefully departed this life, I humbly trust for a better. He begged to see all of us that were on board, which request was immediately attended to, and tho' he could say nothing, yet the look was sufficient to tell us he bade us adieu, and it was affecting to see his old companions in tears and, to one who had long watched him, thus to leave him was more than I could bear, and I therefore left the cabin; the grateful way he had expressed himself for the attentions he had received, marked the goodness of his heart. He begged his clothes and money to be given to his parents with his dying blessing, and wished them to know he had intended going to see them, if he had got home.

8th. Sent another to the hospital, nearly dead of cholera. The 2nd officer is gone ashore ill, and I have 2 cases on board the ship, both recovering after slight attacks. The former a most respectable young man, he has sent on board his watch, gold ring and 19 rupees, with the request that I would inform his father, if he goes, of his death beforehand, and then on our return to give him his things. Oh, 'tis mournful work, thus parting with the partners of a sea voyage. I myself am quite well, and have not the least doubt of escaping the rage of the disorder; if I could manage it, I should like to leave the ship for a day or two, just to get a few happier impressions than this sad job has given me. We expect to be off in three weeks at farthest – even hope two. Therms' range last week 98.

I shall hope to have letters . . . [forwarded] to Calcutta by the first opportunity, with nothing particular in them, only news as to health, happiness, etc. existing at home, directed to Rhamtonoo Das [?] or, perhaps it would be preferable, to the post office. I shall write from the Isle of France about future movements; I should hope this will go no further than thyself, my dear uncle, for it might cause unnecessary pain. Think of me as happy in doing my duty and, if what I have recorded about the Capn. and myself cause an unpleasant feeling, bury it, as I trust I have done. I would have erased same, but the conviction that I had done nothing that you would have been ashamed of me for, induces me to send home all about the matter.

Kind reader, my book is full. I had calculated on a short voyage, the occurrences of which this was to have continued, but since I have had to visit this distant part of the world, and as yet I know not whither I may be bound, I must commence another, not wishing thee to follow me, unless what this contains hath afforded thee amusements: the great object sought in thus recording my little adventures is the pleasure I hope to feel in reading over myself what I have here noticed, which will recall to my recollections days diversified, like the life we lead, with pleasure and with pain. At the same time, I may acknowledge it affords me no small pleasure, thus to give to the different branches of the Beckean family some account of the days spent by one of its most wandering members.

CALCUTTA 5TH MONTH 1827

GLOSSARY OF TERMS USED IN EDWARD BECK'S

DIARIES

Apeak
Beck uses this term to describe what is known in the 20th century as 'Up-and-down' referring to the appearance of the anchor cable just before the anchor leaves the bottom.

Bells
Bells are struck every half hour so that eight bells signifies the end of one watch and the beginning of the next.

Buntlines
Ropes secured to the bottom edge of the sail at suitable intervals and then led up to blocks on the yard above and from there into the mast and down to the deck. Hauling on these ropes may be ordered by 'Bunt up' or by 'Haul on your buntlines'.

Clewing-up
The act of hauling the clews up to the yardarm normally followed by hauling on the buntlines to completely muzzle the sail prior to sending sailors aloft to give the sail a complete stow on top of the yard.

Clewlines
Ropes leading from the clews to the yardarm above and from there to a block under the centre of the yard and from there down to the deck so that the sailors on deck can haul the clews up to the yardarm.

Clews
The two bottom corners of a squaresail.

Compass Points
There are thirty-six points to the compass and these are then divided into quarters. Nowadays the points of the compass are not used except to indicate the direction of the wind. Bearings and courses are given in degrees between 0° and 90° between the four Cardinal Points, North, East, South and West unless a gyro compass or true bearing is being used when the reading is in three

	figures from 000° to 360°.
Crator	A potato – especially an Irish one.
Crossjack	Normally pronounced 'crowjack'. This is the lower yard on the mizzen mast of a full-rigged ship on which up until about 1760 no sail was set due to the fore-and-aft lateen sail projecting forward of the mast below it.

After 1750 when the lateen sail and yard was replaced by a gaff sail and boom ships started to set a square-sail on this yard but kept the name of the yard and named the sail also 'the crojack' as it was normally written.

(Origin: In earlier times the mizzen was known as 'the Jack' and so the yard rigged across it with no sail was named the 'crossjack'. Other yards took their names from the sails which were bent onto them, e.g. 'Topsail yard'.

Dog Watches	These two, two-hour watches are used to produce an odd number of watches in the 24 hours to change the rota each day. Bells in this four-hour period are struck as follows:- 1, 2, 3, 4 then 1, 2, 3, 8.
Graip	A three-pronged fishing spear like a trident.
Heaving-to	The act of bracing the yards on one mast to drive the ship astern while the others drive her ahead with the result that she remains almost stationary when that state is required for launching or recovering a boat or for other reasons.
Holystones	Blocks of soft sandstone used for rubbing the decks to clean them. Beck mentions a big one being called 'The Great Bear' but in the Royal Navy big ones are called 'Bibles' and small ones 'Prayer Books'.

(Origin: The traditional story is that when Royal Naval ships were anchored outside Portsmouth sailors would be sent ashore to steal the tombstones from the nearby churchyards which were made from a soft sandstone that was ideal for the purpose.)

Larboard	The left hand side of the vessel looking forward until around 1850 when that side was renamed 'Port' since the ships main entry port was on that side. In German and certain other European languages it is called 'Backbord'.

Lobscouse	a popular sailor's traditional delicacy usually made up of crushed ships' biscuits and salt pork with other additions according to the cook's choice and availability. (Origin unknown)
Portugese Man-of-War	a very dangerous and poisonous jelly fish with long tendrils.
Reefing	Reducing the amount of sail exposed to the wind by bundling up a special portion with the aid of 'Reefing tackles' and 'reef points'. Some sails are arranged with several reefs so that they can be progressively made smaller by taking in a 'First Reef' and then a 'Second Reef' and then a 'Third Reef', even a fourth.
The Society	'The Society of Friends', generally known at 'The Quakers' and sometimes referred to in these diaries as 'Friends' or 'The Friends'.
Speaking	'Speaking a ship' is to communicate with another vessel at sea by signalling or hailing across the water. For example 'Spoke the *Lord Stewart* this a.m.'
Starboard	The right hand side of the vessel looking forward. (Origin: In Viking and other early vessels steering was effected with an oar (or board) over the right hand side of the stern and this was known as the 'Steerboard' hence starboard.)
Twixt decks	In the 20th century these are normally called 'The tween decks' and means decks below the main deck, especially in cargo holds.
Watches	Ships crews are normally divided into watches with one watch on deck and the other below for a four-hour period as follows:

Midnight to 4 a.m.	–	Middle Watch
4 a.m. to 8 a.m.	–	Morning Watch
8 a.m. to 12 noon	–	Forenoon Watch
12 noon to 4 p.m.	–	Afternoon Watch
4 p.m. to 6 p.m.	–	First Dog Watch
6 p.m. to 8 p.m.	–	Last Dog Watch (NOT Second)
8 p.m. to Midnight	–	First Watch